KNOCKIN' ON
HEAVEN'S DOOR

What would happen if popular culture and the Bible were placed next to one another and treated as though they were the most natural of partners? What if action heroes, the films of Alfred Hitchcock, pornography, sex work, heavy metal music, science fiction and fast food were read against a selection of texts from the Hebrew Bible/Old Testament? This is precisely what Roland Boer carries out in this innovative and provocative book.

Using the work of Michel de Certeau and Henri Lefebvre on popular culture as a theoretical base, as well as that of Fredric Jameson and Slavoj Žižek, Boer engages in a series of readings around certain themes from popular culture and the Hebrew Bible. These include the queer dimensions of action heroes and King David, the sadistic violence of Alfred Hitchcock and the biblical accounts of sacrifice and dismemberment, and hard-core pornography and the Song of Songs.

While these readings may be seen as part of an emerging way of reading the Bible and popular culture – grotesque biblical criticism – the originality of this book lies in the distinctive way in which the themes of violence, sex, noise, food and utopia are interpreted. These themes are also woven together with a fictional detective story in which the main characters of the chapters appear as actors.

Roland Boer lectures in Hebrew Bible at the United Theological College, Sydney, Australia. His previous publications include *Jameson and Jeroboam* (1996) and *Novel Histories: The Fiction of Biblical Criticism* (1997).

BIBLICAL LIMITS

We have to move beyond the outside–inside alternative; we have to be at the frontiers. Criticism indeed consists of analyzing and reflecting upon limits.
  – Michel Foucault ('What is Enlightenment?')

This series brings a variety of postmodern perspectives to the understanding of biblical texts. It challenges the traditional field of biblical studies and invites new partners, including critics of literature, gender and culture, to press the boundaries of a familiar – and unfamiliar – Bible.

EDITORS

Danna Nolan Fewell
Southern Methodist University, Dallas, Texas

David M. Gunn
Texas Christian University, Fort Worth, Texas

Gary A. Phillips
The University of the South, Sewanee, Tennessee

Amy-Jill Levine
Vanderbilt University, Nashville, Tennessee
(Consultant Editor)

ALSO IN THIS SERIES

KNOCKIN' ON HEAVEN'S DOOR

The Bible and popular culture

Roland Boer

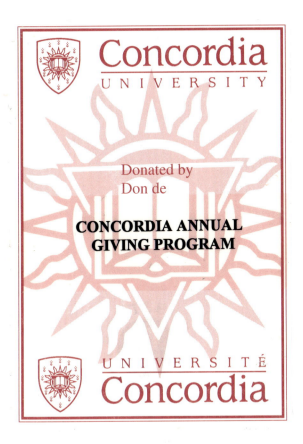

First published 1999
by Routledge
11 New Fetter Lane, London EC4P 4EE

Simultaneously published in the USA and Canada
by Routledge
29 West 35th Street, New York, NY 10001

Routledge is an imprint of the Taylor & Francis Group

© 1999 Roland Boer

Typeset in Garamond by
Ponting–Green Publishing Services, Chesham, Buckinghamshire
Printed and bound in Great Britain by
TJ International Ltd, Padstow, Cornwall

British Library Cataloguing in Publication Data
A catalogue record for this book is available from the British Library

Library of Congress Cataloging in Publication Data
Boer, Roland, 1961–
Knockin' on heaven's door / Roland Boer.
p.   cm. – (Biblical limits)
Includes bibliographical references and index.
1. Bible. O.T.–Criticism, interpretation, etc.
2. Popular culture–Religious aspects.
I. Title.   II. Title: Knockin' on heaven's door.   III. Series: Biblical limits.
BS1171.2.B64   1999
220.6–dc21   98–55198
CIP

ISBN 0–415–19410–5 (hbk)
ISBN 0–415–19411–3 (pbk)

FOR ERIN AND FIONA,
COMRADES

CONTENTS

PREFACE

It seems to me that all those constructed as male desire to be penetrated. This book may be read in part as an exploration of such desires and phantasies. In a culture where masculinity designates penetration, what does it mean for males to absorb, swallow, take in, be penetrated?

Yet, this book also, in related obverse, speaks of my excremental relation with the Bible. For some time now I have felt a distinct horror at the Bible's star status in the western literary and cultural canon, as well as a desire to be rid of the skills I have laboriously gained in biblical criticism. And yet, interpretation of the Bible gives me a curious pleasure; the exercise of biblical criticism provides a strange satisfaction. This is not merely because reflection on and teaching about the Bible keeps me fed, clothed and out of the elements, for the time being at least. As David Halperin observed in our first discussion together, I will never be rid of either the Bible or the Church, although I did not understand the import of this observation at the time. Even though I try to evacuate, to shit it out, I am always full of shit.

Perhaps the Bible functions for me like Freud's 'name of the father', that presence that seems so full of authority and power, but when pressed turns out to be empty and vacuous, a wisp of smoke left behind from an all too rapid departure. Alternatively, my incessant repetition of works of biblical criticism, the obsessive repetition of such activity, indicates, according to Freud, an unresolved trauma to which I return again and again in a futile effort at resolution. In this light, the reader will not be surprised to find a heavy engagement with psychoanalysis in this book, mediated primarily through Jacques Lacan and Slavoj Žižek. Perhaps this is an effort to resolve the trauma I am doomed to repeat. Hence the turn to popular culture.

But there is another source of simultaneous disappointment and delight that comes from living in a country on the fringe of global political and economic power. While home always remains elsewhere, while the possibilities of sustained critical engagement are thin on the ground, there is an enjoyment in being able to soak up a different atmosphere, to be outside, at least in part, the constraints and blinkers of the vast intellectual systems of the academic and cultural superpowers. I hope that some of this antipodality shows through in this volume.

This applies not only to my readings of the Bible but also to the items of popular culture with which I deal. They come from 'outside' Australia in a neo-colonial or post-colonial form (Australia itself is a prime site for post/ neo-colonial investment) – Hollywood film, rock music, McDonald's, Hitchcock, pornography – yet each of these undergoes a mode of appropriation (what I want to call, following Meaghan Morris, 'positive unoriginality') that mutates them in one way or another. This may be in the way the cultural product itself is received (McDonald's becomes Maccas), but it also happens in the piecemeal fashion in which such cultural influences make their way in Australia. A signal of this piecemeal reception is the chapter on Lamentations in which I make use of some work by the Russian Strugatsky brothers, which contrasts with the dominant global/American culture of late capitalism. The most popular science fiction writers in Russia for the past three decades, their work remains extraordinarily difficult to find. A similar mutated and piecemeal pattern applies to the arrival of 'theory' on these shores, where the dictates of long distance book transport, patchy local interest and high prices affect the types of material available.

There is another dimension to the pleasure of these chapters, although it is more of a perverse personal pleasure, a transgressive and painful pleasure beyond pleasure – *jouissance*. For some reason or other action heroes have walked through my ego, heavy metal has thundered in my ears, Hitchcock has lured me with his films (and their inseparable theory), pornography has demanded my gaze, the prostitute has visited my dreams, the male body has mixed my sexual codes, breakfast at McDonald's has become a necessary ritual, and science fiction has reconstructed my utopian imagination. But the strongest mark of that pleasure is the excuse this book has given me to write a story, this time a detective story of sorts, as a metacommentary in the interstices of the main text. However, it is not so much that the story aids in reading the critical text, but that the critical text provides the structural foundation, that it always points towards the story itself, for here lies the thematic and political key of this book.

A word of thanks must go to Scott Stephens, a rare comrade, who critiqued earlier versions of the book. Erin Runions and Fiona Black have provided a continuing communication in which some of the questions I deal with were considered and are still under discussion. Elizabeth Castelli has been, as always, a wonderful friend and encourager, and George Aichele has provided his down-to-earth perspective on my work. Finally, Gary Phillips and David Gunn, as editors of the series, have supported this project from its inception. To all of these people I am deeply grateful.

December 1998
Little Beach, New South Wales

INTRODUCTION

In debt to the Censor

For many readers what I do in this book may seem entirely arbitrary, an example of chronic misreading. For others it may appear as nothing more than a theoretical justification for my baser instincts. While there is a certain willfulness about the sheer anachronism of the exercise I undertake here, as well as moments of caricature of biblical criticism in certain of its more ludicrous manifestations, I do not want to leave the theoretical discussion at the level of arbitrariness, misreading, basic instincts, anachronism and caricature.

The starting point for this volume is a pair of fetishes, two items that entice, engage, obsess: the Hebrew Bible and popular culture. While an autobiographical dimension unavoidably makes its presence felt with such a statement – is not writing inevitably autobiographical? – there is a particular theoretical problem that is raised by the very conjunction of biblical studies and cultural studies. Thus, after considering the critical context within which I labour, I focus directly on the problem itself, which is how one comes to make use of cultural theory or criticism in the space of biblical criticism. In other words, what might conceivably justify the intersection of cultural criticism and biblical criticism, especially across the vast reach of time that separates the respective corpuses on which critical energy is exerted?

Inevitably, there is a broadening critical context for the conjunction of cultural and biblical studies. This context is characterized by two major trends: those religious and biblical scholars who interpret contemporary cultural products, seeking out implicit religious and theological themes[1] and the ways the Bible is represented in such products,[2] and those who interpret the Bible using elements of cultural criticism.[3] And then there are the crossover works that combine these elements in various ways.[4] Of all these efforts, mine comes closest to the final group.

At the same time, this still small flush of publication raises some crucial theoretical questions, given the highly exploratory nature of much of the work. My effort in this book does not seek biblical dimensions in contemporary cultural products as such, nor does it restrict itself to the application of cultural theories to the Bible, nor is it interested in explicit representations of the Bible in contemporary culture. Rather, it juxtaposes biblical and other cultural texts and it does so from the perspective of dialectical Marxism. What are the implications?

The reader will encounter the use of a range of terms and concepts that are part of the constellation of Marxist theory. This is not merely due to the fact that cultural studies remains indebted to Marxism for both its original formation and its continued conceptual and critical apparatus, but also because Marxism is very much part of the intellectual heritage from which I draw inspiration. Apart from Marx and Engels, and apart from the Hegel who peers over their shoulders, Fredric Jameson and George Lukács (the focus of two earlier books – *Jameson and Jeroboam* (1996a) and *Novel Histories* (1997)) have most strongly influenced the critical and political stance taken in this work. Others also play a role – Henri Lefebvre in theorizing everyday life, Louis Marin on utopia, Darko Suvin on science fiction, Alan Soble on pornography, Jacques Attali on noise and music – but the strongest legacy of Hegelian Marxism lies in the practice of dialectical thinking and reading.

It is not often enough in biblical studies that the psychological moment appears, let alone that it is sustained for any acceptable length of time. Fortunately, given my bent for dialectics, the work of Slavoj Žižek provides a source for dialectical psychoanalysis, either when I am on the couch or when I put the text on the couch, seating myself calmly in the half-gloom, asking questions, taking notes, voicing the occasional 'hmmm'. But Žižek's work is not merely dialectical psychoanalysis; it is more specifically dialectical Lacanianism, if I may use such an ugly descriptor. Through a series of spectacular studies Žižek has placed himself at the forefront of those who both interpret and transform Lacan's works. For Žižek the ingredients of such a development include involvement in the transformation of Yugoslavia, an appreciation of the Marxist heritage, and a predilection for popular culture. Behind Žižek and Lacan, of course, stands Freud, whose shadow looms over the whole of this work.

Dialectical Marxism and dialectical Lacanianism are then two of the main foods on which my mind feeds. There is, however, a third that comes from the agglutinate known as cultural criticism. In this case, it is the work of Meaghan Morris and, through her, the inaugural efforts of Michel de Certeau and Henri Lefebvre, who, with their concept of everyday life as an item worthy of intellectual study, must be part of any consideration of cultural criticism.[5] Indeed, it is from this final three that a crucial theoretical problem arises: what role, if any, does cultural criticism have in the domain of biblical criticism; or rather, what is the relation, if any, between these two apparently discrete disciplines?

BAD DEBTS

In response, I have recourse specifically to Lefebvre and de Certeau, although the argument that I derive from their work is a dialectical one. As for Lefebvre, the originator of the idea of 'everyday life', the point that interests me comes from his 'Notes Written One Sunday in the French Countryside,' a chapter of the *Critique of Everyday Life* (Lefebvre 1991). Religion is normally an item of attack for Lefebvre, heretical communist that he was, since it is tied up with philosophical and cultural forms, such as surrealism, that are opposed to everyday life, the life of the lower classes (1991: 127–9). Catholicism and, especially, Protestantism are complex ideologies that produce over-repressive, and eventually terrorist, societies where conflict and opposition are not tolerated (see Lefebvre 1971: 145–7). Yet, the power of religion – for de Certeau the church in France – is such that it permeates everyday life. Although dead, its form infiltrates and continues to influence.

> Theological faith is dead, metaphysical reason is dead. And yet they live on, they take on new life – insanely, absurdly – because the situation and the human conflicts from which they were born have not been resolved. Now these conflicts are not in the realm of thought alone, but in *everyday life*.
>
> (Lefebvre 1991: 141)

As one whose faith is now past, who discarded a commitment that was part of his rural youth, Lefebvre marks here also the continued power of religion over his own life. The church is that which held him strongest, evokes some deep longing for that lost commitment, and yet also makes him line up the church as an enemy of everyday life. It is, in short, that from which he has come, to which he no longer belongs but which still influences him. So also, the forms of religion are everywhere in daily life – 'The ritual gesture when a funeral procession goes by, words of insult, an "A-Dieu" when we part, a wish, a propitious phrase of greeting or thanks ... they are really religious, or potentially so' (1991: 226).

De Certeau exhibits a similar logic, albeit on a different level. My focus is the suggestion concerning the birth of the various disciplines of western scholarship. This may best take its designation from a volume of de Certeau's, *Le christianisme éclaté* (de Certeau and Domenach 1974), the dispersal or shattering of Christianity. The idea takes two major forms, one well trodden by sociologists, the other less used but with much greater potential. To begin with the less threatening argument: after noting, in *Le christianisme éclaté*, the dissipation of Christian discourse into society at large, and the appropriation of religious material by secular institutions and disciplines for 'civil religion', de Certeau traces a similar pattern with the interpretation of the Bible. Initially the church controlled interpretation of the Bible, so that interpretation – signalled by footnotes and marginal glosses – became more important than the biblical text itself. However, with the advent of capitalism, the modes of investigation appropriate to capitalism were used on the Bible. This begins with the claim that the individual is free to interpret the text as he or she likes, and then moves on to methods that are theatrical and scientific. This means

that in the very process of modern interpretation of the Bible there is mod-
elled the dispersal of religious functions outside the religious institutions
themselves (see de Certeau and Domenach 1974: 19–20).

Not a new idea, and if this is all de Certeau can say, then it is not particularly
remarkable. A stronger form of the argument, however, is that religion – specifically Christian theology, since de Certeau, himself a theologian (as well as
historian, psychoanalyst and cultural critic), focuses on Europe – is the originary
discipline that engendered the 'secular' disciplines that grew up and hived off
after the Enlightenment, when Christianity is both abandoned and unveiled
(de Certeau 1988: 179).[6] Historiography, sociology, psychology, philosophical ethics, and so on, all fall under this same logic, the same initial impetus
from theology itself. This is a massive and important thesis, with its own
curious contradiction:

> In every study devoted to it since the eighteenth century, religion has
> always presented this ambiguity of its object: for example, its past is
> by turns explained through the very sociology it has none the less
> organized, and offered as the explanation for this sociology which
> has replaced it. More generally, every society born and issued forth
> from a religious matrix (are there any other kinds of society?) must
> affront the relation that it keeps with its archeology. This problem is
> inscribed within contemporary culture by dint of the fact that reli-
> gious structures have been peeled away from religious contents in
> organizing rational forms of behavior. In this respect, the study of
> religion is tantamount to reflecting on what its contents have be-
> come in our societies (that is, 'religious phenomena'), in the name of
> what its formalities have also become in our scientific practice.
>
> (de Certeau 1988: 176)

The identification of such a contradiction is not to be read as a lament, as a
desire for a lost Christendom, but rather as a dialectical religious historicizing
of western scientific disciplines. It is no longer possible to think of the methods and formalities – 'the ways in which concepts or forms are constituted or
conceived by an act of human thinking' (Brammer 1992: 28) – as religious,
'since they have precisely ceased to be such' (de Certeau 1988: 175). The
forms have been 're-employed', as Ahearne points out (1995: 29), so that
what appear to be similar formal elements between theology and the modern
disciplines now operate in terms of other practices and systems.[7] As non-
religious disciplines that once began in theology, it is now possible to study
religion and theology as though from 'outside'. Thus, sociology analyses a
form of religion or theology through its organization, the nature of its hierarchy, its doctrinal themes and so on, as a type of society; sociolinguistics
interprets theological language as indices of sociocultural transformations;
individual religious affirmations become representations of psychological cat-

egories, and so on – in short, religious claims are understood as symptoms of something else, whether social, historical or psychological, rather than truth claims relating to belief (de Certeau 1987: 192–3). Another way of marking this shift is that religious content hides the conditions of its production. The end result is a 'science des religions' (de Certeau 1987: 195), study of religion that is no longer religious, an adjective which itself becomes enigmatic. Not only does such a change signal the transitions in 'formalities' from their originally religious content, but there is something simultaneously enlightening and inadequate about such post-religious approaches to religion. However, in a characteristic twist, de Certeau notes in regard to such disciplines: 'In a certain way we might consider the time of their religious "filling" as a moment in the history of these cultural forms' (1988: 175–6).

A more particular version of this thesis (and here I pursue the logic of de Certeau's argument beyond his own text) is possible as well: do not contemporary methods of literary and cultural criticism derive ultimately from biblical interpretation? As with religion, whose content is now studied with the methods that originated in theology, so also is the Bible's content now studied with methods that are no longer biblical but have their seeds in biblical studies. That is, the 'formalities' of structuralism, Russian formalism, new historicism, deconstruction, poststructuralism, Marxist literary criticism, ideological criticism, cultural criticism, and so on, are those which derive from biblical criticism, although their content is anything but biblical. If this is granted, then any new discipline, any new approach to the Bible is always already contained in the closed system, since these ways of reading owe their ultimate logic to theology and biblical studies.

It seems that there is an element of the return of the repressed – an idea and methodological option important for de Certeau – in the model of the dispersal of theology and the rise of scientific disciplines. With the suggestion that it is appropriate for these new methods to be used to study religion and the Bible it is as though a whole series of cheques are now waiting to be cashed. Biblical studies has for too long hidden from the consequences of the methods it unwittingly unleashed. And so now it is the revenge on biblical studies that must be enacted.

It is this logic that supplies the theoretical justification for what I do in this book – a reprisal, as it were, via cultural criticism on the Bible and biblical criticism, an accounting of old debts that reluctantly need to be paid.

UNDER THE SIGN OF THE CENSOR

There is, however, a second point of contact between biblical studies and cultural criticism that forms an underlying leitmotif of this work. For this 'point de capiton', this quilting point, to borrow a phrase from Lacan and Žižek, I rely on the work of Meaghan Morris and de Certeau, once again.

Although Meaghan Morris's claim to fame is through a series of studies on Sydney tower, shopping centres, television events, a country motel, and other sites where the everyday lives of people – especially women – intersect, I am interested in one particular paper and in one particular argument. In 'Banality in Cultural Studies' (1990) she breaks through the habitual reference to de Certeau's *The Practice of Everday Life* in nearly every piece of work she has written to offer a more sustained theoretical reflection.[8] And she gets to de Certeau through a dual annoyance in cultural studies itself: one embodied in the 'fatal charm' of Baudrillard's apocalyptic texts, in which everything in its hyper form ends up being its other, in which everything seems to disappear in the whorl of modernity or postmodernity. The other ('vox pop') is the 'banal seduction' of endless cultural studies papers and monographs that seem to rehash the same theme – the subversive promise of even the most degraded activities of popular culture.

In order to get beyond her annoyance at both 'fatalistic theory' and 'cheerily "making the best of things"' (1990: 26), Morris turns to de Certeau's *The Practice of Everyday Life* (1984). Like Fredric Jameson (someone whom Morris rarely cites) in his now famous chapter 'Reification and Utopia in Mass Culture' (1990: 9–34), Morris likes de Certeau's text because it argues 'for a double process of mobilizing the "weighty apparatus" of theories of ordinary language to analyze everyday practices *and* seeking to restore to those practices their logical and cultural legitimacy' (Morris 1990: 26). That is to say, popular culture needs more than its prophets of doom (a sort of elitism that insists on the depravity of mass culture) and its cheer-leaders (those swept away by the anti-intellectualism and populism of popular culture itself). Morris mobilizes a number of key elements from de Certeau's book – polemological and utopian spaces, strategies and tactics, writing and orality – and she notes some difficulties – his 'Everyman' is too much a man (but see Buchanan's criticism of essentializing the subject (1997: 185)) and his reliance on space betrays assumptions of permanency – yet she finds immense promise in the argument that popular culture is a way of operating, of making do. Thus, the most interesting thing cultural studies can do is see how lives are lived and how sites are constructed in the interstices of the vast socio-economic systems.

However, there is a particular thesis of de Certeau that Morris notes and on which I want to focus for a few moments, a thesis that is the dialectical twist at the heart of cultural studies itself. Curiously, this particular argument appears not in *The Practice of Everyday Life* but in 'The Beauty of the Dead: Nisard', co-written with Jacques Revel and Dominique Julia (1986).[9] The argument here is that the repression of popular or mass culture has, from a historical perspective, been that which has provided the very conditions for the study of popular culture itself. Further, it is precisely what has been repressed – the 'other' of popular culture – that may transform the analytical procedures that have been generated out of the repression of that same popular culture.

Charles Nisard, with his *Histoires des livres populaires et de la littérature de colportage* (1854) provides the historical condition and continued possibility for the study of popular culture. Appointed as under-secretary in the Ministry of Police, he was to collect, study, censor, and, where needed, proscribe and destroy the 'street literature' everywhere available in France. In the very process of censorship and policing, the study of popular culture is enabled. It is not only that Nisard used his position to gain access to the literature – it was not merely a ruse – for he maintained the moral condemnation with which the censorship was justified. The 'Commission for the Examination of Chapbooks' was to determine whether these books were contrary to 'order, morality, and religion'. Yet the learned, such as Nisard, would be able to resist their evil influence, thus enabling their preservation, at least as an object of study. All of which leads to the hypothesis: 'these strategies of popular culture take as their object *their own* origin. They pursue across the surface of texts, before their eyes, what is actually their own condition of possibility – the elimination of a popular menace' (de Certeau, Revel and Julia 1986: 128). Yet this inaugural 'murder', the primal violence, is present only as a figure or a trace, as lost origin or 'as the unfound reality', forgotten as an 'object or result of rigorous procedures' (1986: 128). Popular culture, then, becomes a corpse, a body over and through which the scalpel of the coroner/critic incises its own patterns and pictures.[10]

Nevertheless, as a result of Nisard's purge, and many others like it that followed, a select amount of literature and other items of popular culture remained in circulation (those banned would also be highly sought after). On the basis of such material de Certeau, Revel and Julia track a process of idealization of the popular and its connection with the category of 'folklore' (see Schirato 1993: 284). There developed a 'learned nostalgia' (Ahearne 1995: 133) for a constructed realm of the popular. The corpse had now been beautified, sanitized; thus 'the beauty of the dead'. The popular is therefore valorized by those who have constructed the object of study,[11] ignoring and forgetting the more dangerous cultural products that people such as Nisard collected and that remained available. Yet, it is the return of these 'other' elements that interests de Certeau in his work, and this is then the programme of *The Practice of Everyday Life* which may be read, as Kinser suggests (1992: 81), as a reaction against half a century of gloom about ordinary pursuits.

There is also a specific historical dimension to this argument by de Certeau: Nisard's task of censorship and writing took place in the shadow of the 1848 revolutions, the republican days of February and June, and the restoration of the Empire in 1852. Nisard began his task on the last day of November of that year. In fact, the commission headed by Nisard was in response to the political concerns such literature generated, the lampooning of the rich and the divisions such literature would exacerbate. 'The collector's interest is a correlate of the repression used to exorcise the revolutionary danger which, as the days of June 1848 had demonstrated, was still very close, lying dormant' (de Certeau,

Revel and Julia 1986: 124). The repression of popular culture is part of the repression of popular revolutionary currents. Eliminate the danger, censor and then study the body preserved.

In another place (Boer forthcoming) I trace this motif of birth-in-death throughout de Certeau's work, the pattern of preservation and study that arises from repression, of the veneration and reverence for a body preserved, and occasionally cut up and eaten: it appears in de Certeau's study of popular culture, linguistics, orality and writing, heterology, possession and mysticism, in the responses to hagiography by establishment religion, and in the effect of the absent body of Jesus on the church itself. And of course the generation of scientific disciplines and literary criticism that I noted in the previous section have their triggers in the Enlightenment's repression and removal of theology from its position of intellectual and cultural dominance. In each case the pattern differs to some degree, taking on the contours of the issue in question, but the underlying logic remains the same.

If the moment of the censor is that which enables cultural studies, then I would suggest that a similar logic underlies the possibility of biblical studies, although de Certeau himself does not make the connection. Initially, a small selection of religious material is approved and canonized, while the bulk is simultaneously tolerated as useful and censored as a source of error. What was all 'hagiography' to begin with is selected and repressed. Here, once again, is the logic of Nisard: the problem of (religious) literature is that its study is at the same time a process of censorship. So it is that biblical studies is born. The very process of selecting a sacred canon from a wider range of material, the proscription, and at times destruction, of that which is left over is the ground for a discipline like biblical studies. It arises from the simultaneous selection of some literature and repression of the rest. What has been preserved is a little like the dangerous chapbooks kept by Nisard: now that part at least is left and preserved, it may be studied.

Here, then, lies the 'point de capiton', the convergence between biblical studies and the study of popular culture, both of which operate under the sign of the Censor. For cultural studies the moment of censorship is the originating and empowering moment itself: popular culture lives under the proscription of intellectuals, the police – in short, those who set the dominant ideological agenda. It is a proscription that is the reason for study. Similarly, religious literature – hagiography, apocrypha, superstition and so on – operates under a comparable proscription. Here the clerics censor such literature, but in the process they enable its study, preserving some as canon and banning the rest. In this context biblical studies arises. But this also applies to the topics of the individual chapters that follow; in each it is possible to locate censorship as an inevitable and enabling context – for queer studies, Hitchcock and graphic violence, pornography, sex work, heavy metal and prophecy, science fiction and Lamentations, and fast food.

Of course, although de Certeau and I partake of such censorship in our very acts of criticism, we also subscribe to the vital Freudian notion of *le retour de refoulé* the 'return of the repressed', the primal murder and its perpetual guilt, the repression of sexuality and its return in dreams. While this may of course apply to the argument I have traced regarding the possibility of both biblical studies and cultural studies, it is more germane to the tale of what is repressed.

> For the social sciences have analyzed in terms of 'popular culture' the functionings that are fundamental to our urban and modern culture, but that are held to be illegitimate or negligible in the official discourses of modernity. Just as sexuality repressed by bourgeois morality returned in the dreams of Freud's patients, these functions giving structure to human sociality, denied by the stubborn ideology of writing, of production, and of specialized technologies, are returning in our social and cultural space (which they never left in the first place) under the cover of 'popular culture'.
>
> (de Certeau 1997a: 101)

TERMINOLOGY

It remains to deal with a few items of clarification and terminology: Bible, culture, popular or mass culture, high or serious culture, and cultural criticism. A dilemma around which much of my discussion turns is the question of Bible and culture. My theoretical starting point is that the Bible is one dimension of (mostly 'western') culture, and that it is a crucial subunit of the wider cultural phenomenon of Christianity. My understanding of culture is influenced by Marxist thought, in which culture, politics, ideology and the legal system are related in a host of complex ways with each other and then as a block with economics, mediated through the question of social relationships. In this book, 'culture' refers to capitalist culture, or the culture that is characteristic of capitalism. The products of culture that I will consider are more obviously items from capitalist culture, but I also take the Bible as a literary text that has its place in, that is now read as an item of, this culture (and not, say, of feudalism). Having assumed this basic framework, the book may be regarded as an effort to explore the various ways in which the Bible is a part of culture (or at least of those cultures in which it has played a part). Therefore, these essays treat the biblical texts and the texts of contemporary culture in the following terms: an 'application' of features of one part of contemporary culture in order to interpret the Bible, which is now understood as another part of present culture ('Queer Heroes', 'Pawing through Garbage'); an approach to both the Bible and a cultural product using the same methods, which then serves to put both on an even level ('Cows with Guns', 'Ezekiel's Axl', 'Graves of Craving'); the possible foundational role of the Bible, which may now be read as a subtext of culture ('Night Sprinkles', 'Stolen Water'). In other words, I cover three possibilities in the relationship between the biblical texts and other cultural products – the primacy of those other products, the equality of the two poles, and the primacy of the Bible.

While cultural criticism is often used in the broadest sense of the study of culture as such, it seems to me that what is known as cultural criticism, particularly that which has arisen following the pioneering work of de Certeau and Lefebvre, but also Stuart Hall and Lawrence Grossberg, is interested in popular or mass culture. By 'popular culture' I refer in the first instance to working class culture: it is the collection of cultural products that has traditionally been produced and consumed by working class people. In this respect it is part of the class consciousness of the working class. There is a second sense that overlaps with this primary one: the production of material by the ruling classes, giving voice to ruling class ideas and beliefs, for popular consumption. The most obvious forms of this material are those of a nationalist or patriotic odour. Since the material I consider is often part of the overlap between these two senses of popular culture, my reading is less populist than critical. The use of 'mass' or 'popular' for both types of material indicates that these particular cultural products have the largest audience or consumption rate in comparison to other cultural products. It is, in short, what most people consume, including vast sections of the middle class (even though this may be denied). 'High culture', by contrast, is that which has been claimed by the middle class, at least officially. Here belong 'serious' literature, artistic films, and a range of institutions such as the opera, museum, art gallery and so on. (In proper dialectical fashion it is of course the case that critical socialist possibilities sometimes arise from this realm as well.) The terminology of high and serious versus mass and popular signifies a whole range of value judgements that come from the side of high culture. Given these class connections, it is not for nothing that cultural studies, the study of popular culture, arose out of a strong Marxist background. In western capitalism the Bible has by and large been claimed as a major item of 'serious' culture, a constitutive document of the canon of high literature. In the conjunction of biblical texts and those of popular culture, and the theoretical runover between them, I will be breaching the distinction between serious and popular culture. Indeed, Fredric Jameson has argued time and again that the distinction between high and mass culture is a modernist one, and that the collapse of the two is distinctly postmodern.

As for the organization of this volume, the relation between the essays is less one of a consistent argument than multiple connections and overlaps that may be linked in a variety of ways, a description for which the term 'rhizome' is most appropriate (Deleuze and Guattari 1987: 3–25). Thus, themes such as film, sex, gender, violence, death, food, utopia, and the possibility of revolution, recur in different places, somewhat like a rabbit warren or mouse holes. This study is then less like a tree and its roots, or a genetic axis, and more like the subterranean systems of bulbs and tubers, or the relations of rats and ants. 'Queer Heroes' is first, pursuing the queer logic of heroes, sending a trajectory from Hollywood action films through to biblical heroes. In doing so, I seek out the implications of queer theory for biblical studies, as well as ask a few questions of that theory itself. There follows 'Cows With Guns', an interweaving of biblical and Hitchcock texts on graphic violence, interpreted by means of the ideas of sadistic identification and hegemony. 'Night Sprinkles' attempts a small rereading of the Song of Songs as hard core pornography, whereas as 'Stolen Water Is Sweeter, Stolen Bread Tastes Better' searches out the whore stigma in contemporary sex work and Proverbs 1–9. The fifth chapter, 'Ezekiel's Axl', juxtaposes heavy metal and Israelite prophecy by means of anarchism, carnival, ecstasy and hegemony. Science fiction appears in 'Pawing Through Garbage', where the dystopian logic of both the Strugatsky brothers and Lamentations is pursued for its utopian glimpses. Finally, I come to rest at my local Maccas, reflecting on fast food in capitalism and in the Bible with the assistance of Lévi-Strauss.

Yet, alongside the rhizomatic, there is an alternative cohesion to my argument, in that I have organized the chapters in terms of an unfolding, somewhat allegorical, story …

THE EXPLODING ELEPHANT

Part of what Freud was repressing in his embrace of Oedipus were fantasies that structured his sentiments for Fliess – fantasies of male menstruation, anal penetration, and homosexual impregnation.

(Fuss 1995: 7)

The breast … may serve to symbolize the most profound lost object.

(Lacan 1994: 198)

(I pulled the jacket close to my bare skin, pressed the studs together and thrust my hands in its pockets. Although worn and a little grimy from overuse, the wool was still rough and coarse enough to itch and scratch, sending painfully pleasurable sensations through the nerve endings just off my skin's surface. As usual, my nipples enjoyed it the most, scraped and irritated and yearning for more of the crude wool fibres. Lost for a moment in an old pleasure – why did it ever have to end? – I made the most of the walk up the hill, pushing against the westerly wind with my cap peak down to prevent the wind whipping it away. Some of the August westerly squeezed through the openings between the studs in the front, fingering my chest and stomach with cold nails, standing the fine hairs there on end, puckering the follicles in goose bumps. A rare pair of woolen pants clung to my legs. Soon the wind was on my left as I turned right on

Windsor Road, the traffic producing its usual roar, although the fumes were torn protesting off into the east.

Murphy's Garage appeared, the weathered vehicle doors on the battered green building hanging as though they had retired a century ago. The welcome sight of the dilapidated building was marred by the jumble of cop cars, plain and marked, as well as an ambulance. I drew near to a familiar face. 'Michal,' I called, 'what's going on?' She stood back to let me look in through what used to be a fly door. 'Four dead,' she said, 'Old Murphy here, and there's a body, a teenager, behind the baseball reserve, and then two over on Redbank Road, in their thirties, we think.' 'Any connection?' 'None that we can make out, but that's your job.')

1

QUEER HEROES

Queer means QUEER AS FUCK. ... I'm so tired of reading about
what I should be! If I'd swallowed that crap, I'd be married with kids
now, attending church each Sunday morning and sneaking off every
Sunday arvo to the beats under the pretext of pokies or pub-mates.
Not that there's *anything* wrong with that. Some of my queerest fucks
have sported baby-restraints in the back seat.

> (Ted Gott, side bar in Berry and Jagose 1996: 10)

[T]hough your sins are like scarlet, they shall be like snow; though
they are red like crimson, they shall become like wool.

> (Isaiah 1:18)

[T]hey shall have nothing of wool on them ...

> (Ezekiel 44:17)

*(It was the uniforms that had first attracted me, the mean blue, the
pressed shirts and pants, the studs and lapels, stiff caps, leather jackets
and the heavy, steady boots. When I found that the clothing was made of
pure wool, I was enraptured. I wore them without protection, hard up
against my skin. I sought out the roughest wool I could find, railing
silently against the desire of the wool industry to come up with ever
smoother fabrics, less irritable fibres. Walking the city beat was to be in a
continual state of ecstasy. I always seemed to miss the crimes.)*

Are all our heroes queer? It seems so, at least with regard to the action hero,
found mainly in contemporary film, and with regard to the biblical hero.
Both are subject to a play between active and passive roles. In order to situate
this argument, however, I need to detour through queer theory itself. Having
done so, I dwell for a while on action films and their heroes, thereby providing a critical context, a certain exegetical expectation, for reading the story of
David and Jonathan in 1 Samuel 18–20.

ESSENTIALISM, AGAIN ...

I am saying nothing new by observing that queer theory is a part of the debate between constructionism and essentialism (or at least the proponents of

13

these positions). Constructionism – that one's identity is constructed out of the myriad social, cultural and linguistic cross-currents in which one lives – may in one sense be regarded as part of the long process of disenchantment and denaturalization that begins with the Enlightenment; whereas religion was the first, sexuality is one of the last to feel its effects. It would seem that constructionism has taken the field, the arguments and analyses making use of constructionism moving in to ever more areas of research as essentialism retreats in disarray. Indeed, the prime polemical task now seems to involve identifying the stench of the decaying essentialist corpse hidden in the basement of one another's writing.[1]

The specific contribution of queer theory, which partakes of but is not to be completely identified with constructionism, is to focus on the operation of the heterosexual/homosexual binary and on the politics of knowledge and difference. According to Seidman (1996), queer theory arose in the context of the New Right backlash of the 1980s, to which the response was a more radical politics of difference influenced by poststructuralism and Lacan. Over against the unified homosexual identity there was posited a multiple, unstable and regulatory process.

> Queer theory is suggesting that the study of homosexuality should not be a study of a minority – the making of the lesbian/gay/bisexual subject – but a study of those knowledges and social practices that organize 'society' as a whole by sexualizing – heterosexualizing or homosexualizing – bodies, desires, acts, identities, social relations, knowledges, culture, and social institutions.[2]
>
> (Seidman 1996: 13)

Thus, the contentious edge of queer theory is the attack on identity politics and its implicit essentialism that had been crucial for lesbian, gay and bisexual activism from the sixties onward, especially after the Stonewall riots of 1968.[3] (Here also is the mark of the Censor on queer theory and activism.) Indeed, some of the important early texts of queer theory equivocate on precisely this dilemma – to follow the direction of much underground consumption of popular culture and seek a referent for queer readings in the semi-concealed gay or lesbian identifications of the various stars, film directors, writers and so on; or to strike out in an anti-essentialist direction with the risk of losing one's moorings in the hard won space of gay, lesbian and bisexual cultural interpretation that had been established. A prime example of such an ambivalence is Alexander Doty's *Making Things Perfectly Queer* (1993, especially 17–38),[4] but it also bedevils collections such as *Out in Culture* (1995), edited by Doty and Cory Creekmur. In both cases there is a desire to embrace the poststructuralist logic of queer theory but there is also a wariness of the apparent fluidity of the identities thus attained, a wariness manifested in the search for fixed reference points in the sexual identity of individuals.

What attracts me about queer theory is the type of reading tactics it enables, especially that of 'queering the text', of reading straight texts and cultural products as queer.[5] This means that the search for a firm referent is only a small part of queer readings. Its larger programme is to bypass or outsmart the straight Censor and discover a wealth of divergent sexual constructions in any one text. There are two debts for such a tactic, one to camp and the other to the swirling discussions of performativity.

Despite the fact that the cultural products – both biblical and contemporary – with which I am dealing are not quite campy enough (although Abraham or Samson or Yahweh as high camp would be infinitely more attractive), the underlying logic of camp is what I draw upon. Identified, desexualized, depoliticized, privatized and with the connotations of homosexuality minimized in the landmark essay of Susan Sontag (1994: 275–92)[6] – in which she argued for Camp (capital C) as an unintentional 'sensibility' rather than an 'idea' – the study of camp has sought to turn the tables on conventional readings of camp: whereas the gay, lesbian and bisexual dimensions of camp were seen as one aspect (and a small one at that), subsequent critics have argued that camp is primarily a queer activity that has been coopted by straight society (Robertson 1996: 4). Camp generates a 'sense of too-muchness, the excess, or inappropriateness, produces a sudden self-consciousness in the viewer, but one that needn't dissolve the basic meaning of the gesture' (LaValley 1995: 63). It is characterized by the appropriation and redefinition on terms of gender, sexuality and so on, of cultural products – like stars, fashion and genres – that come from an earlier moment of production but have lost their cultural force. While there has been some debate over the territory and ownership of camp – is it a gay male preserve (Meyer 1994)? is there a feminist camp (Robertson 1996)? and what about straight camp (Creekmur and Doty 1995)? – the agreement lies with its queerness. Yet, camp is also used again and again in straight cultural products: in doing so, however, these cultural products partake, albeit unwittingly and therefore more powerfully, of gay, lesbian, bisexual and transgender assumptions. 'In other words, camp has the ability to "queer" straight culture by asserting that there is queerness at the core of mainstream culture even though that culture tirelessly insists that its images, ideologies, and readings were always only about heterosexuality' (Creekmur and Doty 1995: 3).[7]

Perhaps the most successful way an anti-essentialist or constructionist position has been developed is in terms of understanding identity as performance or masquerade, as the staging of identities in particular ways and for particular audiences. Judith Butler, following on from Lacan, is of course most closely associated with such arguments in relation to gender (1990; 1991; 1993), but the argument has made its way into other areas as well. Butler has been criticized for excluding questions of class and economics from her materialism (Ebert 1996; Hennessy 1995; on a different level see Dean 1993), but she has tempered the voluntariness of the theatrical metaphor of performance (see

Butler 1993). Yet, it is precisely this theatricality that stands out when the item under discussion involves acting, particularly acting that foregrounds masculinity or femininity (Holmlund 1993). For this reason I am interested in the performance of masculinity in action films.

Queer, camp, performance – all that remains is to invoke the work of Eve Kosofsky Sedgwick, especially her *Epistemology of the Closet* (1994), where the argument is no less than that twentieth century western culture has been shaped by the desire and effort for, yet inability to achieve, homo/heterosexual definition. It is precisely this effort at definition and the mutual dependence of both sides of the slash that I pursue in my readings of action film heroes and the figure of David. In both cases there is the denial of a queer subtext while simultaneously foregrounding the queer turn itself.[8]

> *(Although I am not a leather person myself, there were some who were a little more than mildly excited about law enforcement leather. Not only were there the obligatory jackets made of cured, black, heavy cowhide, but some of the boots could lace or zip almost all the way up your calves. And then, for the motorcycle units, full leathers were available – tight pants, jackets, boots, gloves, even the occasional leather cap under the helmet. The various leg braces, back supports, corsets, shoulder guards and vests added another dimension again. Whenever I saw one of these guys, I couldn't help thinking of Tom of Finland.)*

'MY OWN PRIVATE KEANU'[9]

> For it is *deviance* from the demands of strict straight/heterosexual paradigms (however they are defined in a given time and place) that most often defines and describes our sexualized and/or gendered pleasures and positions in relation to movies, television, videos, and popular music. Indeed, many so-called straight mass culture texts encourage 'deviant' erotic and/or gendered responses and pleasures in straight viewers.
>
> (Doty 1995: 85)

> Don't play no faggots.
> (Sylvester Stallone to Perry King in Howes 1993: 5)

It seems that mainstream commercial films, along with bestseller novels, have inherited the strong generic expectations that formerly belonged to folklore and the realm of oral culture. This is not to say that genre is exclusively the domain of popular culture in the postmodern moment, but that the strictures of genre are much stronger when the question of profit becomes more explicit. (By genre I refer not so much to a relatively stable set of features but rather to a convergence or intersection of features from other genres, which are themselves intersections of so many others.) Experimental, less financially successful films are then set over against the crassness of mainstream commercial film in the belief – whose justification always seems to escape me – that such films are more authentic or worth serious intellectual attention.

Thus, the action film – the epitome of all that is anti-SNAG, it would seem – begins with an incident, sometimes a minor one, that soon escalates into a potential disaster of global dimensions. The hero, inevitably a social misfit, is then called upon, often from retirement, in order to take on an old foe whom he understands better than any other (is there not a hint of Hegel here?). Alternatively, the hero happens upon a situation in which he then becomes involved in order to avoid harm to (good) people. There follows a range of sequences, requiring varying degrees of violent conflict, in which hero and villain wear each other down until closure is achieved through a fight to the death. The hero, although battered and almost broken, wins through, the gladiatorial combat saving the group/town/city/nation/earth.

However, the fundamental feature of the action hero is the play between activity and passivity, between being the subject and object of the verb, which is both 'to gaze' and 'to strike out'. This ambivalent play is embodied in the fetish of male bodies in action films.[10] For a generic feature of the action film is the moment of bodily exposure, when the hero shows his body for visual consumption, willfully or not. It signifies at first glance an assertion of male muscular presence, a seriousness of the business at hand. Normally, such a strip-down takes place for exercise or training, or for the business end of the film when some 'real' work needs to be done – in disposing of bad guys and engaging in some punishing hand-to-hand combat with the arch-villain.[11] Yet, at the same time this active body is bared to be gazed upon and ogled.

What is noticeable about the male torsos shown on screen is their hairlessness. The hirsute bodies of older heroes, like Rock Hudson, have given way to depilated pectorals and abdominals. It is not so much the distinction from animality, like Enkidu's shift from hairy wild man/animal to smooth human in the *Epic of Gilgamesh*, but rather that depilation in western cultures is conventionally a female trait. The removal of hair is, then, not only a civilizing move, but also a feminizing one.

(I had always preferred the hairy gendarmes: a deep five o'clock shadow, bushy nostrils, fine dark hair between the cheeks and around the nipples, long and greasy on their heads.)

The removal of hair brings about an intense focus on the skin. In a similar way that the conventionally depilated female draws visual attention to the skin, so also does the depilated hero. But there is another angle on the skin that comes as it were from inside: in the same way that the removal of external foliage reveals that which lies beneath, the alteration of the shape and the size of the muscles 'beneath' draws attention not so much to the muscles themselves but to the skin that they form. (In fact, it is only the voluntary and striated muscles, not the smooth and involuntary muscles, that seem to be of interest.) Although the talk is always of muscle size and definition, and although there is a wide interest in body-building circles in muscle anatomy, it is ultimately the skin itself that counts. Thus, before a posing session, body-builders will seek to produce a cling-wrap effect, reducing as far as possible subcutaneous fat and water so that the skin will cling as closely as possible to the muscles themselves. In the end, it does not really matter what is under the skin – muscle, silicon, collagen – so long as the desired shape is achieved.

And what is interesting here is the shape of that skin. For body-builders seek immensely rounded skin shapes. The curving shoulders, rippling backs, bulking upper and forearms, shapely thighs and calves, and the reduction of the penis for male builders – all of these give off a series of contradictory messages in relation to dominant conventions regarding body, or rather skin, shape. For the rounded and curved shapes of male body-builders evoke the now older western expectations of the curved female, with large breasts, fuller arms and thighs, and a small waist. Indeed, the desire for silicon implants in male pectorals mirrors the use of such implants in female breasts. Further, in female body-building, but also in gay body-building, the desire is not so much for rounded bulk, but for definition, for the 'cut' body, in which the angles are sharper and the lines more angular – older conventions for males are now appropriated for women and gay men.

These bodies are, finally, there to be looked at, gazed upon, admired. Like the female pin-up, built male bodies demand the gaze: is not the whole purpose of body-building, with its posing routines and competitions, finally to have the body looked at and assessed? The skin, rippled, stripped and cling-wrap tight, is nothing but a screen upon which the action figure is projected and looked at. This skin/screen is therefore an object of passivity: the beefcake has everything done to him. Yet, the particular genre of film that is projected upon this skin/screen is the action film, as though to counteract the passivity of the body-builder and cinema itself. As Tasker (in a rare moment of insight) suggests, 'the muscular male hero is caught by the camera, he is both posed and in motion at the same time' (1993a: 77). This is the crucial contradiction of action film (and, I will suggest below, of the story of David), which is too easily connected with the contradiction of masculinity and feminity.

(The station gym of course had a steady stream of jocks. Although the older ones had gone to seed, cigarettes and beer guts, the younger ones sweated out their reps. Money was a little tight, so it was mostly free weights, but the sight of jumbled leathers, woollen uniforms, boots, caps, and gloves in the locker room was enough to draw me in. Small moustaches, cropped hair, sweetly sweating and pumped bodies greeted me on each entry. And then there were the showers ...)

In this light we can understand the unveiling of hero bodies in action films. So, when Jean Claude van Damme, Dennis Rodman and Mickey Rourke reveal their torsos in *Double Team* (Hark 1997), the codes are very mixed: the intentional messages of male virility dissipate before codes that identify such bodies as in some way feminine. They are, in other words, both heroes and sissies all at once. The skin that we see, depilated and shaped to curve, is one that is as much feminized as it is masculinized. Further, these bodies present evidence of hard 'work' to get them built, yet also ask to be looked at and desired. And how many bodies like this have I seen in action films – Sylvester Stallone, Arnold Schwarzenegger, Jean Claude van Damme, Dennis Rodman, Val Kilmer, Rutger Hauer, Dolf Lundgren, Steven Segal, Chuck Norris, Mickey Rourke, Mel Gibson, even Dean Cain as Superman in television's *Lois and Clark*? The heat of competition has been felt by those with softer, more squishy, or thinner bodies: thus the later bodies of Kurt Russell, Michael Douglas and even Clint Eastwood have more shapely skin than their earlier manifestations.

> *(Law enforcement and machismo were synonymous at this station, as elsewhere. We were big men, protecting the law, intimidating with our physical presence, proud of our ability to squeeze a confession out of the most innocent looking suspect. But we did it with grace, poise, and flexed lats.)*

Thus far I have collected a few bodies at work, rounded, shaved, ambiguously masculine, passive and active. But this is only the beginning of an argument, so some more work needs to be done before the queer logic of these films becomes apparent. One action hero I have not mentioned thus far is Keanu Reeves (although his repertoire is not purely action): Keanu also bares his torso in most of his films, but there is a deeper ambiguity about all of this. For Reeves takes with him rumours of gay proclivities that have never been made public: he is in many respects the classic closet gay (everyone knows but pretends not to, while the closet knows everyone knows but pretends, with them, that they don't know). Although he has made a film in which he plays a hustler – *My Own Private Idaho*, a remarkable remake of *Henry IV, Pt II* in terms of a road movie by Gus van Sant (1991) – even here a distinction is made in the surreal scene in the sex shop, where he speaks from a *Male Call* magazine cover: 'It's when you start doing it for free that you start growing wings ... you grow wings and become a fairy' (Van Sant 1993: 107). Later, when River Phoenix (Mike) declares his love in a mostly improvised dialogue for Reeves (Scott), the latter replies 'Two guys can't love each other ... I only have sex for money' (Van Sant 1993: 160), a sentiment reinforced in the later sex scene of Scott and Carmella. Yet the very need to make such a distinction begs its arbitrariness. Despite efforts to cast him in romantic or dramatic roles (*The Devil's Advocate*, Taylor Hackford 1998) Reeves has had a substantial number of gay fans since his brief appearance in the ice hockey film *Youngblood* (1986, starring Rob Lowe). Admitting his limits as an actor, they have followed him through the boy–man appearances in *River's Edge* (1987), *Permanent Record* (1988), *Bill & Ted's Excellent Adventure* (1989) and *Bill & Ted's Bogus Journey* (1991), and then felt let down by his attempts to play an adult role in Coppola's *Dracula* (1993) and Branagh's *Much Ado About Nothing* (1993).

Yet, it is precisely in the action films that Keanu's greatest gay appeal lies, according to Paul Burston (1995: 34–5). In fact, I want to suggest that Keanu Reeves embodies in many respects the ambiguities of the male action hero. Cast as a straight action hero, he is not so much the anomaly but the underlying logic of such queer heroes.[12] Thus, in *Point Break* (Bigelow 1991) he plays FBI agent Johnny Utah who investigates a group of surfing bank robbers headed by Bodhi (Patrick Swayze); a fellow cop describes Reeves as 'Young, dumb and full of come'. A campy spoof of the buddy action movie, in which the key clue is a tan line on a surfer's bare ass, Reeves and Swayze develop an intense erotic bond; '(d)espite the fact that homosexual acts never fully enter the picture, it remains the queerest thing that Keanu has committed himself to' (Burston 1995: 34; see Tasker 1993a: 162–4). In *Speed* (De Bont 1994) Reeves is the butch LAPD cop Jack Traven who comes in to solve the problem of the runaway bus, on which a bomb is set to explode if the bus drops below 50 mph. The gay coding here comes to the surface when, as Žižek suggests (1996: 27), it takes the violence and narrow escape of the ending to put Keanu, by accident, in the arms of Sandra Bullock. Only such force is able to achieve the hetero Hollywood couple.[13] Similarly, in *Chain Reaction* (1996) it takes the explosion of the cold fusion hydrogen reactor to get Reeves and Rachel Weisz (Dr Sinclair) finally to embrace. Yet he is virile, muscular, daring, strong and brutal when he needs to be – all the features of a good action hero. 'With his gym-toned body and number two crop, Keanu's appearance in *Speed* is the best facsimile yet of all that gay men desire: an action man with gripping hands and eager, come-fuck-me eyes' (Burston 1995: 35).[14]

The deeper queer logic of action films placed in sharp relief by Keanu Reeves may be located with relative ease by anyone with a reasonable diet of such films. For example, in the big-budget revival of the action formula of the 1970s – *Action Jackson* (Baxley 1988) – Action (Carl Weathers playing a rare black male lead) is rehabilitating Sydney, a drug addict and prostitute. She asks him, for the third time, whether he wants a fuck, only to receive a negative reply from a semi-naked Jackson. 'You gotta be either queer or a cop?' she says. 'Well, I'm not queer' he answers.[15]

The most significant group of action films are those with a pair of males who team up to deal with the bad guys – the conventional buddy film, often a western (paradigms here are The Cisco Kid and Pancho, the Lone Ranger and Tonto, Butch Cassidy and the Sundance Kid) or a cop film (the inaugural pair being Batman and Robin).[16] For example, *The Last Boy Scout* (Scott 1991), has the white and black team of Bruce Willis as down-and-out detective Joe Hallenbeck and Damon Wayans as the flamboyantly dressed (leather pants, red leather jacket) footballer Jimmy Dix. They work together to uncover high level corruption. Early in the film the initial conflict between the two dissolves into cooperation, articulated in a dialogue that is nervous about gay associations.

> 'Say man,' says Jimmy, 'you ever play ball? You gotta good build.'
> 'You a fag?' asks Hallenbeck.
> 'No, I'm just trying to break the ice.'
> 'I like ice; leave it alone.'
> 'You're a lot of fun to be with,' Jimmy responds.

The attempt to dispel the homoerotic dimensions of their association merely serves to foreground it all the more. As Fuchs suggests, 'the cop–buddy team must always deny and fulfill what Eve Sedgwick terms "male homosocial desire", the continuum from homosexuality to homophobia and back again' (Fuchs 1993: 194–5). The destruction of villains and buildings at the climax of the film functions then as a psychosexual display, an externalization of their erotic attraction and a resolution of differences; yet, at the same time, suggests Fuchs, these 'resolutions' foreground the irresolvable tensions of homoeroticism and homophobia: this is the 'buddy politic' (1993: 196).[17]

Another pairing is equally queer: the action hero and his opponent. Normally, they are indistinguishable in physical prowess, sharpness of reflex and in muscle mass, so it is the softer side that sets the hero apart. In between the regular destruction of human bodies, the hero shows signs variously of compassion, understanding, world weariness, humour and concern, over against the villain's obligatory cruelty and hardness. The fight to the death itself is often highly orgasmic and homoerotic. Protagonists that resolve their differences not so much through a fight to the death but through conflict for top spot appear in *Top Gun* (Scott 1986), in which the homoeroticism of flying jackets, male military locker rooms, flying jargon ('this guy's hot on my tail', 'this boy's all over me', 'my dick, my ass') and male bonding are thick on the ground. The major bonding scene at the end of the film is between the Cruise character Maverick and the blond boy Iceman (Val Kilmer).

(Perhaps my favourite beat was with the bicycle unit. Although the bikes were standard issue and nothing to salivate over – how were we ever going to catch a speeding cyclist? – we had to wear, thankfully, the regulation cycle unit gear of tight wool shorts and short-sleeved shirts. Rolled up like muscle-T's, with our boots clamped into pedals and woollen shorts rubbing back and forth we pedalled rhythmically around Parramatta, watching one another's shapely thighs. A light layer of sweat made the shorts even more prickly. Although we went in pairs – Jonathan and I, Keanu and I, Jonathan and David, David and I, Keanu and Jonathan, Keanu and David – we never resolved any of the major threats to the world.)

The queer logic of action films, the homo/hetero definition that Sedgwick identifies as crucial, the active/passive play, registers most sharply in the buddy film *Double Team* (Hark 1997), starring Jean Claude van Damme[18] and the flamboyant Dennis Rodman, an already distinctly camp basketball persona before his work in film. (As with many buddy action films, such as the *Lethal Weapon* series (Donner 1987; 1989; 1992; 1998), homoerotic tension is displaced onto race (see Tasker 1993a: 45).) Rodman is the queer double of Van Damme (Quinn), who finds Rodman in a gay nightclub in Antwerp, dressed in purple pants that cut low at his navel and a short silver top that barely covers his breasts. His hair varies between orange, yellow and white, and he has various pieces of metal in tongue, nose, ear and navel. At the same time he is well-muscled – shown off later when he strips off his shirt to rescue Quinn's wife and newborn baby boy from the villain Stavros (Mickey Rourke). It is almost as though Quinn's hetero status must be asserted through being a breeder, since the teaming between him and Rodman is distinctly homoerotic – they 'accidentally' embrace on two occasions. The film is one of the best examples of my argument about the queer underside or alter-ego of the action hero. Here queer and straight have been split apart and given different but closely intertwined character roles, although they fill the single character slot of the action hero. To borrow an idea from Edelman (1995; also Dowsett 1996: 26), in *Double Team* the double character signals a simultaneous repression of the anal – such a refusal being constitutive of heterosexuality – and its acceptance and eroticization.

DAVID THE 'COCK COLLECTOR'

> … it was less David's music than his buttocks which relieved the King. … He let my father King Saul make love to him when that was my father's need; he lay with my brother Jonathan, letting him kiss his feet, his thighs, his wrists, his throat; and in the night in which I lost my restraint and spoke to him in anger, he came to me, later, and took me. (Princess Michal to Ethan ben Hoshaiah, historian)
>
> (Heym 1972: 35)

> Young, dumb, and full of come.
>
> (Fellow cop on Keanu Reeves in *Point Break*)

The story of David and Jonathan in 1 Samuel 18–20 is in some respects an obvious text with which to make a connection to the queer logic of action films. In fact, my reading of action heroes provides a context, a frame of mind, from which this story may be read. Apart from reading it as a paradigmatic case for biblical heroes, the text demands attention since there is a chequered history of interpretation of this story at both a popular and more critical level. In what follows there are five areas: the reception of the text; David as action hero; his relations with Saul's family; his relationship with Jonathan; and a subtext of sexual signifiers. Throughout I am interested in the significance of the passive/active distinction. The underlying question, of course, is not only whether David is a queer hero, but whether he is a *fucking*, or a *fucked*, hero.[19]

The bulk of attention in the research of male-to-male sexual acts (there are no explicit references to female-to-female acts) in the Hebrew Bible is directed to those texts where it is explicitly mentioned – the stories in Genesis 19 and Judges 19, and the prohibitions in Leviticus 18:22 and 20:13 (see, for example, the revisionist debate in Boswell 1980: 92–102 and Boughton 1992; also Niditch 1982; Stone 1995; 1997). However, 1 Samuel 18–20 has its own share of interpreters, both within and outside biblical criticism. Fewell and Gunn (1993: 148–151), as well as Schroer and Staubli (1996), have attempted to explore what has long been denied in biblical scholarship but has had a currency in popular gay readings of the text (see Howes 1993: 172) and in the work of John Boswell (1995).

Most commentators on 1 Samuel 18–20 have been circumspect, preferring the closet of biblical criticism (these critics will peer above the following text at various points). By contrast, Fewell and Gunn point to the history of artistic interpretation – Donatello, André Gide's play, Stefan Heym's *The King David Report* (1972) – over against biblical critics, who, they feel, have played fast with the text, politicizing Jonathan's 'love' and not that of his sister Michal. In fact, David seduces and uses everyone, including Jonathan. A 'homosexual reading', they feel, has 'many anchor points in the text' (1993: 149). Even though Jonathan lives out a 'heterosexual role', fathering children, his 'primary sexual orientation is homosexual', or possibly 'bisexual' (150). Schroer and Staubli (1996) want to romanticize a little more, suggesting the story provides a model of male-to-male love, comparable with male-to-female love.

The problem here is that the reading of Fewell and Gunn assumes too much, particularly in universalizing ideas such as the 'homosexual role', heterosexuality and bisexuality. The research mentioned at the beginning of this chapter should caution against any such assumptions, given the construction of these categories in the last century. Before this there were sexual acts between people of the same sex, but the social and cultural systems by which such acts were understood vary considerably.[20] For instance, in his work on Classical Greece, David Halperin has argued that sexual penetration and socio-economic status were intertwined. Penetration was something adult males, full citizens, did to various non-citizens such as women, children, foreigners, and slaves; it reflected the respective social status of penetrator and penetrated, pleasure being the prerogative of the former. Thus, relations between adult males challenged the social and cultural order and, although they may have happened, they were not acceptable.[21]

Ken Stone has argued for a comparable construction of sexuality in the

Hebrew Bible, making the connection with the honour/shame pattern of Mediterranean societies and restricting penetration to women. He concludes, in a reading of Genesis 19 and Judges 19, that 'male homosexual contact serves metaphorically for other sorts of unequal male–male power relations. Sexual penetration signifies social submission' (Stone 1995: 97).[22] The implications for a reading of the story of David and Jonathan are significant: who is penetrated and who is the penetrator? But this assumes that Stone's construction of sexuality in the Hebrew Bible is valid. Halperin is not so sure, for in 'Heroes and Their Pals' (1990a: 75–87) he compares the stories of Gilgamesh and Enkidu in the *Epic of Gilgamesh*, David and Jonathan in 1 Samuel 18–20, and Achilles and Patroclus in the *Iliad*. He argues that these stories, coming from roughly the same period (the turn of the last millennium BCE, that is, some 500 years before the Athens of his other studies), make use of kinship and conjugal terminology and imagery to depict friendship. As far as Achilles and Patroclus, his main focus, are concerned, he uses the confusion of the later Greeks (who tried to understand their relation as a paederastic one yet were confused by Achilles' superior social position – suggesting he was the dominant partner – over against his youth – suggesting a role as submissive youth) to caution against trying to impose categories from our temporal and social locations regarding the construction of sexuality onto those not our own, or even to avoid transposing assumptions about one period and attributing them to others. For David and Jonathan this means that 'friendship' – itself a construct – between males may well be homosocial and homoerotic, imaged as kinship and marriage, and yet does not imply male-on-male sexual acts.

Halperin's cautions need to be heeded, although questions remain about the certainty of historical reconstruction of the texts and their origin and social context. Indeed, there are two ways in which such research may be read and used: one as an effort to construct various facets of ancient sexuality using the texts as (somewhat recalcitrant) witnesses; another as the attempt to construct the texts themselves as queer. In the end it is the second option I follow, and in this light the crucial point of the work of both Halperin and Stone is that in the ancient Mediterranean (Greece for Halperin, Israel for Stone), penetration signifies male, dominant, citizen, and active, whereas being penetrated signifies female, subordinate, non-citizen and passive. It is precisely the question of penetration that serves as a key for my reading of the story of David and Jonathan, a reading that thereby picks up the active/passive ambiguity of the action hero.

(I suspect it was the skirt and growing bust that crossed some clearly felt although unarticulated border. The woollen clothes, the leathers, the hair, the gym, the blissful days pedalling around town, the masculine masquerade – all of these were fine, but skirts and tits on a man were not. For some reason, law enforcement and transvestites did not mix. There was no real hostility, just a quiet blocking out from regular activities,

thousand metre stares, an absence of talk. Before long, the paperwork for my discharge was through; I cleared my locker and left.)

So, is David, the son of Jesse, to take his place beside Arnold Schwarzenegger, Sylvester Stallone, Steven Segal and Keanu Reeves? He shares the collection of corpses, a muscled body, superior fire power, and a knack of coming out on top. His career begins auspiciously enough: a giant slain in 1 Samuel 17 with a stone and the giant's own sword – although this reverses the usual man-to-man combat that comes at the close of conventional action films. Before chapter 18, then, David has already established himself as a hero beyond peer, the giant-killer of Israel. Yet, he has only a few verses prior to this been introduced as the one secretly anointed by Samuel (1 Samuel 16:1–13), and then as the soother of Saul's torment by the 'evil spirit from God' (1 Samuel 16:14–23). Indeed, he is recommended by 'one of the young men' (1 Samuel 16:18) for his smooth music, its ability to assuage the foul spirit of Yahweh afflicting Saul. So, in chapters 16 and 17 of 1 Samuel there is already a curious pairing: David is both lyre player and giant-killer, gentle crooner and macho man, 'skilful in playing', says the same young man in Saul's service, 'a man of valour, a warrior, prudent in speech, and a man of good presence; and Yahweh is with him' (1 Samuel 16:18).

By chapter 18, when David (re)enters Saul's service, he is immediately successful 'wherever Saul sent him' (1 Samuel 18:5). His popularity and success, far above Saul's, spur the women to sing and 'make merry': 'Saul has killed his thousands, and David his ten thousands' (1 Samuel 18:7). What is notable here is that David's heroics in 18:5–7 immediately follow the first covenant of love with Jonathan in 18:1–4 – the two dimensions seem to be intertwined. While Jonathan divests himself of his clothes (1 Samuel 18:4) David is immediately successful in war (18:5). David's hero status is elevated with more success in war in 1 Samuel 18:13–16, a result of which is that 'all Israel and Judah loved David' (18:16). Further military success only serves to enhance his popularity: in 1 Samuel 18:30 he responds to a Philistine attack,[23] while in 19:8 he launches an assault. (A more Freudian resonance comes from the gathering of 200 Philistine foreskins in 18:25–9, but I will return to this below.) He strides through Jerusalem as though he were an action film star, for 'his fame became very great' (1 Samuel 18:30). In fact, Jonathan was his greatest fan, far beyond Saul, who 'loved' David 'greatly' (1 Samuel 16:21), or the people and servants who 'loved' him (18:16, 22), or Michal who 'loved' him (1 Samuel 18:20, 28), beyond even the narrator who finds him 'ruddy', 'good looking' and bestowed with 'beautiful eyes' (1 Samuel 16:12). Like the people's, Jonathan's adoration of David seems to be related directly to his fighting prowess: in 1 Samuel 18:1 he 'loves' David immediately after the killing of Goliath, and in 1 Samuel 19:5 he protests to Saul, bringing up Goliath again: 'he took his life in his hand when he attacked the Philistine,[24] and Yahweh brought a great victory for all Israel'. In this material David is quintessentially active, taking the initiative, killing Philistines, attracting attention. He is clearly an action hero.

> *(I had had a good track record: a solid string of arrests and convictions, mostly for difficult crimes with queer leads. Yet this seemed to carry little weight in the end.)*

At the same time, David's active role seems to be wholly contained in his miltary prowess. In all else, he is chronically passive. Although it is sometimes understood as seduction (Fewell and Gunn 1993: 148–51; Heym 1972: 35), the texts mention that various people 'loved' David; nothing more is written, especially of David's actions and thoughts in this regard. Polzin (1993: 191) speaks of the narrator keeping the inner life of David 'opaque'.[25] What I want to stress here is the passivity of David in these relationships: he is the passive receptor. In the case of Saul, it seems to be love and then hate: his 'love' of David, taking him from his father Jesse to be permanently with Saul (1 Samuel 16:21–3) soon turns into hatred. David's success as an action man triggers a desire by Saul to kill him, the evil spirit of Yahweh now seemingly activated by the lyre playing, or at least it no longer seems to have the effect it once had (1 Samuel 18:10–11).[26] 1 Samuel 19:9–10 connects harp and evil spirit a little more closely, although not in a directly causal sense. Indeed, Gillet (1990) has argued that the text exhibits Saul's homosexual desire for David – again desire is directed towards David – and the transferal of that desire first through his daughters and then through Jonathan.

> *(The station chief in particular, Saul, took a distinct dislike to me, although he had once made a pass at me. His bouts of depression and rage didn't help, and there were rumours of his coprophilia about. Once he found out about the hormones, I was regarded as a potential public relations disaster for the whole force.)*

Further, Jonathan is not the only progeny of Saul to be infatuated with David: Merab is offered to David as an incentive to fight more Philistines in the hope that he would be killed (1 Samuel 18:17–19), although there is no mention of her love. In the end she is not given. Then Michal 'loved David' (1 Samuel 18:20). An attempt to use a daughter to trap David backfires twice – once in the bridal price of 100 (David obtains 200) Philistine foreskins (1 Samuel 18:25–7), and again when Michal helps him escape Saul's hit squad (1 Samuel 19:11–17). The over-riding desire of Saul is to be rid, excrementally, of David, but there is also a drive to set up male-to-female connections as traps. Yet both liaisons are unfruitful – Merab's never takes place, while Michal's early affection fades away into impotence, bitterness and the absence of children (see 2 Samuel 6:16, 20–3). Over against both of these, Jonathan is the only offspring of Saul whose relationship with David flowers. Jonathan, as it were, presents an ideal version of the relationship with David that seems beyond Merab and Michal. This is reinforced by Jonathan's absence from the text between 1 Samuel 18:4 and 19:1, which is precisely the textual space devoted to Merab and Michal, as well as David's elevation to proper hero status before Jonathan returns in 19:1. As his sisters exit, Jonathan moves in to replace them.

Along with Saul and his offspring, biblical critics have also been taken with David. Hertzberg, for instance, finds the story 'the most beautiful description of a friendship which the Bible offers us'. 'David', we are told, with a hint of infatuation, 'is evidently a man with particularly attractive features, as we are shown here and often elsewhere; he takes hearts by storm, and everyone falls for him' (Hertzberg 1964: 154).

What, then, of Jonathan? Is this relation the real buddy-politic of the story? Most commentators see in the relation between Jonathan and David a transfer of political power, of the kingship which is assumed to be rightfully Jonathan's. Various signals in the text encourage such a reading: Jonathan's stripping of his clothes and weapons – robe, armour, sword, bow and belt (1 Samuel 18:4) – and the giving of them to David is read as a symbolic transfer of power (so, for example Jobling 1978: 4–25); and of course Saul also strips off in a prophetic frenzy, divesting himself of his power (1 Samuel 19:24). (Here, undoubtedly, is the comparable moment of torso uncovering I noted earlier in action films, although it is not the hero David who does so, but Jonathan and Saul.) With such a reading Saul concurs, saying to Jonathan in a fit of rage, 'For as long as the son of Jesse lives upon the earth, neither you nor your kingdom shall be established' (1 Samuel 20:31).[27]

Yet, there seems to be much more to the relationship. Some biblical critics hedge their bets. So, Brueggemann speaks of 'loyalty' and 'complete commitment', and that David is, in a somewhat loaded phrase, the 'passive recipient' of Jonathan's devotion (Brueggemann 1993: 232). McCarter argues in an effort at neutrality that the issue is 'inseparable devotion'. Jonathan, in other words, is so taken with David that he becomes vitally 'devoted to him in affection and loyalty' (1980: 305).[28]

It is as though the impotent and unfruitful marriage between David and Michal (whose impotence is signalled by the bridal price of a heap of blood-caked Philistine foreskins[29]), Saul's daughter, comes to fruition with David and Jonathan, Saul's son. The text is full of references to the affection that Jonathan felt for David, narratively triggered, as I have noted above, by his heroic feats, particularly the great inaugural feat of slaying Goliath, as well as the Philistine battles. And yet, David is also 'prudent in speech' (1 Samuel 16: 18), for the immediate narrative connection is between Jonathan's affection and David's words to Saul: 'When he had finished speaking to Saul, the soul of Jonathan was bound to the soul of David, and Jonathan loved him as his own soul' (18:1). The statements continue throughout the remaining three chapters: 'because he loved him as his own soul' (18:3); 'Saul's son Jonathan took great pleasure in David' (19:1); 'Your father knows well that you like me' (20:3, David to Jonathan); 'Jonathan made David swear again by his love for him; for he loved him as he loved his own life' (20:17). And then there is the final narrative act of parting: 'and they kissed each other, and wept with each other; until David magnified himself'[30] (20:41). It is notable that the great weight of reference is to the affection of Jonathan; only in passing is anything said of David, giving an oath in 1 Samuel 20:17 and weeping and kissing in 20:41. Only in the lament at the death of Saul and Jonathan in 2 Samuel 1:19–27 is there a hint of David's affection, although here it takes the form of grief or distress: 'I am distressed for you, my brother Jonathan: greatly beloved were you to me; your love to me was wonderful, passing the love of women' (2 Samuel 1:26).[31] Yet even here, David is the passive recipient of affection: he speaks of Jonathan's 'love' for him, while Jonathan is only 'beloved' to him – the passive verb form is telling. Jonathan is, it seems, the active partner in this relationship, David the passive one; Jonathan the penetrator, David the penetrated.

(I managed to hold on to some friends, though. Michal found nothing objectionable, preferring to identify with fringe types. And Jonathan, the chief's second-in-command, took exception to my expulsion, challenging his call and supporting me wherever he could. I spent some time at his place when I first moved out; no money, no home.)

David and Jonathan make two distinct covenants together (1 Samuel 18:3; 20:16), although Polzin stresses the covenantal language of the whole of chapter 20 (Polzin 1993: 192, 264–5[32]). In the first it is Jonathan who makes the covenant with David. There is no indication about what this covenant might be or mean, except for the statement 'because he loved him as his own soul' (1 Samuel 18:3). It seems to include Jonathan's stripping, but once again the meaning is unclear. The second covenant – is it an elaboration of the first? – is between Jonathan and the 'house of David', and here Jonathan vows 'May Yahweh seek out the enemies of David' (1 Samuel 20:16). There follows 'Jonathan *made* David *swear* again by his love for him' (1 Samuel 20:17, emphasis added). These covenants are then reinforced on three other occasions, first by David in 1 Samuel 20:8: '[Y]ou *have brought* your servant *into* a covenant of Yahweh with you' (emphasis added). Then there is an elusive comment by Jonathan: 'As for the matter about which you and I have spoken, Yahweh is (witness [Greek Bible]) between you and me forever' (1 Samuel 20:23). Third, at their separation in 1 Samuel 20:42 Jonathan says 'Go in peace, since both of us have sworn in the name of Yahweh, saying, "Yahweh shall be between me and you, and between my descendants and your descendants, forever."' Even here, where there is reference to a mutual covenant, the statement itself is made by Jonathan. Whenever David refers to the covenant, he casts himself syntactically as its passive recipient.

Apart from a cautionary note about how to understand the word 'love' (*'hb*) in the text, especially against a late twentieth century construction of the word, it is important to note the function of covenant here. Although covenantal language seems to be based on treaty arrangements between political parties or leaders in the Ancient Near East, in the Hebrew Bible the prime reference for covenant is between Yahweh and various individuals, mainly patriarchs and kings, and the people of Israel. Without pursuing a whole tedious (at least for one who grew up on a diet of Protestant covenantal theology) discussion on covenant, it is worth noting that such covenants rarely, if ever, take place between equal partners. One is always stronger, more dominant, than the other, and the covenant stipulates the terms of such an unequal arrangement (a little like S/M agreements). Thus, Yahweh requires obedience and proper worship in return for blessing and prosperity. Similarly, the covenants between David and Jonathan signal such inequality. The question is whether, as Polzin suggests (1993: 191), it is Jonathan who wants the covenant to preserve his own offspring from David, the one with power, or whether Jonathan instigates the covenant in order to protect David from his father (1 Samuel 20:8).

Is this a case of the use of a certain (theological) way of speaking to signify a relationship of sorts between two males, as indeed it is for one between men and that other male, Yahweh? For one of the relationships that is often neglected in readings of these chapters is that between Yahweh and David. From Yahweh's search, through Samuel, of David in chapter 16, it is repeatedly pointed out that David is Yahweh's anointed. Even Yahweh, it seems is enraptured: 'Yahweh', we are told, 'does not see as mortals see; they look on the outward appearance, but Yahweh looks on the heart' (1 Samuel 16:7). Yet, when David arrives, Yahweh responds, apparently, to his appearance: 'Now', the narrator gasps (giving vent to a narratological desire to penetrate), 'he was ruddy, and had beautiful eyes, and was handsome. Yahweh said, "Rise and anoint him; for this is the one"' (1 Samuel 16:12). Yahweh is not averse to admiring attractive youths. After this it is made clear that 'Yahweh was with him' (1 Samuel 18:14; see 16:18; 18:12, 28). David is his boy. Once again David is the object of attention, this time from an active Yahweh who seeks him out.

(Jonathan, I must admit, was keener than I was about the setup, wanting to make it permanent. I wasn't so sure, staying a couple of weeks and eventually moving on to one squat, and then another, technically homeless. There were plenty of places around Parramatta where one could hole up for a while, stay warm and dry, and even invite the occasional friend around. My favourite was on an old, large, industrial site hard by the freeway. It had been cleared and awaited development, but meanwhile the grass grew long and the old machine shed in the far corner, all brick and tile but divested of machinery, made a fine shelter.)

29

All the same, I have not located any explicit reference to sex, although my search has been for the active/passive dynamic. There is strong affection, intense feelings between two males, although this may be no more than an effort to speak about the nature of male relationships, using terminology from elsewhere – love, covenant, kinship (the 'brother Jonathan' of 2 Samuel 1:26). Yet the passive (in regard to love and affection) and active (with reference to military exploits) split is quite clear.

What of the words themselves, especially the verbs? Is there room for a transgressive misreading, a search for the linguistically repressed that outsmarts the Censor? Although the word for 'take pleasure in' or 'desire' (*ḥfṣ*; 18:22, 25; 19:1) may be read queerly, a couple of words in the first few verses of chapter 18 are more suggestive. 'Jonathan', we are told in verse 1, 'was bound to the soul of David.' The root *qšr* has the basic sense (in *qal*) of knot or tie together; in the verb form used here (*niphal*) it bears the sense of 'to commit oneself to' or 'to be joined together' (compare Nehemiah 3:38/4:6). Not only is there a delectable suggestion of bondage, but the verb also hints at a plumbing connection at the same time. Further, verse 4 contains a verb referring to what Jonathan does with his clothes and weapons. Normally the form (*hithpael*, which appears only here) of *pšṭ* is read as 'strip oneself', but it has the sense cluster of 'spread out', 'stretch' or 'extend'. Thus, a secondary reading emerges here for the reflexive sense of the verb: to extend or stretch oneself, that is, to achieve an erection; and to spread one's self, or perhaps cheeks. Does not this suggest both active and passive roles, penetration and being penetrated? Two verbs, then, with multiple possibilities, one (*qšr*) evoking commitment, bondage and fucking, the other (*pšṭ*) including stripping, spreading out and erection. Jonathan's divestment of his vestments and the making of the covenant takes on some nuance.[33]

But there are other images of penetration that are not tied to verb forms. I have already mentioned the Philistine foreskins, a pile of bloody flaps, carved from their slaughtered hosts one by one and delivered to Saul. Symbolically, David is the 'cock collector', one who acquires penises and their symbols. Such a symbolic castration folds back, however, on David himself: in being the bridal price for Michal, an unproductive marriage, the foreskins also signify David's symbolic castration, preferring, as he does, to be penetrated rather than to penetrate (Michal, it seems, should have made use of a strap-on dildo). And then there is Saul himself, who wields a futile spear. Twice (18:11; 19:10) Saul attempts to pin David to a wall with a spear while David is making music. Here the Hebrew word *nkh*, to strike or pierce, is another verb that signals penetration, this time more violently, rending the body in the process. Jonathan also is the subject of a spear throw (20:33, same verb) from Saul after their exchange over David. Once again images of penetration are part of the male relationships, but here it is signally fruitless, for Saul seems to be shooting blanks at both son and lover. The spear misses, repeatedly, bearing out Lacan's notion of the phallic signifier: that the phallus, as distinct from the penis, actually indicates the absence of the penis, or at least penile activity. Finally, Jonathan shoots an arrow past his 'boy' (20:21 etc.) or 'young man' (20:22) or 'little boy' (20:35) with coded messages shouted out for David (1 Samuel 20:35–40; see also 1 Samuel 20:18–23). Another phallic signifier? This one also misses its mark, although it was never intended to make contact, except verbally (Polzin (1993: 193) reads the arrow as a mark of Jonathan's straight speech that has more truth than he realizes). After the arrow incident David and Jonathan meet, weep and kiss, never to meet again.

David, it seems, is a chronic collector of cocks. Philistine foreskins for Michal and Saul, spears from Saul (and one directed to Jonathan), and arrows from Jonathan, as well as verbs that turn on the question of penetration. At the same time, these phallic signifiers fail to hit the mark. Does David have an 'anus dentata', biting off, swallowing and consuming all that is directed or thrown at him? Does his anus threaten to consume all that it receives? The curious thing about this queer action hero is that he is the passive one in 1 Samuel 18–20; everyone does things to him, admiring, selecting, anointing, loving, making covenants, throwing spears and firing arrows. Perhaps this should be read as not only an accumulation of power, but also of sexual power. Jonathan too is strangely active and passive. Fewell and Gunn (1993: 151) argue that Jonathan is identified with women, both by Saul (1 Samuel 20:30) and David (2 Samuel 1:26), yet Jonathan is the one who initiates most of the action. David is overwhelmingly a passive receptor, a role that, according to all the schemas of sexual relations, indicates subordinate status, a secondary role, a disinterested partner. He is fucked, it seems.

Let me return to an earlier point, in which I suggested that David's rise as a hero in 1 Samuel 18–20 is interwoven with his emergence as a queer sexual being. The question then is whether there is more than the mere placing of David's military and queer exploits side by side in this narrative? I want to suggest that, like the actions films I considered above, there is an internal logic to the 'queer' dimensions of this story, namely, that the hero David, the model of a great king and an example for all the other kings to follow in the books of Kings, must have a highly ambiguous sexual presence in these stories. The ideal hero is the ideal queer. He is, like the action hero, both an initiator of action and a passive receptor, the active hero and the penetrated sexual part-ner. This doubleness, this Freudian repression, is marked in the text by the perpetual verbs of hiding (19:2; 20:5, 19, 24, 25), absence (20:27), covering (19:13), uncovering (20:2), stripping off (18:4; 19:24), nakedness (19:24), eluding (18:11; 19:10), removal (18:13) and fleeing (19:12, 18; 20:29).[34] Of course David becomes a key figure in the development of messianic expecta-tions, the hope for the ideal king, the super (queer) hero. David, and for that matter other biblical heroes, may better be seen as a sort of biblical Herakles (see Loraux 1990), whose gender identification and sexuality are highly am-biguous, both as a virile man and lover and as a 'feminine' passive figure.

In the end, though, my reading of 1 Samuel 18–20 has been set up by Saul,

31

of all people, for his words, his reported speech, in 20:30–1, connect both the political and the sexual in the relation of Jonathan and David: 'You son of a perverse, rebellious woman!' he says to Jonathan, 'Do I not know that you have chosen the son of Jesse to your own shame, and to the shame of your mother's nakedness? For as long as the son of Jesse lives upon the earth, neither you nor your kingdom shall be established' (1 Samuel 20:30–1a).

(Every now and then, work mysteriously came my way. Jonathan was still in a minor position, but it would have been Saul who cleared it. I got word through Michal, or Jonathan, or Mary, or Keanu or David. In fact, David and Keanu had, I heard from Jonathan, struck up a relationship. But for me there was always some pay, especially for the queer cases, the ones with odd twists and interesting sexual angles. And I could wear skirts or pants as I chose, buy the hormones and grow some decent breasts.)

CONCLUSION

> Another way to argue this would be to point out that queerness (precisely because of its 'invisibility') has managed to pervade popular culture to such a degree that it hardly makes sense to draw distinctions between what is 'mass culture' and what is 'queer subculture'.
>
> (Burston 1995: 120)

Keanu Reeves, it appears, provides the 'truth' of David, the queer hero and forerunner of the messiah. In the same way, David constitutes the 'truth' of Keanu Reeves and action film heroes. They are both ambiguously active and passive in a distinctly sexual sense. Indeed, it may be that the story of David and Jonathan should be rewritten as the story of David and Keanu.[35]

(So, the wind penetrated the door of Murphy's garage, pushing through its gaping boards and around the open edge, forcing it wider. Amongst the old batteries, cans of nuts and bolts, greasy engine parts and tyres, a pile of old blue overalls lay in the corner, blood dried black on a greasy grey head.)

2

COWS WITH GUNS[1]

Sadistic hegemony, Hitchcock and biblical dismemberment

All fat is Yahweh's

(Leviticus 3:16b)

You eat the fat, you clothe yourselves with the wool, you slaughter the fatlings …

(Ezekiel 34:3)

[T]he Law itself is the ultimate perversion.

(Žižek 1992: 222)

(As I bent over to look more closely at the crumpled body of old Murphy, Michal explained, 'He was found early this morning by a customer. Our guess is that he's been dead for a couple of hours. A big blow on the head.' The yellowed grey hair was matted with blood, and half of his head was caved in. Something else caught my eye, a bloody patch at his crotch. Noticing my gaze, Michal added, 'He's been castrated. His toes and fingers are gone as well. And take a closer look at what is pinned to his chest.' A scrap of paper was stapled to his left nipple with a yellow 'M' scrawled on it. Now I knew why Jonathan had dropped by my squat with word of a new case for me.

'What about the others?' I asked.

'You'll find them interesting, if a little gruesome. Let's go and have a look.')

Violence, insisting on a more direct audience here, recurs in different formats at various places in the remaining pages. It has already appeared in the action hero's resolution of the nation's/globe's/universe's problems and threats. My focus in what immediately follows is the work of Alfred Hitchcock – a signal moment in contemporary popular culture and cultural criticism – and some texts of the Hebrew Bible. As with Chapter 1, I am seeking 'a point de capiton', this time in the ideology and structure of violence in both corp(u)ses.

Why Hitchcock? Is there is not more violent material on which I might reflect? Not only are Hitchcock's films crucial for the establishment and development of popular cinema – spanning as he does the realist and modernist phases of silent film, the high modernism of the black and white talkies and the postmodern innovations of the 1960s and 1970s (see Jameson 1990: 155–7) – but they also play a crucial role in cultural criticism itself, let alone film studies. Indeed many of the methodological moves in film criticism are founded on studies of Hitchcock (for feminism, see Mulvey 1989: 2, and the useful survey by Sloan 1993: 15–42[2]). Further, in a thread that carries through from the preceding chapter, there is a distinct queer interest in Hitchcock's work (Corber 1991, 1993; Price 1992; Roth 1992).[3]

Yet, Hitchcock's work has not always enjoyed such critical attention, being written off for most of his career as a producer of light entertainment.[4] Here the first signals of the Censor's presence may be deciphered, namely in the disparagement of popular work such as Hitchcock's by critical commentators. But Hitchcock himself also fought with censorship, especially in political form. Films critiquing hanging,[5] depicting the 1926 General Strike,[6] or the anarchist siege in Sidney Street, London,[7] were either axed or modified. 'Again and again I have suggested authentic ideas to my production chief, only to be told: "Sorry, Hitch, but the censor'd never pass it"' (Hitchcock 1995: 198).[8] The inability to pursue more sociological themes pushed him into fiction, where many of those themes reappear in ruses to bypass the Censor.

The Censor also appears at a deeper level in the basic logic of violence that I trace. It begins with two common themes in Hitchcock criticism: the barely concealed presence of deviance and disorder in the normal, everyday world in which we live; and the manipulated identification of the audience with certain characters. I give both themes a dialectical twist with the assistance of Lacan and Žižek via hegemony and sadism. Hegemony appears more directly in a comparison between the Hitchcock texts of *Rear Window*, *Rope* and *Shadow of a Doubt* (where the murders takes place off screen), and the biblical texts of Leviticus 1–7 and Genesis 22 on sacrifice. It is the turn of sadism with *Dial 'M' for Murder*, *Psycho*, *Torn Curtain* and *Frenzy* (where death is graphically portrayed), and the biblical stories of the Levite's concubine (Judges 19) and the slaughter of Agag (1 Samuel 15).

For the first group, and for the theme of a deviant underside, the issue turns on the relationship between that ideological horizon by which violence is defined and the violence of the very establishment and persistence of that horizon.

Žižek's dialectical Lacanianism brings him to the insight that it is not so much the violence that we recognize that is the main problem: it is that which we no longer recognize. This goes past the more conventional observations concerning covert violence – that dominant social formations sanction certain types of violence and not others – to argue that it is precisely the absence of violence that is most suspicious. In fact, the highest form of

violence is that which coincides with the absence of violence: it is this supreme violence that 'determines the "specific colour" of the very horizon
within which something is to be perceived as violence' (Žižek 1994: 204).
This of course means that hegemony, in its very concealment of violence
and claims to ideological dominance, is the location of supreme violence. In
other words, the arrogation of the decision as to what is and is not violence
is an attempt to remove oneself from scrutiny. In making the determination,
in setting the criteria by which violence is recognized, the one who legislates
in this way appears to be removed from the processes so identified. But this
is a simultaneous effacement of the violence of the establishment and main-
tenance of that hegemonic power. The field within which one says 'there it
is' is itself the primary violence which needs to be disrupted and broken up.
And once this is done the violence and corruption of that normality, of the
Censor itself, becomes everywhere apparent.[9]

> *(Not one of the codes of the Law we were supposed to enforce while I was
> in the force were kept by us. As keepers of the Law we needed to break it
> to enforce it, always driving fast, making acquisitions in the cause of
> justice, relishing the S/M potential of our jobs.)*

As for sadism and audience identification, the key text is Lacan's 'Kant with
Sade' (Lacan 1990), particularly the diagrams outlining the twist of the Sadean
fantasy (62–5). From here I draw the suggestion that what begins as the sadist
inflicting harm on the subject, and in that way finding pleasure (this is the
Will-to-Enjoy), ends up construing the sadist as subject of that harm (for
Sade this was his repeated imprisonment, arranged by his mother in law, and
eventual commitment to an asylum by Napoleon). In Lacan's formulae, the
sadist as subject (S) becomes the barred subject, $. Žižek takes this argument
and applies it to Hitchcock:

> First, he [Hitchcock's 'sadist'] sets a trap of sadistic identification for
> the viewer by way of arousing in him/her the 'sadistic' desire to see
> the hero crush the bad guy, this suffering 'fullness of being' .... Once
> the viewer is filled out with the Will-to-Enjoy, Hitchcock closes the
> trap by simply realizing the viewer's desire: in having his/her desire
> fully realized, the viewer obtains more than he/she asked for (the act
> of murder in all its nauseous *presence* ...).
>
> (Žižek 1992: 222)[10]

Apart from exploring a similar logic in the biblical texts, the question is how
these two positions – the effaced violence of hegemony and sadistic desire –
may be connected with each other, for if that is possible then the ahistoricism
of the argument on sadism may be significantly historicized by that on
hegemony.

(We walked down the street, eastward from Windsor Road and away from the ridge line. Poisonous oleanders guarded the first one hundred meters or so, concealing the banks of the road cutting. The houses were mostly old fibros, built and settled on parcels of land allotted to World War II veterans. Without a footpath, we walked on the road, turned left and then right on Elizabeth Crescent. Here the fibros gave way to Housing Commission brick bungalows, small two bedroom houses built in clusters around the whole Sydney area for people unable to buy their own, their ubiquity belying the fable of home ownership. Street-wise kids played cricket on the street, a few dogs wandered about and out of work parents talked. On the curve of the Crescent the baseball ground opened up, doubling as a flood basin.)

'THE CRACKING OF MUNDANITY'[11]

> Some of our most exquisite murders have been domestic; performed
> in simple, homey places like the kitchen …
> (Hitchcock, quoted by Goodwin 1981: 227)

Many of Hitchcock's films begin with, or are constituted by, an off screen murder. Apart from the three that I will discuss, there are the murders in *The Lodger*, the body washed up in *Young and Innocent*, the suspicious death of the general in *The Parradine Case*, the murder behind the curtain in *Blackmail* and of the husband in *Stage Fright*.

In some respects these are the easier films, the off-screen murder exerting, as it were, a gravitational force on the action yet staying just below the horizon. Thus, in *Rear Window*'s wonderful evocation of apartment life in New York's Greenwich Village of the 1950s, the suspected death and dismemberment of Thorwald's wife is at first entirely unbelievable (and never definitively proven (Julian Smith 1992)). With his suspicions aroused as he is woken by a scream and crash from across the courtyard,[12] the voyeuristic[13] and immobilized Jefferies (James Stewart) tries to convince his fiancee, housekeeper, the police, and of course the viewers – all of whom desire with Jeff the dismemberment of Thorwald's wife. The 'murder' is notable for the contradictory theories that arise to explain it (see Ferrara 1985: 25–16): Mrs Thorwald has been cut up and put in a large trunk tied up with rope, or she has been buried in the garden, or she was dismembered and removed in Thorwald's sample case. In fact, the theme of dismemberment appears in the form of speculation on the part of various characters at different points: in response to Lisa's, 'It's more than a little ghoulish to be disappointed that a man did not kill his wife', Jefferies asks, 'Just how would you begin to cut up a human body?' Stella, over breakfast, asks, 'Now just where do you suppose he cut her up?' In a cannibalistic moment that we have come to expect from Hitchcock, Jeff tries to eat bacon and eggs while Stella worries that the hypothetical trunk might begin to leak. Later she suggests that Mrs Thorwald is 'scattered all over town'. Finally, Jeff, reflecting on the absence of evidence in the garden over which the dog was killed, speculates that Thorwald removed his wife 'in sections' in the sample case. Thus, by the time detective Doyle tells Jeff that 'Thorwald's ready to take us on a tour of the East River' and that 'a hatbox' has something interesting in it, the assumption is clear, although not finally proven.[14] The only death is of course that of the dog itself, which we see dead, but not killed, because it 'knew too much', as Lisa says.

The point here is that everyday life, the quotidien, goes about its own way (signalled by the continuation of all the little everyday lives at the close of the film) apparently – at least for *Rear Window* – oblivious to the violence that is part of its fabric. In fact, the very difficulty of identifying the violence, of pinning down the killer, except through voyeuristic speculation, signals its slipperiness. Is it just the imagination, the snooping, of Jefferies, Lisa and Stella, or is there something tangible that one struggles to grasp, the difficulty of doing so being constitutive of that order that defines violence in the first place?[15]

(Behind the back diamond we dropped down some rocks into a small gully by a stream that drained from the baseball ground. Lantana and rubbish crowded out the creek below the old eucalypts. A couple of people were left beside the creek, preparing to clean up the site. I recognized one or two, nodding a greeting to Abraham, a senior officer I knew. A body bag lay on the ground beside a torso in a red t-shirt. The whole body was there, except none of the parts were connected. The head lay off to the side, a beard and long blond hair above the gory neck; the arms were at odd angles, hacked off at the elbows, and the legs had been severed just above the knee, torn jeans still on upper and lower parts. Again, on the left nipple was stapled a piece of paper with a yellow 'M'. Noticing the blood soaked crotch, I asked Michal, 'Any theories?'
'Not yet.')

Rope is a little more interesting in this regard, since here oblivion to the murder – its last orgasmic moments hanging over into the beginning of the film – by the guests at the party is structurally related to the murder itself. The body of David Kentley lies in the chest – 'a ceremonial altar for a sacrificial feast' in the words of Brandon – from which the murderers Brandon and Philip, and their cleaner/cook, serve the food (chicken and paté, in a distinctly cannibalistic touch) for their party, ostensibly to bid farewell to Philip who needs to practise for his big piano concert, but also to bid farewell to the dead man in the chest. And it is not merely the thrill of pulling off the trick for the 'murderous gays': the tension of the film and the perpetual threat/anticipation of discovery relies precisely on the opposition between the ignorance of the guests – David's father and aunt, his girlfriend and her former beau, and their old housemaster Rupert Cadell (James Stewart) – and the ruse of the hosts. No death, no party; no body, no tension. In *Rope* the connection has been made between violence and normality, between death and the everyday. The violence of the murder is constitutive of the normality of the party itself, all of which then unravels at the end with the discovery of the crime by Rupert, and his horror at seeing his ideas of the Nietzschean superman put into practice. A distinct contrast with *Rope* that simultaneously enforces my argument is *The Trouble with Harry*, where Harry's body is so foregrounded that it becomes a focus for the airing of petty hates, secret likes and proposals of marriage. It too is the base upon which everyday life is possible, especially since Harry was universally hated.[16]

What is interesting here is the ambivalence of Hitchcock himself over *Rope*. Either he disavows it[17] or focuses on technique (Hitchcock 1995: 275–284; Truffaut 1986: 259–66), the elided ten-minute takes that made it his 'most exciting picture'. Yet there may be something more here, for the narrative which works around continuous camera takes and the barest of editing entraps the audience and makes it complicit in the murder committed at the beginning of the film.[18] Our complicity is wrought with the dramatic irony – we know what the situation is – and then with our appreciation of the morbid jokes and double entendres. So, by the time we get to the crooked candlestick,

> … out of a natural instinct for neatness and order, we *want* that candlestick straight. And then we realize that our wish masks a hidden, impure desire: we want the crime kept a secret; we want the killers to get away with it. Brandon casually straightens the candle, we breathe a sigh of relief, and so we are trapped.
>
> (Bauso 1991: 237–8)

Here already there is an intersection between hegemonic violence – the body in the chest as the very reason for the party – and sadistic identification.

> *(The pieces were gathered in the bag and carted away as we walked down the gully to the road below. Jonathan appeared, toiling up the slope. 'How are you going, cocksucker?'[19] he greeted me.*
> *'Get stuffed,' I replied affectionately.*
> *'I was told you were up here,' he said.*
> *'You didn't warn me about this lot,' I challenged him.*
> *'Then I would have spoiled it for you,' he replied. 'What do you reckon?'*
> *We turned right and set off up the hill and past the larger houses of Mary Street, discussing theories. The westerly wind was battering the*

turpentines, and now it bore some moisture, small drops were flung in our faces and against clothes that clung to our bodies like another layer of skin, every bulge and crevice emphasized. I was reminded of the slow-motion images of sprinters in their tights. Redbank Road was about two kilometers away, so we had some time to reflect.)

In *Shadow of a Doubt*, a film that 'seethes with repression' (Kay Sloan 1985: 92), the connection I am pursuing becomes explicit. 'Hitchcock turns the wholesome family life of … middle America belly side up and finds it crawling with unresolved psychic conflict' (Kay Sloan 1985: 92). Here it is the perspective of the young girl, Charlie (Teresa Wright), that proves crucial: at first idolizing her 'Uncle Charles' (Joseph Cotten), after whom she has been named, she comes to a slow realization that the world is a much uglier place below the surface. For Uncle Charles turns out to be someone who preys on widows, gets them to fall in love with him and then arranges their deaths in order to inherit their money. It is the crucial emerald ring given to Charlie by Uncle Charles, with the initials (BM to TS) of another, unknown, person on it, that triggers Charlie's suspicions. They are confirmed by Graham, the detective, and then by Charles himself, who attempts to kill her with the 'accident' of the car exhaust in the garage and then finally on the train.

In the Til Two Lounge Uncle Charles acknowledges Charlie's knowledge, although now he takes a different tack:

> What do you really know? You're just an ordinary little girl living in an ordinary little town. You wake up every morning of your life and you know perfectly well that there's nothing in the world to trouble you. You go through your ordinary little day and at night you sleep your untroubled, ordinary little sleep filled with peaceful, stupid dreams. And I brought you nightmares. You live in a dream. You're a sleep-walker, blind. How do you know what the world is like? Do you know the world is a foul sty? Do you know that if you rip the fronts off houses you'd find swine? The world's a hell. What does it matter what happens in it? Wake up Charlie. Use your wits. Learn something.

In Uncle Charles's words the effaced violence of hegemony finds a distinctively Hitchcockian expression. How can people in their nice houses, on their nice streets, with their nice friends, pass judgement on his acts of violence that allow him to live as comfortably as they? For their lives are no different from the one he lives, except that the violent structure of their everyday life has been overlaid and denied with myriad half-forgotten justifications. And then they presume to designate that which is unacceptable, *qua* violence, in their world. In naming something such as Charles's life as murderous and violent, the normal and everyday enables the effacement of its own violent establishment and continuance. They are not merely connected in some loose way; they stand in a dialectical relation, since the one relies on the other for its status. As Barton comments, 'Hitchcock's films persistently uncover the "nonself" within the "self", the gothic deviancy lodged within realist normalcy' (Barton 1991: 87).[20]

However, Charlie and Uncle Charles are not so much two sides of this moral dialectic as bearers of the dialectic within themselves. She is morally grey, as Bannon argues (1985: 60), calling evil to herself by inviting Charles and sending him away to continue his murders, until she accidentally kills him. Uncle Charles, the widow murderer, is of course an extremely likable villain, in proper Hitchcock tradition. The dark ambiguity of *Shadow of a Doubt* is established in the opening sequence, contrasting the *film noir* environment of Uncle Charles in Philadelphia with a parallel series of shots of Charlie in Santa Rosa, the 'cheery world of sentimental Americana' (Rothman 1982: 180). Yet it is in the ending, as Rothman argues, that this ambiguity is finally played out: was the death of Charles, eulogized at his funeral for the gift of blood money to the town before he left, really an accident?

Shadow of a Doubt is sometimes evoked when a theological reading of Hitchcock rears its much criticized head. In 1957 (reprint 1979), Rohmer and Chabrol argued that a Catholic world view permeates Hitchcock's films, making an explicit appearance in *I Confess*. Despite the excesses of the argument, there would seem to be a grain of truth here, particularly if Žižek's (1992) development of this argument is appreciated. For Žižek suggests that it is Jansenist Catholicism that is important for Hitchcock, in which a God who demands unbearable obedience to a hard Law also presides over a world in which evil and good are inextricably bound up with one another (so *Rear Window*, *Rope*, *Shadow of a Doubt*). Strongly determinist, like Calvin's Protestantism, humans ultimately have no control over their fate – evil and good appear without warning and for no apparent reason – no matter how hard they may try, how much penance they may do, or how many sacrifices they may make.

('*It seems to me that the murderer is deranged; hence the castrations*', *suggested Jonathan.*

'*Why here, in quiet Northmead?*' *asked Michal.*

'*Just the place for it*', *I replied*, '*although I think the castrations are not really deranged. Either they are a false trail, or the killer is collecting genitals, moveable phalluses even*'.

'*Moveable phalluses?*' *said Michal.*

'*Yeah*', *I replied* '*read Judith Butler, although this is a misreading of her argument.*'

'*So you think these might be classed as sex crimes?*' *Jonathan asked me.*

'*No, I would like to read the sexual as political here*'.

'*What about the yellow M's on the paper?*' *asked Michal.*

'*Beats me*'.)

The ability of the status quo to efface its reliance upon violence in order to continue to exist has its dialectical obverse in the banality of ubiquitous, sanctioned violence. It is, in other words, either everywhere or nowhere, and these two possibilities will turn out to be part of the same situation. The violence that effaces itself through its very banality is that of sacrifice, especially in Leviticus 1–7, although this sacrificial violence may itself be regarded as displaced, as in the story of Abraham and Isaac (Genesis 22). Do these texts, then, realize the 'truth' of the Hitchcock films I have discussed?

Rather than identify the violence that is marginalized and therefore undesirable, Leviticus opts for the routinization of violence in everyday activities like sacrifice. And in these chapters such routinization has already gone a long way. Here we find an elaborate mechanism,[21] with various grades of sacrifice – not all of them involving animals, although most do – linked to various types of offences and/or festivals. I am especially interested in the slaughter, dismemberment and sacrifice of the animals in Leviticus. Thus, in the description of the burnt offering for atonement in 1:1–17, the animal may be a bull (1:5), sheep or goat (1:10), turtledove or pigeon (1:14). The bull is to be 'slaughtered before Yahweh' (1:5), the blood splattered against the altar (1:5), the animal flayed[22] and dissected (1:6), and then the various parts – head and fat (1:8), entrails and legs (1:9) – burnt on the altar (1:9). Similarly, the sheep or goat is dismembered (1:12) and the bits and pieces – head, fat, entrails, legs and other parts – arranged and burnt (1:13). The bird, a little small for such detailed dismemberment is to be dealt with by having its head twisted off (1:15), the blood squeezed out against the altar (1:15), the crop removed and thrown away (1:16) and the body torn open by holding its wings (1:17).[23] At the close of the description of each type of animal is intoned 'a burnt offering, an offering by fire of pleasing odour to Yahweh' (1:9, 13, 17).[24] Yahweh is then not only butcher but also cook, a beer in one hand and skewer in the other, turning the steaks of the Lamb of God on the Barbecue.[25]

(We passed along Moxham's Road on the way to Redbank Road and the smell of barbecueing meat entered our nostrils. An evening meal seemed to be in preparation. With the locals a tradition had arisen whereby one did not merely turn up with some steaks or sausages for the hot plate; instead, the host would acquire in some way or another a live cow or sheep or goat, depending on the size of the party. With the guests all present on the front lawn, the bleating or lowing animal would suddenly be confronted by one of the women, large knife in hand, which she slashed across the animal's neck. Amidst a cheer, the animal then collapsed to the ground, was drained of blood and carved up into cookable sections. Noone was permitted to leave until the whole animal had been dissevered, cooked and ingested. Front lawns in the whole area had large dark patches of blood on them.)

41

After a considerate moment for vegetarians in 2:1–16 (a tofu slab on the grill), the triple procedure repeats in chapter 3 for the offering of well-being, except that the animal may be male or female, and only certain body parts are to be offered – for cattle and goats the fat around the entrails, kidneys and their fat and the appendage of the liver (3:3–4, 14–15), ditto for sheep except that the tail is to be included (3:9–10).[26] And then, with some variation but an overwhelming similarity, chapter 4 covers sacrifice for unintentional sins of the priest (4:3–12), the whole Israelite congregation (13–21), the ruler (4:22–6) and the individual Israelite (4:27–35). In each case the fatty parts – entrails, kidneys and liver appendage – are sacrificed on the altar, while the rest is burnt up 'outside the camp' (4:12, 21) in the case of priest and whole people. As the litany of reasons for sacrifice progresses, the detail of each procedure diminishes, referring instead to the procedural similarity with the other offerings (4:10, 20, 26, 31, 35; 6:17; 7:7), and an increased focus on the possibilities for incurring guilt. Indeed, so banal have become the sacrificial guidelines that the narrative slides towards a battle for allocation of body parts between Yahweh and the priests. Although entitled to various portions of animal bodies and grain offerings from specific sacrifices (6:16–18; 7:6; 7:8–9, 14–18, 31–6), even those that have a contagious holiness (6:24–30), the priests are not permitted the fat or the blood: Yahweh has a fat monopoly, it seems, a liking for cholesterol that mocks the dangers for humans. 'You shall eat no fat of ox or sheep or goat. … You must not eat any blood whatever' (7:23b, 26a). 'All fat is Yahweh's. It shall be a perpetual statute throughout your generations, in all your settlements: you must not eat any fat or any blood' (3:16b-17).[27]

If the banality of sacrifice comes through in the shift in content to arguments over food distribution, then style also plays a role. The sheer repetition of the form – with minor variations for the preparation and burning of particular animals for particular types of offering – has a deadening effect upon modern readers, an effect that has been described, after its construction in the eighteenth century, as 'boring' (see Spacks 1995). The descriptions themselves are what we might term 'clinical', outlining the various procedures for killing, cutting up, skinning, giving out portions depending on the sacrifice. Yet, the stark descriptions of animal parts and the ritual guidelines are curiously soporific, their 'simple, almost monotonous sequence' (Noth 1965: 19, like Noth's own prose) speaking of the everyday normality of such dismemberment.

In the end, the hegemonic violence of Leviticus 1–7 operates at a number of levels. Apart from the quotidien banality of such slaughter, dismemberment and burning, the liturgical rhythms and slaughterhouse punctuality of sacrifice move in two other directions – the theological system of sin, and human sacrifice. In regard to sin, it is not only the idea that a deity requires sacrifice in order to assuage sin and guilt that is of interest, but the ideological construction of sin, guilt and atonement. The very notion that humans live with a fundamental inadequacy, that they are inherently sinful, would seem to be a highly pervasive ideological system, a hegemony, in other words, whose constitutive violence is rendered banal and unremarkable through sacrificial systems. Yet, the very need to sacrifice – to propitiate and render predictable an unpredictable deity – bears closely upon the theological reading of Hitchcock, where a Jansenist Catholic God brings not only inexplicable misfortune on people, but also presides over a world where good and evil are intertwined. Propitiation, while trying to render such a God predictable, recognizes by its very structure the arbitrariness of the deity.

Second, the glaring omission in Leviticus 1–7 is human sacrifice. Human sacrifice, cannibalism and the complexities of its denial appear starkly in Genesis 22, the Akedah, the sacrifice of Isaac, which should be read as the missing section, now as Haggadah, of Leviticus 1–7. Here is found, especially with the later modifications to the E account (adding the final words of the angel of the Lord in 22:15–18), a process of hegemonic concealment that shows all the contradictions of such concealment: Abraham's hand is averted at the last moment by God's command that he desist (22:11–12), turning the elaborate sequence into a test: 'now I know that you fear God, since you have not withheld your son, your only son, from me' (22:12). Absolute fear of (faith in?) God should be prepared for human sacrifice, the best human possible, but in the end that is not required by God, elided as it were by the ram in the bush, which is 'offered up as a burnt offering instead of his son' (22:13). Yet, as Levenson points out in response to arguments that this text speaks of Israelite opposition to child sacrifice, Abraham was not only never commanded to sacrifice the ram as he was his son, but 'it is passing strange to condemn child sacrifice through a narrative in which a father is richly rewarded for his willingness to carry out that very practice' (1993: 13). Further, the source critical suspicion that in Genesis 22 may be found the various layers covering an initial story of sacrifice reinforces my argument, although in inexplicable fashion traces of the earlier story remain, such as 22:19, where we read, 'so Abraham returned to his young men' – alone and without Isaac. Only after Abraham meets the young men do the plurals return: 'and they arose and went to Beer-sheba; and Abraham (on his own!) lived at Beer-Sheba' (22:19). As Zuckerman suggests (1991: 19), Genesis 22:6, 7, 12 and 16 take on a more ominous tone in the light of 22:19. Thus, in the later text, the violence that is signified and denied (human sacrifice) in favour of that which is sanctioned (animal sacrifice) only serves to indicate the originary and enabling violence (human sacrifice) that has been concealed, forgotten and denied by naming it as something other than what *we* do. Sanctioned violence is then a substitute for human sacrifice, namely the sacrifice of (one's best) animals.

('Did you hear,' said Jonathan, 'that Bloodwood Necropolis is having an Open Day with a huge Barbecue?' Bloodwood was the oldest and largest

of Sydney's crematoria, a veritable city of the dead with roads, hills and small suburbs within.

'I wonder what they are cooking on the Barbecue?' I mused.

'Not something I was planning to attend', said Michal. 'Who is the Open Day for? Potential customers, or long standing patrons?')

In many respects the process of sacrifice in Leviticus 1–7 and the Akedah in Genesis 22 exhibit the features of hegemony, which is the contested terrain of ideological dominance, always attempted by the ruling classes and always contested by those ruled. Not only does the battle over hegemony (itself a dimension of class struggle) manifest itself in purely ideological terms, such as religious discourse in the Hebrew Bible, but also a crucial dimension of hegemony is the concealment and naming of violence. Thus, to be able to identify what is violent is a hegemonic act, carried out by the ruling classes, since it entails a concealment of the originary and perpetuated violence of the establishment of the ruling classes themselves. It is this that I see operating in Leviticus 1–7 and Genesis 22, as well as *Rear Window, Rope* and *Shadow of a Doubt.*

In this respect, sacrifice in Leviticus 1–7 and Genesis 22 realizes the 'truth' of the films I have discussed, since it is not merely that the violence is hidden but that its ubiquity renders it hidden through its banality. But then, Hitchcock's films show the 'truth' of the biblical texts, since the very structure of that hegemony rests on its enabling violence. One of the best expressions of the simultaneous effacement and ubiquity of hegemonic violence may be read in a scene at an assembly line in Detroit left out of *North by Northwest*:

> I wanted to have a long dialogue scene between Cary Grant and one of the factory workers as they walk along the assembly line. ... Behind them a car is being assembled, piece by piece. Finally, the car they've seen being put together from a simple nut and bolt is complete, with gas and oil, and all ready to drive off the line. The two men look at it and say, 'Isn't it wonderful!' Then they open the door to the car and out drops a corpse!
>
> (Hitchcock in Truffaut 1986: 392–3)

THE GRAPHIC MARQUIS (DE SADE)

> Of course, to enjoy making terrifying films is bound to suggest a form of intellectual sadism, and yet it can also be quite wholesome.
>
> (Truffaut in Truffaut 1986: 295)

But how might the question of hegemonic violence be connected with the other methodological concern that I noted earlier, that of sadistic desire? In

Lacan's 'Kant With Sade' he argues that the Marquis de Sade realizes the logic of Kant's own system, the truth he was too afraid to name: that the depth of radical evil is constitutive of human existence. There is at the heart of the human endeavour a sadistic drive, perhaps best expressed in Kant's saying: 'in the misfortunes of our best friends, there is something which is not altogether displeasing to us' (Kant 1960: 29). De Sade was in the end correct: human beings like to inflict violence on others, or see violence inflicted on others, especially those who are identified as enemies or hateful in some sense. Of course, the twist is that that same violence is returned upon the sadist. The problem here is to avoid the universalizing tendencies of psychoanalysis, to historicize such an argument. One way is through the connection with hegemonic violence.

To begin, once again, with Hitchcock: in a number of films – *Sabotage*, *Psycho*, *Frenzy*, *Dial 'M' for Murder* and *Torn Curtain* – the violence takes place 'on screen', as it were. A boy, two women and two men are the subjects of the killings. The biblical texts I will discuss depict their killings 'in text', a woman in Judges 19 (the Levite's concubine) and a man in 1 Samuel 15 (Agag).

(Redbank Road drew near as some drops of rain rode the angle of the wind. I was thankful for the wool for a very different reason now – its ability to retain body heat. 'Looks like the media are here', said Michal.
    'Why? What's different about this killing?' I asked.
    'You'll see', said Jonathan.)

Contrary to Rothman's argument (1982: 250) that Hitchcock's films become more graphically violent over time, the killing of Stevie in the early *Sabotage* remains a point of critical contention.[28] After identifying with the boy, the viewer is then made distinctly uncomfortable by his accidental death when the anarchist bomb he is carrying for his brother-in-law, Verloc, blows up the bus. But this serves only to increase viewer sympathy with his sister, Mrs Verloc, who kills her husband over dinner with a carving knife.[29] (He becomes the meat, never to be eaten, that she has just been carving.) Sympathy for her is built up through the involuntariness of her act and through the callousness of Verloc over the death of the boy. By this time, we sadistically will his death at her hand and do not hold her responsible. 'Here, we weren't trying to frighten anyone; we had to make the viewer feel like killing a man, and that's a good deal tougher' (Hitchcock in Truffaut 1986: 147). Crucial to viewer involvement was the montage cutting sequence at the dinner table,[30] a technique, initially developed by Eisenstein, that was to be refined for the shower scene of *Psycho*. The technique, along with the specific staging of shots, has the effect of making the viewer feel part of the action (Garrett 1991: 30), while the subjective or point-of-view shot generates viewer sympathy (Cooke 1990: 196).

Yet, in *Sabotage* there is already a link between sadism and hegemonic violence, for after Stevie is given the package containing the bomb which must be delivered before its detonation time, there is a suspense sequence of the sort that made Hitchcock's fame. Stevie is held up by a toothpaste/hair oil sales-man (becoming a temporary model), and then must wait for a royal procession before finally boarding the fateful bus. What interests me here is the conjunction of the royal procession and the anarchist's bomb: sanctioned violence meets that which is named terrorism, except it is in the hand of the boy. In part, the royal parade (state power) causes the boy's death by holding him up (he dies at 1.45 pm because he does not get to Piccadilly on time), thus effecting a transferal between hegemonic violence (the soldiers protecting the royal carriage) and terrorism – i.e. what appears peaceful (the state) is inherently violent. The sadistic desire to see Verloc killed is then generated out of this hegemonic violence.[31]

(A number of television trucks and film crews were held at bay by some uniformed cops. I thought I glimpsed a rotund old man with protruding lips in suit and hat crossing the road and disappearing into the jumble of vehicles. 'Isn't that …?' I began, but held myself back.)

While there is a structural and technical continuity between *Sabotage*'s dinner table and *Psycho*'s shower scene, the difference is the ' "enforced" identification with a psychopathic killer' (Allen 1986: 55) in *Psycho*, for after the death of Marion (Janet Leigh) viewer sympathy, with nowhere to go, subtly shifts to Norman Bates (Anthony Perkins) himself.

Of course, the sequence that has generated perhaps the most critical discussion of Hitchcock, and one that enables the sympathetic transition from Marion to Norman, is the shower murder. One of the best known moments in screen history,[32] it has also been regarded as the classic expression of male-to-female violence.[33] Yet, it is also highly ambiguous, a mix of sadistic enjoyment and profound distress,[34] an act carried out by a disturbed killer who is constructed as a woman, his mother, at the moment of killing. (In fact, it first appears to be women-to-woman violence.) A crucial factor in sympathy for Norman is his apparent insanity, taking on the persona of his mother.[35]

By killing off his main star, Janet Leigh, halfway through the film, Hitchcock broke Hollywood protocol (although he had done a similar thing with *Sabotage*). Not only did the montage 'give the impression of a knife stabbing a victim' (Hitchcock, 1995: 146),[36] but it also, through the cinematic cutting used to achieve the shower scene, cuts the film in two, moving from Marion to Norman (Edelman 1995: 160–1).[37] Robin Wood (1989: 146), largely responsible for the initial elevation of Hitchcock in English language film criticism, finds the breaking off of identification with Marion the most brutal element. We have no option but to identify with Norman after we have been emptied of the terror of the shower scene.[38] And this identification is sealed in an apparently small moment in the film: when Marion's car, with her corpse wrapped in the shower curtain in the trunk, is sinking into the marsh where

Norman has driven it at the back of the hotel, it pauses a moment, threatening to arrest its slow decline. Involuntarily, viewers wish the car on its way, thereby hoping that Norman will not be caught. After the pause, the car continues and sinks, but by this time we have been taken in.[39] Following such a sadistic identification, the murder of Arbogast seems justified and the persistent investigation by Samuel and Lila is perceived as a threat to Norman.

> (There was even a priest present. 'What's he doing here?' I asked.
>   'Police chaplain', replied Jonathan.
>   I knew that they called out the chaplains on bad cases, although this one, Lee Vite was his name, had a gruesome reputation for relishing the worst crimes at which to provide spiritual comfort.)

Is there a biblical text that intersects with *Psycho*? It seems to me that Judges 19, the so-called story of the Levite's concubine, may well express a comparable logic, for here a woman is also killed brutally. The key text for my purposes comes close to the end of the story (19:29): 'When he had entered his house, he took the knife, and grasping his concubine he cut her up, according to her bones, into twelve pieces and sent her throughout all the territory of Israel'.[40] It is not clear that the unnamed[41] woman is dead after the pack rape in Gibeah (although the Septuagint is clear on this); all that is written in response to the Levite's 'Get up, we are going' is 'But there was no-one answering' (19:28). Thus the Levite may well be read as complicit with her murder, killing her as he dissects and dismembers.[42]

The story is almost universally dismaying for biblical critics, with minimal efforts at salvage.[43] Even with efforts to understand the logic of the text,[44] to which I will turn in a moment, it is read as a negative example, as a sign of how bad things have become,[45] as an example of how misogynist the biblical text can be,[46] as 'the most horrible story of the Hebrew Bible' (Bal 1993: 209). Yet, what is interesting about these readings is the way reader identification or sympathy is firmly attached to the unnamed concubine, as it is to Marion in *Psycho*. So the knife may be read in a similar fashion as well: its penile penetration and dissection in rape and dismemberment also severs reader identification with the woman and subtly shifts it to the Levite (in the same way that Norman gains our sympathy).[47] As the body itself is butchered and written, becoming a letter embodying a message (so Bal 1993: 224), identification shifts to the writer, the Levite. This is important for the remaining story, for the Levite now seems to be an agent of revenge and the reader urges him on to punish the Benjaminites of Gibeah. By the time the story winds down in chapter 21, the impression is that the Benjaminites have been justly punished for their crime, and that Israel has been lenient in allowing a few to survive. But it is the delay in slaughtering the Benjaminites that hooks the reader: the first two victories of the Benjaminites create a moment of tension, comparable to the pause of the sinking car in the swamp in *Psycho*. We hold our breath for a moment or two, breathing a sigh of relief when the car continues sinking, when the Benjaminites finally get defeated. In the same way that we hold out for Norman, so also we barrack for the Levite.

The twist in all of this is that such support for the Levite transposes itself back into the narrative before he dismembers the concubine. Here is the grisly 'truth' of this text, the twist that shows up reader complicity, for to back the Levite is to wish the concubine dissevered, to assume that the 'crime', the 'outrage', has been done not against the woman, but against the Levite himself.[48] So also with Marion's stabbing in *Psycho*: both biblical text and film engage us 'as an accomplice – a role which [we] find more and more repellent as the film[/text] proceeds' (adapted from Keith Cohen 1989: 147).

In this story, the sadistic impulse intersects with the struggle over acceptable and unacceptable forms of violence. Here dismemberment seems to be the acceptable violence – not one Israelite raises an eyebrow – and the rape by the 'sons of Belial' (19:22) / 'lords of Gibeah' (20:5) unacceptable. Also acceptable is the armed punishment of Gibeah with 400,000 troops, although the hegemony thus sought is not without cost (40,000 Israelite dead in the first two battles (20:21, 25)). Is not this a clear marker of the difference between the violence by which social order and hegemony is maintained and that which is named 'outrage' by that same hegemony? This suggestion is reinforced by the connections between the dismemberment of the concubine and sacrifice. An old interpretation, revived with a twist by Bal, it notes that the terms used in 19:29 are 'the proper terms for cutting up the carcass of an animal' (1 Samuel 11:7; 1 Kings 18:23, 33) and for the ritual 'cutting up of the victim for sacrifice' (Leviticus 1:6, 12; 4:28; 8:20 (Moore 1908: 420; see also Hamlin 1990: 167)). For Bal (1988:119–27) the whole story is sacrificial, echoing Genesis 22, except that it is a systematic anti-sacrifice, in which the gift is given up, the rape is defiling and the dismemberment is desacralizing.[49] But, as I argued above, sacrifice itself, in its very banality, points to the ubiquity of hegemonic violence.

For the final stage of my argument I consider three scenes in *Dial 'M' for Murder*, *Frenzy* and *Torn Curtain* over against 1 Samuel 15. In these texts the notion of sadistic transfer – the sadist becomes the victim – is clearest. In *Psycho* the sadistic transfer works through identification with Norman and the discomfort that such identification with a psychotic killer brings. In Judges 19–21 a similar process operates with the Levite. However, in this last collection of texts, the sadistic transfer happens at the moment of graphic violence itself.

In *Dial 'M' for Murder*[50] the murder scene embodies the sadistic transfer, for the would be murderer himself ('Captain Leslie') is murdered by Grace Kelly. In this case sympathy lies with Grace Kelly, and our desperate wish that she does not fall into the trap set by her husband, Tony (keen on her life insurance), that she escapes the stranglehold, is realized when she manages to stab the murderer with a pair of scissors. The initial stabbing is full of the audience's Sadean sympathy, but as he falls backwards, towards the camera, he rams the scissors, now foregrounded in close up (and originally in 3D), further into his back in a grisly fashion.[51] The twist of the scissors as they are ground deeper in is also the twist that shows up our involvement in murder, revulsion at the scene signalling a sadistic self-awareness. But suddenly, we are the sadistic victim, for the start we feel at the scene is the jab of the scissors in our own backs.

(The chief who had thrown me out of the force was there. Saul was fielding media questions, speaking a lot without saying anything, answering the same question in a different way each time he answered. The experienced reporters present found themselves taken in and admiring him. His only match was an old persistent reporter, Samuel, who refused to take Saul's crap and always pushed him on why the police seemed to be avoiding their duties. Of course, Saul behaved as though I didn't exist.)

Comparable to the rammed scissors of *Dial 'M' for Murder* is the slaying of Agag in 1 Samuel 15. A brief sentence in 15:33 carries the weight of the preceding narrative events upon it: 'And Samuel hewed Agag in pieces before Yahweh in Gilgal.' This is Samuel's last act, apart from grieving over Saul (15:35), before the anointing of David in 1 Samuel 16. Yet Saul is the focus of the chapter in which Samuel's frustration slowly rises. Through a tedious, painful process, Saul persists in seeking a way around Samuel's condemnation for having failed to follow the order to obliterate Amalek (1 Samuel 15:3).[52] Samuel finally gives in, acquiescing to Saul's request to return and worship with him (15:30). And then, immediately after the notice that 'Saul worshipped Yahweh' (15:31), an extremely frustrated Samuel commands that Agag be brought to him. Is Samuel to complete the ban on Amalek that Saul failed to carry out himself? Is Agag here the first sacrifice of the things saved from destruction? It seems that the king of the Amalekites stands in for the king of the Israelites.[53] There is a difference between the versions at this point on the issue of Agag's words in 15:32, with the Qumran (Hebrew) and Septuagint (Greek) versions having one text and the Masoretic Text (Hebrew) another. But does this not reflect the ambiguity of Saul's own status? Having worn Samuel down, would Saul also say, 'Surely the bitterness of death is past' (MT); or, in the face of Samuel's condemnation and rejection, would he say 'Surely this is the bitterness of death' (Qumran/Septuagint)? Not merely content with a sword thrust or a slit throat, 'Samuel hewed Agag (Saul) in pieces before Yahweh in Gilgal'. The image is one of aging prophet hacking away at the body of Agag in a frenzy of rage, frustration and grief. Yet, the words come as a shock at the end of the story, an over reaction that twists the knife as it were, for the reader's sadistic impulse. But it also signals the sadistic transfer for those who identify with Saul, for the ambiguity of the Agag/Saul identity implicates the reader, from whom lumps of bleeding and quivering flesh begin to splash on the text's page as Samuel's sword hacks the reader in pieces as well.

> (*Bloody hunks of meat were strewn over the front lawn, splattered over the steps and smeared down the front hallway. 'I thought you would like this', said Jonathan. I said nothing in response, merely looking about. Lying in the doorway to the kitchen were the remains of the body, a badly hacked up torso with one leg still attached. The head was at the back door, and the limbs scattered in small pieces throughout the small house. Only the left nipple was intact, another note stapled to it, another 'M'. In the oven in the kitchen was the head of another body, skin partially flayed, a bloody pair of scissors nearby, but otherwise not touched. She had been gassed, and yet another note pinned to her left nipple.*
>   '*The other one's male', said Michal in response to my look, 'but we can't find his balls anywhere.'*)

The culmination of all of this is in the killing of Mrs Blaney in *Frenzy* and of Gromek in *Torn Curtain*. Mrs Blaney's murder by Bob Rusk (Barry Foster) is, for Rothman, 'the most heartbreaking passage in Hitchcock's work' (1982: 250); for Modleski it is 'infinitely sad, pathetic, among the most disturbing scenes cinema has produced' (1988: 113). Responsible for a series of 'necktie murders' in Covent Garden, Rusk, who, as he says to the dating agency, likes masochistic women,[54] lures women to a hotel room and brutally kills them with a necktie. Mrs Blaney's murder, however, is shown from beginning to end, without being eroticized as in *Psycho* (so Modleski 1988: 113), generating a profound discomfort through the vivid depiction of a slow and brutal death.[55] Similarly, in *Torn Curtain* there is a gruelling, drawn out, ten minute sequence in which the Paul Newman character wrestles with Gromek, all the while aided by the rural woman who pours scalding soup on him, hands Newman a carving knife that breaks off against the victim's neck, and lastly hits Gromek's legs with a shovel while Newman drags him to an open oven, where he is suffocated, the camera focusing on his twitching fingers that finally come to a rest. As with *Sabotage*, the death happens in domestic space with appropriate items: a pot of soup, a carving knife, a shovel and then the gas oven. And it must take place silently, for the taxi driver is waiting outside. Gromek (Wolfgang Kieling) is a political and ideological enemy – an agent of communist East Germany – who must be destroyed, since he stands in the way of the survival of the Newman character, who himself must escape with the crucial formula in his head. Not only is Gromek politically unlikeable for a majority of the audience, but he appears as a sly, conniving police agent.[56] It is almost too easy to wish Gromek's death (he in fact asks for it), so the sadistic transference is all the more marked. Once the sadistic wish is expressed, it is relentlessly turned on the viewer, who now becomes the sadistic victim. 'We are implicated – *we* are

killing Gromek – and Hitchcock spares us no discomfort for our complicity' (Wood 1989: 202). Or rather, it is we who are slowly being killed,
burnt, stabbed, and gassed.

CONCLUSION

One of the features of Hitchcock criticism is how much the auteur himself
has pre-empted critical reception of his work (shown by the amount of
words in this chapter from Hitchcock's mouth). Pithy statements and comments seem to have a knack of re-appearing in the form of critical readings.
The dominating, divine presence of Hitchcock is of course a relic of modernist concerns with the author,[57] but there is a curious twist provided by
the biography by Spoto (1982). For here is found more than we ever wanted
– misogyny, sadism, rape fantasies, bathroom and other fetishes about sex
and the body, guilt, anxiety, a mother fixation, phobias about women, people, the world, and a drinking problem late in life. Although for Spoto
Hitchcock was out of control,[58] I would rather argue that not only is this a
surfeit of the auteur, but that we should expect nothing else. Are not the
contradictory dimensions of all these elements simultaneously revealed *and*
concealed in his films?

But does not Spoto's description belong as much to Yahweh as to Hitchcock,
who, in the words of Rothman, is

> impotent in the face of the possibility that we will fail to acknowl-
> edge him. He cannot openly express the pleasures and terrors of his
> role, cannot compel our recognition. Insofar as he is human, he must
> wish – whether consciously or not – to avenge himself on those viewers
> who fail to acknowledge him. The fantasy of unleashing violence on
> the viewer who condemns him to his condition of impotence is built
> into the conditions of his role.
>
> (Rothman 1982: 107)

All we can do, like Rothman (so Modleski 1988: 118), is submit to such a
being.

There is one final dialectical turn to make here, and that is to suggest that the
sadistic violence of Hitchcock's films and the biblical texts is none other than
the return of the repressed (to borrow a phrase from Freud) of effaced hegemonic
violence. It is as though the ubiquitous violence that no one sees forces its way
through in sadistic violence, turning to make the sadist the victim.

(I rolled a cigarette and looked about, avoiding the jagged pieces of flesh.
Abraham appeared, having come over from the site of the second murder.
'We have identities for three of the bodies, although the mincemeat is a

bit harder to reconstruct. Apart from old Aaron Murphy, there was Isaac Moses up by the baseball ground. This place is where Melekh Agag is supposed to be living, so we guess that those are his bits and pieces all over the place. As for the woman in the oven, we don't know; Agag's girlfriend, maybe. If so, her name was Merab.'

'Do you know anything about them?' I asked.

'Not much', he said, 'except that they were all involved in the local porn industry.'

Now this was home territory for me, since I had worked for a time in various roles – theatre hand, stunt cock, video editor, actor and director – in the Parramatta industry. And if anyone knew what was going in porn, it was Sue Lammith. I hadn't called on Sue for a long while.)

3

NIGHT SPRINKLE(S)[1]

Pornography and the Song of Songs

The truth, in this sense, is that which runs after truth – and that is
where I am running, where I am taking you, like Actaeon's hounds,
after me. When I find the goddess's hiding place, I will no doubt be
changed into a stag, and you can devour me, but we still have a little
way to go yet.

(Lacan 1994: 188)

Make haste, my beloved, and be like a gazelle or a young stag upon the
mountains of spices.

(Song of Songs 8:14)

*(Sue's place was about an hour's walk away in the early evening. I needed
to think, so I set off, passed through the crescendo and smell of Cumberland
Highway, the back of the vast, jumbled postmodern children's hospital,
the disused gaol built with convict-cut sandstone and over the sluggish
brown Parramatta River with urban debris decorating its sides. On the
southern bank Sue's light was on; I knocked on the arched door. Surprise
and delight saw me in and seated in an office overloaded with film
editing equipment, papers, clothes and a battered fridge. From a small
southern window I could just make out the chequered neon sign at the
police station across the intersection.)*

If popular culture has a symbiotic relationship with censorship – as de
Certeau would have it – then pornography, especially hardcore,[2] must be
the most brazen of the whole lot (see Michelson 1993: 274–300). Political,
religious and feminist sparring over pornography inevitably anti-climaxes
with reflection on the (de)merits of the Censor. But what these debates
miss is that it is precisely the Censor that author-izes pornography itself (so
Kendrick 1996).[3] From the celebrated first moment of pornography – Pietro
Aretino's *Sonnetti lussuriosi* (1527),[4] popularly known as 'Aretino's postures',
a collection of sonnets to accompany some engravings of sex positions by
Giulio Romano – the Censor has been present. In Aretino's case, the publication was banned by the Church, the engraver imprisoned and Aretino
barely escaped death.[5]

This curiously intimate relation between censorship and pornography was still rocking back and forth in the so-called 'porn wars' of the 1980s. Thus, Andrea Dworkin (1981)[6] and Catherine MacKinnon (1989), with their desire to have antipornography criminal legislation introduced in Minneapolis and Indianapolis in the USA, gave birth to the oppositional Feminist Anti-Censorship Task Force (FACT). In England a few years later FAC, Feminists Against Censorship, was shaped in order to head off similar moves there (see Feminists Against Censorship 1991; Matrix 1996; Williams 1989: 23–33). Of course what the whole conflict requires (but what is not possible here) is an analysis that has as its model Marx's *Eighteenth Brumaire of Louis Bonaparte*. Items in such a group session would include the deviant cause-and-effect position (effectively destroyed by Cameron 1992; see also Koop 1987),[7] the quantitative studies investigating this question (Allen, D'Alessio and Brezgel 1995; Childress 1991; Cowan and Dunn 1994; Fisher and Grenier 1994; Heilbrun and Seif 1988; Jervey 1983; King 1993;[8] Kutchinsky 1992; Lawrence and Herold 1988; Padgett, Brislin-Slutz and Neal 1989; Segal 1990; 1993; Trostle 1993; Wilcox 1987), the two contradictory commissions (1970 and 1986) in the USA that respectively rejected and then affirmed the cause-and-effect argument (Einsedel 1989; Williams 1989: 14–23), the Williams Report in England in 1979, violence (Durbin 1996: 54; Linz, Donnerstein and Penrod 1987; McConahay 1988: 63; Slade 1984), the troubled distinction between erotica and pornography (Nead 1993),[9] and between obscenity and art (Williams 1993a), and the complete neglect of gay, lesbian, bisexual, transvestite, S/M, genderfuck and other healthy non-sexist queer practices (Bensinger 1992; Evans and Gamman 1995: 41; Henderson 1992; Kipnis 1993; Lau 1993; McClintock 1993; Patton 1994; Pendleton 1992; A. Smith 1995; Smyth 1990; Watney 1987; Waugh 1995; Williams 1989: 184–228). But it is the cause-and-effect argument that has dominated the scene, tied up with the idea that pornography is based on domination itself (Finn 1996: 34–65, 81–95; Hansen, Needham and Nichols 1989). And it is this that has formed the backdrop to the inadequate debate in biblical studies on pornography and pornoprophetics (Brenner 1995; 1996; Brenner and Van Dijk-Hemmes 1993: 168–193; Carroll 1995; 1996; Exum 1995; Setel 1993). The domination position has undergone systematic attack from many angles (Irving 1992; Ferguson 1991; McConahay 1988; Mainil 1992; Ross 1993; A. Smith 1995), including an exquisite response by Judith Butler:

> Such a rigid determinism assimilates any account of sexuality to rigid and determining positions of domination and subordination, and assimilates those positions to the social gender of man and woman. But that deterministic account has come under continuous criticism from feminists not only for an untenable account of female sexuality

as coerced subordination, but for the totalizing view of heterosexuality as well – one in which all power relations are reduced to relations of domination – and for the failure to distinguish the presence of coerced domination in sexuality from pleasurable and wanted dynamics of power.

(Butler 1994: 7)

The delectable arena of (especially queer) S/M, here identified by Butler in her final sentence, has of course been an object of absolute censorship, and, significantly, of the harshest legal penalties – the sexual subversion of the techniques of enforcement is thereby recognized (see McClintock 1993: 219–22; Watney 1987).

Pornography is then necessarily political and ideological: to speak about it is to take up a political position (Brigman 1983; Cameron 1992: 3; McConahay 1988: 36; Watney 1987: 76).[10] It seems that one must either side with the Censor or against: as for me, any drive to outsmart the Censor is worth the effort. For pornography has always had some sort of intercourse with political radicalism, from its earliest uses by Aretino and those who followed him as political and religious subversion (see Hunt 1993a: 35–8;[11] Weil 1993), connections with anarchism and the proletariat (Arcand 1993: 115–23), the French Revolution (DeJean 1993; Hunt 1993b), English radicalism of the 1820s and 1830s (McCalman 1988: 204–37),[12] to government inquiries and the affront caused by fringe porn today.

In its own way, the split over allegorical and literal readings of the Song of Songs engages a similar dialectic to the one I have touched on above, for allegorical readings have allowed the Song entry past the Censor into the canon and into the history of interpretation. Produced in part by the allusive poetic language of the text, its allegorical preservation has then stirred the desire for literary readings. Allegory may be regarded as the ruse by which the Censor was fooled.

> (*Sue had been working for some years now in the old Presbyterian Church which she leased when the congregation moved to a new site. Her office was the former vestry, and the main sanctuary the studio with its cameras, sets and stained glass in the background. After we had caught up on the last few years, the ashtray had been filled and the fridge depleted of beer, she asked, 'You looking for work?'*
>
> *'No, I'm chasing a lead.'*
>
> *Her facial muscles altered, the smile faded. 'Some of your actors were found dead a few hours ago.' Just then someone pounded on the door. She hesitated, realized her light was on, and went to answer it. A moment later I was introduced to Solomon Wiseman,[13] one of her directors.)*

EJACULATOR MEETS THE SLUT GODDESS[14]

That's three to four times as many adult book stores as McDonald's!
(Goldman 1983: 124)

Let me begin with Michel Foucault, particularly his division between *ars erotica* and *scientia sexualis*. For Foucault, *ars erotica* is an earlier tradition that passes on its esoteric truths from master to pupil through a long process of skilled and severe initiation, experience and discourse, leading to 'an absolute mastery of the body, a singular bliss, obliviousness to time and limits, the elixir of life, the exile of death and its threats' (Foucault 1990: 58). *Scientia sexualis*, by contrast, comprises 'procedures for telling the truth of sex which are geared to a form of knowledge–power strictly opposed to the art of initiations and the masterful secret' (58). It arises out of the medieval confession, 'which in the Christian West was the first technique for producing the truth of sex' (68). But what is stimulating about *scientia sexualis* is that its rise is tied up with the rise of capitalism[15] and the modern world, with the Renaissance, the scientific revolution, the Enlightenment and the French Revolution. But this is also when pornography thrust itself forward: 'Writers and engravers of pornography came out of the demimonde of heretics, freethinkers and libertines who made up the underside of those formative Western developments ... . Pornography was not a given; it was defined over time and by the conflicts between writers, artists and engravers on the one side and spies, policemen, clergymen and state officials on the other' (Hunt 1993a: 11).[16]

(Sue and Solomon were part of Parramatta's colourful demimonde, a group that included pornographers like Sue, drug pushers, ecoterrorists, occasional communists, ferals and sex workers. Apart from films and videos, Sue produced magazines, books and internet porn.)

Thus, it might be argued that the emergence of the literal[17] and the decline of the allegorical reading of the Song[18] coincides with the slow transition from *ars erotica*, of which the Song is one of the earliest documents, to *scientia sexualis*, with the rise of modernity per se. If I add to this de Certeau's argument that those items of the modern world I have just listed have their impetus from Christian theology and, I would add, biblical studies, then it seems that the Song itself – especially with the turn to a literal, sexual reading because of disillusion with allegorical interpretation – is part of the invention of pornography.[19] Pornography may then be understood as gaining its enabling power from the simultaneous breakup and founding role of theological and biblical traditions. This is enhanced with Foucault suggestion that *ars erotica* and *scientia sexualis* are more dialectically related, the latter being in some way a sublimated form of the former (1990: 71). So it might be asked: is not a pornographic reading of the Song a sublimated version of an allegorical one?

For Weaver, writing on 'Pornography and the Religious Imagination', the Song of Songs is 'one of the most erotic poems in ancient literature' (1989: 73). But it is also one of the most pornographic poems of contemporary literature. It is as though a literal reading generates an archaeology of present pornography.

('Who's dead?' Sue asked.

'Isaac Moses and Melekh Agag, and an unknown woman with Melekh', I replied.

'That's probably Merab', said Solomon, 'she and Melekh have been spending some time together.'

'There was also an old garage owner,' I said, 'Murphy, but I don't believe he worked for you.'

'Actually, he did a few films for older audiences', Sue responded.

I told them about the deaths, the condition of the bodies, the notes and the castrations. 'They might have been castrated because they worked for me', Sue suggested.)

In such an archaeological delving, the first act involves the tongue, for the Song spills out a whole vocabulary of sex. In place of the obligatory Hebrew 'to know' (*yd'*), there are 'pasture' a 'flock' (1:7, 2:16; 6:2) or 'kids' (1:8), 'lie down' (1:7), 'embrace' (2:6; 8:2), 'hold' (3:4), 'hold captive' (7:6/5), 'stir up' (2:7; 3:5; 8:4), 'awaken love' (2:7; 3:5; 8:4), 'ravish' (4:9), 'come' (2:8; 4:16; 5:1), 'come up' (3:6: 4:2; 8:5), 'arise' (2:10, 13), 'lead' and 'bring' (8:2), 'knock' (5:2), 'open' (5:2, 5, 6; 7:13/12), 'bud' and 'bloom' (7:13/12), 'gather lilies' (6:2), 'give forth fragrance' (1:12), be 'sweet to my taste' (2:3), 'feed' (2:16; 4:5), 'eat' fruit (4:16; see also 5:1), 'drink' (5:1), 'pour out' (1:3), 'bathe' feet (5:3), 'thrust' a hand into a hole (5:3).

Apart from the myriad possibilities of the sexual act itself, the various connected items – genitalia, fluids, orifices, protrusions – also have a wide secondary terminology. Thus, we find liquids and spices such as 'wine' (1:2, 4; 5:1; 7:3/2, 10/9; 8:2), 'oils' (4:10) and 'anointing oils' (1:3), 'perfume' (1:3), 'nard' (1:12; 4:13–14), a 'bag of myrrh' (1:13), 'myrrh' (3:6; 4:6, 14; 5:1, 5, 13), 'frankincense' (3:6; 4:6, 14), 'nectar' (4:11), 'honey' (4:11; 5:1), 'milk' (4:11; 5:1, 12), 'saffron' (4:14), 'calamus' (4:14), 'cinnamon' (4:14), 'aloes' (4:14), 'fountain' (4:12, 15), 'living water' (4:15), 'flowing streams' (4:15), 'wet with dew' (5:2), 'night sprinkles' (5:2), 'the juice of my pomegranates' (8:2); some of which are notable for their fragrances (4:10, 11, 16).[20] The sexual body is variously a 'garden' (4:12, 16; 5:1; 6:2; 8:13), a 'vineyard' (1:6; 2:15; 7:13/12; 8:11), an 'orchard' (4:13) and a 'nut orchard' (6:11), or an apple or fig or palm tree (2:3, 13; 7:8–9/7–8; 8:5). Further, plants and fruits function as euphemisms for sexual zones and organs[21], their ripeness a signifier of sex (Munro

1995: 80): 'cluster of henna blossoms' (1:14; see also 4:13), 'crocus' (2:1, 2), 'lily' (2:1, 16; 4:5; 5:13; 6:2; 7:3/2), 'flowers' (2:12), 'vines' (2:13; 7:9/8, 13/12), 'blossoms' (6:11), 'grape blossoms' (7:13/12), 'wheat' (7:3/2), 'fruit' with a sweet taste (2:3), 'choicest fruits' (4:13), 'raisins' (2:5), 'apples' (2:5; 7:9/8), 'pomegranates' (4:3; 6:7, 11; 7:13/12) and 'mandrakes' (7:14/13). Animals also stand in for sexual designators: 'flock' (1:7, 8; 4:1; 6:5), 'kids' (1:8), 'gazelles' (2:7, 17; 3:5; 7:4/3; 8:14), 'wild does' (2:7; 3:5), 'foxes' (2:15) and a 'stag' (2:17; 8:14). And then there are the orifices and their barriers described as parts of human dwellings: 'tents' (1:5, 8), 'curtains' (1:5), 'wall' (2:9; 8:9, 10), 'window' (2:9), 'lattice' (2:9), 'doors' (7:14/13; 8:9), 'boards of cedar' (8:9), 'mother's house' (3:4; 8:2), 'chamber of her that conceived me' (3:4; see 8:2), a 'palanquin' with 'posts of silver', 'back of gold' and 'seat of purple' (3:9–10). Various landforms suggest body parts, both the bits that stick out such as 'mountains' (2:8, 17; 4:8), 'mountain of myrrh' (4:6), 'mountain of spices' (8:14), 'hills' (2:8), 'hill of frankincense' (4:6), 'peak' (4:8), and those that open up, such as 'clefts of the rock' (2:14), 'covert of the cliff' (2:14) and 'blossoms of the valley' (6:11). Finally, some miscellaneous items may designate sex: 'column of smoke' (3:6), 'litter of Solomon' (3:7), 'sword at his thigh' (3:8), 'alarms by night' (3:8), 'wood of Lebanon' (3:9) and 'jewel' (4:9; 7:3/2). Even with the *wasfs* – love poems in which the body of another is described metaphorically – the descriptions of facial features function as displaced references to the nether regions – 'eyes' (4:1; 5:12; 6:5), 'hair' (4:1; 5:11; 6:5), 'teeth' (4:2; 7:10/9), 'lips' (4:3, 10; 5:13; 7:10/9), 'mouth' (4:4), 'cheeks' (4:3; 5:13; 6:7), 'head' (5:2, 11; 7:6/5). 'Hand' (5:5) and 'feet' (5:3; 7:1/3) work in a similar way.

Both sex and death – the two great drives of Freud's later writings – generate a host of secondary signifiers; although the specific terminology may change, the Song generates a specific lexical category, a linguistic register associated with the naming of sexual acts and anatomical parts. In this respect it is a partner to the use of technical and medical language in the pornography of the eighteenth century, since such language was otherwise avoided (Frappier-Mazur 1993: 206), and of obscene terminology in the twentieth century. Such a list, to which the reader may quickly add, might begin with 'fuck', 'bang', 'hump', 'nail', 'pussy', 'cunt', 'flaps', 'cock', 'schlong,' 'cum', 'jism', 'blow-job', 'hand-job',[22] but it also brings to bear a range of resignified terms from other discourses such as 'greek', 'french', 'english', 'glory hole', 'golden shower', 'water sports', and 'rainbow shower'. And then there is the semi-technical terminology that includes coitus, fellatio, cunnilingus, analingus, rimming, felching, coprophilia and so on.

Such a generic feature produces what Goulemot terms a 'metaphorical excess' (1994: 66) in pornography and what Grossberg depicts as 'exoticism' in the Song (1989:56–7). Along with its unusual syntactic conventions,[23] the vocabulary of the Song discharges a sexual strangeness, perhaps even a deviance that is enhanced by the associations with sadism and masochism (5:4, 7), bestiality (see the animal references above), incest (1:6; 3:11; 5:1; 6:9; 8:1), intergenerational sex (3:4; 6:9; 8:2) and paedophilia (8:8–9). Indeed, to be entered by the Song is a little like being entered by the Marquis de Sade.

> (*'Melekh and Merab did a lot of fetish stuff for me', Sue went on, 'you know, leather, vinyl, rubber, body parts. They specialized in doing things you wouldn't dream of with plants and food. As for Isaac, he did the really kinky stuff, most of it illegal.' Solomon leant against the old ecclesial brick and lit a smoke.*)

There is, however, another tendency to which the language leans – fetishism, the 'specific excess of perversity' (Goulemot 1994: 66), the intensification of desire in a piece of the body, in clothing, in food, or in an external object, whether animal, vegetable or architectural[24] in order to highlight sexual difference (see Kuhn 1985: 35–40). In other words, to use Freudian terminology, I am speaking of libidinal investment, an intense sexual charge invested in the whole range of items I have listed above – spices, plants, food, fruits,[25] flowers, animals, buildings, geography and body parts themselves – which may now be reread as a vast catalogue of fetishes. While the fetishism of contemporary pornography makes use of similar toys, it differs in its focus on clothing, such as rubber, leather, vinyl, wool and so on. Although one is reminded of Tom of Finland's drawings in the Song's fetishization of military dress and armament (3:8; 4:4; 6:10), the effect of the nature fetishes is to turn the various flora and fauna into body covering.

Yet, it is not merely the items to which the language refers that constitute fetishes, for, as Frappier-Mazur (1993) argues, there is a paradoxical relation between the obscene word and truth. The twist in her argument is that this works only in the sense that the truth in question is a simulacrum or fetish. That is, the word itself becomes the fetish, the locus of desire, rather than the object to which it refers. Cast free from and replacing their referents, the fetish–words of the text may trigger imagination and phantasy: 'The truth of the obscene word is that it manifests the dependence of eroticism on the imaginary' (218).

This brings me to a third zone, the conjugation of realism and phantasy. It seems to me that the Song is as much concerned with 'the real thing' – despite the ambiguity that lies deep in such a wish – as contemporary pornography, especially hardcore. In the Song it is important that various types of sucking and fucking have, textually, taken place, preferably more than once. While in a literary text this is not so much signified by mere description but by the linguistic and metaphorical excess I have been tracing, and specifically by the vocabulary of sex such as 'pasture a flock' or 'gather lilies', in a filmic text a distinct set of practices construct a similar realistic effect. Thus, viewers of contemporary pornography feel ripped off if the real thing hasn't taken place, if it can be noticed that the actors are faking it; 'porn's televisual techniques construct – indeed its appeal in part hinges on – a "real" person performing within the limits of his or her own body, unenhanced by special effects … or stunt men, the body with all its scars, stretch marks, lopsided balls, and un-matched breasts' (Patton 1991: 377 and 379; see Kaite 1995: 48). This of course requires suspension of the knowledge that this is, after all, acting, but then cinema itself is no different. In still photography, penetrative sex (the 'meat shot'), whether anal, vaginal or oral, often requires that the tip of the penis/dildo/tongue be inserted, so that it can be seen that it is really being inserted, and not, say, bent back and hidden (see, for example, Faust 1980: 18). At the same time it is only the tip, so that the phallic protusion may still be seen, although it is occasionally completely buried (see Kaite 1995: 48). Similarly, for cunnilingus, rimming and felching, the tongue normally touches the clitoris or labia or anal rim, or its tip penetrates vagina or anus. It is rarely inserted completely, nor does the mouth obscure the vagina or anus from view. The same applies to fisting, although here there is a slight variation: for 'real' fisting the hand must not merely be half-way in the orifice, it must have disappeared, although still attached to a wrist which then serves as evidence: 'Oh shit, her hand really is all the way in there.' The work of tongue, penis, dildo or fist must be 'real', or, as Williams suggests for porn film, visible (Williams 1989: 94). The ultimate aim, the orgasm, must also be real, and the evidence for that can be registered by the generic function of the 'money shot',[26] the external ejaculation of male or female[27] into the air, on a partner's back, breasts, in his or her mouth, or elsewhere on the body. The prevalence of a whole subgenre of still photography which features the 'cum shot' is also part of this argument, as are golden showers or water sports. In most pornography women rarely ejaculate, so the more ambiguous thrashing and groaning takes its place.

> (*'Didn't old Murphy have trouble with the come shots?' I asked. 'He was old when we were kids.'*
>
> *'He was just a bit slower', Sue said, 'but it was worth the wait. Merab, if that's who you found, beat them all with her come shots, though. It's a shame she's dead.' I was starting to regret it too.*)

Do we not also find the money shot in the Song? While 4:13 (see below), 4:15 and 5:5 may be read in that way, the largest group of terms refer to liquids: wine, oils, perfume, nard, myrrh, nectar, honey, fountain, living water, flowing streams, night sprinkles, and the juice of pomegranates. Yet, the Song seems to go much wider than the restricted concern with ejaculation, evincing a central role for fluids, especially bodily ones.

Of course, the paradox here is that the need to see physical evidence, as well as the sounds (Williams 1989: 121–6), of sexual pleasure produces a display that is hardly 'real'. The orgasm rendered visible is 'problematic and paradoxical' (Smyth 1990: 156).[28] The catch is that the 'realism' sought after, in both the Song and pornography, must follow stylized patterns in order to be identified as 'real'. In the Song and written pornography there are the conventions of poetic and narrative linguistic construction and the meta-phorical excess of the language, while in visual pornography there are the appropriate positions to afford the viewer maximum exposure, the right sounds, shots and clear evidence of sexual climax. There is, in other words, a high level of technical artifice to make hardcore seem realistic, including poor film stock, editing and acting. Pornography, as Arcand points out, is both 'truth and lies' (1993: 174).[29]

> ('But who would want to kill them', I asked, 'apart from a psychopath?'
> Sue looked to Solomon, who hesitated a moment while stubbing out a
> cigarette. 'Well, they all used to meet as a group, along with some others,
> in one of the brothels near here. No-one seems to know what for, but it
> wasn't sex.')

But it is possible to go deeper, for the realist artifice, the effect of the real, the 'interminable quest for realism' (Williams 1989: 124), of the Song and writ-ten/visual pornography is precisely the tip of contact with phantasy. Pornography functions as a phantasmic repository: it 'is not so much realist as it is a mirror for activities we imagine but cannot observe ourselves en-gaged in' (Patton 1991: 377). It provides a base on which to build phantasies but it can't determine those phantasies (see Ross 1993: 240), even though the phantasies themselves are culturally, pornographically, and, with the Song, biblically, constructed (see Slade 1982: 153). Yet, rather than set realist desire over against phantasy, I would suggest that it is precisely the effect of realism in pornography and the Song that enables phantasy, and that it is the need for phantasy that produces the effect of the real. Phantasy is not that which con-ceals a dreadful reality; rather, it articulates the subject's traumatic relation to enjoyment, that is, to that which can never be acknowledged, integrated, or fulfilled – the 'real' (see Žižek 1994: 178).

The conjunction of phantasy and the real stimulates another zone that requires attention. It would be a mistake to see the traumatic phantasy struc-ture of pornography and the Song as somehow sundered from 'real' sex, which is then the ideal, natural human activity that is degraded through pornogra-phy (so, for instance, Blonsky 1992: 103–124; Gagnon 1988; Griffin 1981[30]). Masturbation, images, narrative and poetry, simulated or virtual sex, insofar as they produce phantasies, are not so much substitutes for the real as the real thing themselves. Actually, sex with 'real' partners is a substitution for mastur-bation, for simulated sex, for phantasy itself. 'Lacan's thesis that "there is no sexual relationship" means precisely that the structure of the "real" sexual act (the act with a flesh-and-blood partner) is already inherently phantasmatic – the "real" body of the other serves only as a support for our phantasmatic projections' (Žižek 1994: 210; see also Dean 1993: 11). This means that peepshows express the reality of sex: the dancers, dressed in phantasy costumes, dance behind a screen (on which the phantasy is projected) which is opened for a few seconds at a time when a coin drops in the slot (see Dudash, 1997; Funari, 1997).[31]

This dialectic of the real and phantasy shows through in a different way with the relation between narrative and 'real' sex. What is meant here is that the desire for the 'real', the generic expectation that in some way 'genuine' sex will take place, removes the possibility of narrative progression. The story is merely the pretext for the act itself, a vehicle for the sexual numbers (Williams 1989: 130), and the two would seem to be mutually exclusive (see Goulemot 1994: 141; Michelson 1993: 43–4; Žižek 1991a: 111). Too much narrative progression diminishes the pornographic focus.[32]

There is, however, another 'narrative', which is that of the rhythm of sexual episodes themselves.[33] This other narrative achieves, in conventional pornography, closure through the money shot; yet this type of (repeated) closure negates any closure of the narrative proper (see Pendleton 1992: 156–8; Slade 1982: 159). If I adjust my terminology, then it is the narrative of sex, the stages, combinations and sequences of acts, that excludes the possibility of another narrative – that of story or plot – gaining any foothold. This generic contradiction may account for the absence of any sustained story apart from the sex in the Song. Thus, although poetry is less likely to bear narrative sequences, and despite efforts to determine such a sequence in the Song (Goulder 1986), the Song is distinctly plotless. This means also that the assumption of one pair of lovers (pursued most thoroughly by Landy 1983; see also Wendland 1995[34]) – functioning as an alternative unifier of the Song – must also be discarded (so Brenner 1989: 28–9[35]); as with pornography, sex takes place with a range of partners and combinations. Even the poetic structure, a final refuge for unity, is basically 'open and loose' (Grossberg 1989: 70; Keel 1994: 16–17; contra Deckers 1993 and Exum 1973; Landy has a bet both ways, 1983: 33–58).

> ('They had been meeting regularly for some time', continued Solomon, 'although it was always on a different night at a different time. It really looked like they were trying to avoid the police, especially the secret types.'
>   'Well, if they were plotting anything', I said, 'then they seem to have kept it a good secret.' The neon sign on the police station across the road gazed at us, unblinking, through the small window of Sue's office.)

A third partner to the contradictions of realism/phantasy and narrative/sex is the friction between the explicit and the concealed. A feature of the Song is the way the various efforts at making the sex explicit only serve to conceal it further; the very means by which sex is indicated as taking place only frustrate such a process of indication. In the Song this problem opens out primarily through the language that is used: the various phrases and terms used to indicate body parts, fetishes, desire, fucking and bodily fluids are those which only yield up their load after a series of rereadings – the sexual codes need to be known or surmised before the explicit sex becomes clear. This not only defeats the desire for the explicit representation of sex, but would seem to be constitutive of it. Similarly, in pornography, the most explicit representations cannot help but conceal. In written pornography the language functions in the same way as the Song, whereas in visual pornography the standard scene of penis/dildo/tongue/hand in some orifice only serves to conceal the penetrating item at the very moment of penetration: it is as though mouth, anus and vagina not only hide the penis, but that they now have their own protrusion – the woman gains a penis[36] (flesh or otherwise) or phallic tongue, the man or woman a tail or a limb or an oversize tongue (see Kaite 1995: 48). It is no longer clear who possesses what, or who is being penetrated. Concealment also unites.

Apart from the variations on the crotch shot, often at angles that take some practice in themselves – and are a common source of cramps for models and actors – so that the camera may have as clear a view as possible, the effort to peer into orifices, especially the anus and the vagina, merely reinforces the processes of concealment.[37] Even nipple sucking, cunnilingus or rimming, apparent exceptions, succumb to the explicit/concealed contradiction, for as soon as the tongue touches nipple or labia or clitoris or anal rim, these sites of contact are concealed from view by the tongue itself. Indeed, it seems that some form of concealment is necessary in order to assert that the 'real thing' is taking place: explicitness requires a hidden clitoris, anal rim or nipple, a buried or swallowed penis, dildo, hand or tongue.

('They did their best to keep their meetings concealed', offered Sue, 'or at least to look like they were doing something else, like going to the brothel for sex.' Sue was looking tired, the lines on her face a little deeper than when I had seen her last.)

Finally, the Song in its pornographic throes incessantly repeats itself.[38] Apart from the perpetual terminology of sucking and fucking (see above) and its episodal return (1:7–8, 12; 2:3, 8, 16; 3:4; 4:5, 16; 5:1–6; 6:2, 11; 7:6/5, 13/12; 8:2), there are the repeated *wasfs* (4:1–5; 5:10–16; 6:4–10; 7:2/1–6/5),[39] the repetition of key terms such as wine, lily, myrrh, garden, trees, and gazelles, and the multiple sexual partners. 'The Song teems with phonological, lexical, syntactic and imagistic associations – inextricably bound with no logical order' (Fox 1985: 71[40]). Although it may refer to the repetitive nature of sex itself, there is something in the dynamic of desire that such repetition signifies. Michelson (1993: 42–3) argues that repetition function as an aphrodisiac, lending itself to the buildup of erotic excitement. Yet I prefer the suggestion of Jacques Lacan and Slavoj Žižek that the prime purpose of desire is not fulfillment but the replication of desire itself: desire seeks not its consummation but the eternal prolongation of desire. The desire of desire is to remain unconsummated, for once it is sated, desire ceases. Or, the search for satiation, the object of desire is empty, void. Therefore, desire remains unfulfilled, perpetually repeating itself. And so the repetition of the Song and of contemporary pornography may be understood. For in pornography the most persistent feature is the desire for yet more images, more films, more hardcore representations. One story or picture or film may satisfy for a time, but there is always a pressure to read another story, another magazine, borrow another film, or visit another web-site. Apart from this, the sheer number of stories, images and films available attests to this repetition, the desire to replicate desire itself, 'desire in the second degree, desire of desire' (Lacan 1992: 14).

SCHLONG OF SCHLONGS

[O]ne thing is for sure: if you don't have come shots, you don't have a porno picture. Plan on at least ten separate come shots.
(Ziplow 1977, quoted by Williams 1989: 93)

The question, then, is what happens if we take a 'literal' reading to its logical extreme?[41] Is it merely about sucking and fucking, or is there more? A casualty of such a reading must be the metaphorical intercourse between love and sex, for the two are never connected in pornography and, I would suggest, in the Song. It seems to me that the Song is not so much concerned with active penetration, for the poetry gives out to phantasies of being penetrated, of opening out and accepting. 'What does', asks Waugh, 'a passive penetration fantasy or a submissive fantasy look or sound like?' (1995: 315) Indeed, the most prevalent phantasy 'perversion' in pornography is the male desire to give up gender identification and play the role of the female (May 1981), that is, to take on the role of transvestite.

('Do you want to see the last film in which they all acted, apart from old Murphy?' asked Sue.
'I'm not sure if it will help', I replied. 'Then again, at least I will be able to see what they looked like in one piece.' Sue led me into the former sanctuary; in a corner was a large video screen. I settled down in an old plastic chair with a beer, the various city lights refracted through the stained glass above.)

'The Schlong of Schlongs' read the flickering credits, 'Director: Solomon Wiseman. Starring Sue Lammith as herself, Merab Saul as Sharon Rose, Eve Adam as Beth Rabbim, Solomon Wiseman as Hermon Senir, Melekh Agag as Frank Incense and Isaac Moses as Leb Bannon.' A scene opens with a female (*Sharon*) wanting to fuck, but with a man already spent from too many partners. 'Let him kiss me with the kisses of his mouth' (1:2), she wishes. The woman talks, evoking an image of the king pursued by women with lust in their bodies – 'therefore the maidens love you ... rightly do they love you' (1:3–4). But she also is accustomed, it seems, to seeking pleasure from these 'maidens' as well as the man she has her eyes on. She daydreams for a moment, remembering a swinging session in the king's chambers (1:4), although it is unclear whether the king in her memory is the man she desires now. Nor is it clear where the 'wine' and fragrant 'anointing oils'[42] come from (1:2, 3), or the 'perfume poured out' (1:3): from his cock, their cunts, mouths, or whatever. Indeed, water sports do not seem out of the question.

Next it is a black beauty (*it was Sue herself*) who speaks, promising a story of interracial sex with its interlocked pale and black skins, dark purplish pigmentation wrapped around a light pink and bluish veined cock. 'I am black and beautiful', although she holds back a view of her beautiful ass, blocking the gaze (1:6), concealed behind the 'tents of Kedar', the 'curtains of Solomon' (1:5). She, the narrator, has not been idle, fucking around since an early age – 'my own vineyard I have not kept!' (1:6) much to the annoyance of her 'mother's sons', even though they also tried to fuck her. Yet, the black beauty has her eyes on a man, although neither he nor she has been idle: 'tell me ... where you pasture your flock, where you make it lie down at noon?' she asks him. But she has been 'beside the flocks' of his companions, sucking and fucking both male and female companions to her heart's content. (*Fortunately, the use of condoms and dental dams is everywhere in evidence.*) The two finally manage to get away, with him, Hermon 'Stunt Cock' Senir, telling her to 'follow the tracks of the flock', to track down his cock, and to 'pasture your kids beside the shepherds' tents' (1:8). (*Now there will be a pack of fucking shepherds, I think to myself. At least there will be plenty of wool, but I am to be disappointed.*) There are, it seems, the two of them for a moment, although he projects a phantasy of a 'mare among Pharaoh's chariots' (1:9), wanting to mount a horse. But what he is really interested in are her 'jewels' and 'ornaments', 'gold' and 'silver' (1:10, 11), her anus between her 'cheeks' (1:10) and her cunt.

Having met, and she having drawn him away from others who want him, the two set to work on the couch (1:12). It turns out that he is a king(-size) after all. She thrusts her flaps in the air, letting him smell the 'fragrance' of her 'nard' (1:12) as he goes down on her. She begins to groan, her cunt juices mingling with his saliva; he rims her anus, inserting his tongue. They shift position, moving to tit-fucking, his 'bag of myrrh ... lies between my breasts' (1:13), he is like a 'cluster of henna blossoms' (1:14). She grabs her nipples, twisting them and squeezing her mammaries together over his cock. The camera pans backwards, giving a wide angle view: the two are in a forest, on a bed of grass surrounded by cedars and pines (1:16–17). But now it is her turn and in a crotch shot she opens out like a flower[43], a crocus (2:1) or lily (2:1, 2), to his searching tongue. He moves it slowly and gently around the rim of her anus, taking in its rich flavour, moving then along each of the external labia, touching her clitoris as he passes. Then he sucks hard, drawing out all her loose cunt flesh into his mouth. She begins to come, but then she turns and takes his cock in her mouth, like an 'apple tree among the trees of the wood … his fruit was sweet to my taste' (2:3).[44] (*It seems to me that she's smoking a huge, fleshy-coloured, cigar, although it does look a bit like a tree trunk between her teeth.*) As she comes, her labia sucked deep into his mouth, as though he were at a 'banqueting house' (2:4), he withdraws and shoots his load into her lips, mouth and face – 'sustain me with raisins, refresh me with apples; for I am faint with love' (2:5). While she groans loudly as she shoots her load onto his face, eyes and hair, his cum leaks down her face and drips down her chin, evidence of the real thing.[45] Having 'embraced' (2:6) and swallowed, she warns the 'daughters of Jerusalem', themselves dying for a gazelle or doe, not to 'stir up or awaken love until it is ready' (2:7) or … you will get a face full of cum.

(*I must admit that my appetite had been whetted, since I like to use my own tongue and mouth.*)

Repetition now sets in, with the next fuck cycle underway (2:8–17). Beth Rabbim and Leb Bannon make their appearance here. (*I haven't heard of them, but both of them have kinky reputations.*) It begins with a long tongue darting over Beth's very ample breasts, 'leaping upon the mountains, bounding over the hills' (2:8). As the camera pans out, somewhat shakily, the large pink nose and muzzle of a 'gazelle' (2:9) come into view. Beth has her eyes closed and groans, enjoying the rough tongue of the animal. But now a 'young stag' (2:9) walks over, sniffs Beth's face and then her cunt. Its huge cock is distended as it gazes at Beth's mons venus, pondering her interwoven pubes: 'Look, there he stands behind our wall, gazing in at the windows, looking in at the lattice' (2:9). (*Oh my God,*[46] *I think, he's not going to fuck her, is he?*) But now both stag and gazelle morph into satyrs,[47] with human heads, arms and chests, but animal lower bodies, legs and genitals. Leb, the stag, speaks: 'Arise, my love, my fair one, and come away' (2:10, 13). At first Beth thinks he is talking to her clitoris, but then she realizes he means her as a whole. She gets up, while the half-man, half-stag talks about spring, the rising sap and the mating season. Fetishes abound, as he evokes 'flowers' and 'turtledoves' (2:11), 'figs' and blossoming 'vines' that 'give forth fragrance' (2:13). (*The very thought of spurting vines is a phantasy all on its own, I think to myself.*) The three of them find a place, among the rocks, while Leb looks for her anus, or 'face', between her ample ass cheeks, 'in the clefts of the rock'. She farts, after he has asked to 'hear' her 'voice' and he sniffs deeply of the aroma, 'for your voice is sweet and your face is lovely' (2:14). Leb pulls a couple of 'little foxes' out of his bag, about to insert them up her anus, like gerbils, but they run away. And now they fuck, Leb 'pastures his flock among the lilies' (2:16)[48] for the whole night 'until the day breathes and the shadows flee' (2:17). While Leb pumps in and out of her ass, the 'young stag on the mountains of Bether', the half-man/half-gazelle doubles up in her cunt. Inevitably, they both withdraw and spray cum all over her ass and tummy.

(*I remember that Annie Sprinkle finds nothing more exciting than watching sex with animals, but I am not an animal person myself except for the feel of fur on my skin, so the phantasy leaves me a little nonplussed.*)

Two brief scenes follow, one a desperate search in the throes of desire and lust (3:1–5) and the other an ode to the phallus. (*Here is a little plot, I reflect; not too much, I hope.*) A solitary man[49], Frank (*so that's what Melekh looks like whole, I thought*), lies in 'bed at night', seeking 'that which my soul loves' (3:1), groping around the bed but not finding what he is looking for. 'Maybe I left it outside', he thinks, in 'the city, in the streets', or 'in the squares' (3:2), but he still can't find it. As he searches further, he comes up against the bed posts, the 'sentinels', whom he asks for what he has lost: 'Have you seen that which my soul loves?' (3:3). But then, with a sigh of relief, Frank finds it, holds it and will 'not let it go'. He brings the dildo up, smears some lube on it and slides it up his pucker, 'into my mother's house' (3:4), stimulating his prostate and groaning with relief. He comes, with thoughts of the 'daughters of Jerusalem', 'gazelles' and 'wild does', but the relief is temporary, for he has stirred up and awakened love before it was ready (3:5).

A cut to a new scene begins, concentrating on the stunt cock of Hermon. A voice-over speaks, a male voice, lost in wonderment as Hermon's cock slowly begins to rise: 'What is that coming up from the wilderness, like a column of smoke?' (3:6)[50] It has been cleaned of smegma; the aroma of all the usual flora negated, since it has been 'perfumed with myrrh and frankincense, with all the fragrant powders of the merchants' (3:6). Enraptured, the voice exclaims, 'Look, it is the litter of Solomon!' and the pubic hair is like the 'sixty mighty men of the mighty men of Israel' (3:7). A fade out replaces Hermon's pubes with a phantasy of muscled warriors in leather skirts with leather shields, 'each with his sword at his thigh' (3:8). (*These are the sorts of soldiers I would like to meet!*) Now Hermon is really getting wood, like the 'wood of Lebanon' (3:9). Another fade out turns this cock into a pillar 'of silver' (3:10), a construction item in the palanquin of Solomon (3:9–10). The voice calls to the 'daughters of Jerusalem' to 'look', to admire this magnificent phallus, this 'crown with which his mother crowned him' (3:11). Leb appears and sinks slowly onto Hermon's huge schlong, sliding up and down as the scene fades.

(*I'm getting a bit tired of all these schlongs; isn't there any relief?*) Without any introduction a fourth scene begins (4:1–15),[51] focusing on the beautiful body of Beth Rabbim. Another voice-over breaks into the scene, but now it is a woman, and she savours Beth's body, running her tongue over Beth's eyes, veil, hair, teeth, lips, mouth, cheeks, neck and breasts. But the phantasies are of a grotesque body[52]: an image grows on the screen, with doves for eyes, goats for hair, ewes for teeth, doubled over, thread for (lizard) lips, pomegranates for cheeks, a tower for a neck, and fawns or gazelles for breasts (4:1–5). The image flips over to pubic hair, labia and ass cheeks. But the real fetish here is with the mammaries, dripping milk in anticipation of childbirth. The voice becomes a body (*Sharon*), giving Beth's magnificent breasts a treat. Sharon moves from one to the other, hastening 'to the mountain of myrrh and the hill of frankincense' (4:6), circling one and then the other, teasing nipples to erection with her tongue and mouth. Beth herself finds voice, calling Sharon 'my bride' (4:8, 9, 10, 11, 12), 'my sister' (4:9, 10, 12). Calling on Sharon to 'come with me', she calls her from 'the peak of Amana, from the peak of Senir and Hermon, from the den of lions, from the mountains of leopards' (4:8)[53]. Beth, it seems, has sensitive nipples (*like mine, although there is no rough wool here*) and she has orgasmed through her nipples alone: 'you have ravished my heart' she tells Sharon (4:9), but now it is Beth's turn to pleasure Sharon, unleashing a festival of liquids. Sharon's 'love' is better 'than wine', 'the fragrance of' her 'oils than any spice' (4:10). Beth begins her work, drawing 'nectar' with her hand and tongue from within Sharon's creamy 'lips', 'honey and milk' are inside, moistening Beth's mouth and nose. But still Sharon has not come, she is 'a garden locked, a fountain sealed' (4:11). Finally, with Beth's assistance, she lets loose, quickly and repeatedly, spraying, sprinkling her own cum over Beth's tongue and face:

> Your ejaculation[54] is an orchard of pomegranates
> with all choicest fruits,
> henna with nard,
> nard and saffron, calamus and cinnamon,
> with all trees of frankincense,
> myrrh and aloes,
> with all chief spices.
>
> (4:13–14)

Once she has come, Sharon lets loose a long stream of piss, a golden shower, 'a garden fountain, a well of living water, and flowing streams from Lebanon' (4:15). Beth's mouth is open, tasting the pungent brew, much like a morning piss, savouring its taste. By the time Sharon has finished, Beth is dripping from head to toe, soaked with Sharon's cum and piss.

(*This is not too bad, I ponder, at least there is no plot to distract from the sex.*) The camera fades in to a scene with Sue Lammith lying in the open, her beaver prominent. She calls on the 'north wind' and the 'south wind': 'blow upon my garden that its fragrance may be wafted abroad' (4:16). The next cut is to Frank, sniffing the air like a hound dog, following his nose to 'his garden', to 'his choicest fruits' (4:16). He tops the rise on which Sue is spread-eagled, and he eats her out, eating his 'honeycomb with his honey', drinking his 'wine with his milk,' gathering his 'myrrh with his spice' (5:1). Sue, it seems, is as juicy and fluid as Sharon. Frank eats and drinks, 'drunk with love' (5:1). Yet this is only the beginning, for his engorged cock is ready, throbbing, knocking (5:2). 'Open to me', he says (5:2), but she is not ready, for she has been working on his cock, touching its head with the tip of her tongue and then swallowing it whole, deep throating him again and again. She leaves saliva all over the head and even on his pubic hair: these 'locks' drip 'with night sprinkles' (5:2). Along with the saliva, the head of his cock has a drop of pre-cum on it, it is 'wet with dew' (5:2). Sue wants to fuck, for she has already undressed and fucked, bathing her 'feet' in preparation (5:3). Now his cock enters her waiting cunt, but he withdraws this 'hand' and slowly works in another, his left hand: he 'thrust his hand into the hole'[55] and Sue's 'innards yearned for him', his hand moving back and forth in an ecstasy reminiscent of the ultimate orgasm of chilbirth. She is loose and open now, Frank's hand stimulating her cunt; so she grabs his cock and he sprays cum all over her hands – her 'hands dripped with myrrh, [her] fingers with liquid myrrh, upon the handles of the bolt' (5:5).[56] The S/M tendency of this scene develops further, for as she 'opened to [her] beloved' she 'turned and was gone'. (*OK, I was mentally leafing through my Lacan, finding the place on the insatiability of desire.*) The hand, the man and the schlong are gone, and her searching and calling yields no results (5:6); instead, 'the sentinels found' her, tied her up, 'beat' her and 'wounded' her, leaving her without her 'mantle' (5:7). The S/M of fisting has given way to that of bondage, beating and pain. (*Is this coerced domination or the desired and pleasurable dynamics of power? It is hard to tell.*) But Sue seems to get off on this, for, as she tells the sexy 'daughters of Jerusa-lem', 'I am faint with love' (5:8). And the 'daughters' reply, asking what is so special about her 'love' (5:9) that she can take her pleasure elsewhere; in reality, she cares little for him – he is but a cock and a hand.

A very different scene follows, in which the body of a man (Frank) is the object of the gaze, languorously perused by people whose gender is indeterminate.[57] A queer voice runs over the body, enjoying it like a picture from a queer pornzine. The voice likes his ruddiness (5:10), head, black hair, eyes, cheeks, lips, arms, body, legs and speech. But, as with the earlier scene on the female body, this body is both fetishized and grotesque, its head becoming gold, hair a raven, eyes doves, cheeks beds of spices, lips lilies,[58] arms gold, body ivory and sapphires, legs alabaster columns.

As this slow scene closes, the randy 'daughters of Jerusalem' finally get in on the action: 'which way has your beloved turned', they ask Beth, 'that we may seek him with you?' But they are too late, for a cut finds Beth's 'beloved' already fucking, completely unfaithful to her. Leb is pasturing 'his flock in the gardens' of Frank, he gathers 'lilies', pasturing 'his flock among the lilies' of Frank's anus (6:2).

Another idle scene follows (6:4–10), slowing down the pace after the earlier S/M. Again it is a body, again a gaze, although this time it is Sharon's velvet skin that is under scrutiny. And again a queer voice savours the body, this time a woman's voice.[59] The camera moves over a grotesque, fetishized body once more, except that this time it is celebrated by 'sixty queens and eighty concu-bines, and maidens without number' (6:8; see also 6:9). Even her mother adores her body, finding her 'perfect' and 'flawless'. Sue's queer voice becomes enraptured, desperately wanting Sharon, who 'looks forth like the dawn', is 'fair as the moon, bright as the sun, terrible as an army with banners' (6:10).

So she descends to Sharon's cunt, her 'nut orchard', her 'blossoms of the valley', her budding 'vines' and her 'pomegranates in bloom' (6:11). Sue turns out to be a 'generous giver',[60] fulfilling every 'fancy' (6:12).

Finally, it is Sue's body that everyone wants to see, the daughters of Jerusalem calling on her to 'return' so they can watch her 'dance' (6:13/7:1). This time the camera focuses not on her 'face' before fading to her ass and cunt; it begins below, with her 'rounded thighs' (7:2/1), moves up to her 'navel'[61] and 'belly' (7:3/2) and then up to her breasts, neck, eyes, nose, head and hair (7:4/3–6/5). But this is a highly desirable body, with large thighs, rounded belly, smoky eyes and a 'Lebanese' nose;[62] yet it is also fetishized, the scene fading into a construction of sculpture, pottery, wheat, lilies, fawns and gazelles, an ivory tower, pools, a gate and a mountain.

A brief scene (7:7/6–10/9) sets up the final one. Two bodies are entwined, at least one of them is a female 'lover' (7:7/6) who is like a 'palm tree' (7:8/7). The fetish here is on the breasts, transposed into fruit that must be eaten – 'clusters' on the palm tree or on the vine (7:8/7–9/8).[63] But it finishes with a swallow, this time of the woman's ejaculate, that is like the 'best wine', 'going smoothly, gliding over lips and teeth' (7:10/9).

The final scene lives up to generic expectations: although it is somewhat amorphous, it fulfills the normal expectation for an all out orgy.[64] And indeed we find a whole range of people here – brothers (8:1), mothers (8:1–2, 5), daughters of Jerusalem (8:4), a little sister (8:8), then the director, Solomon, makes an appearance (8:11–12), vineyard keepers (8:11–12), those 'who dwell in the gardens' (8:13), and a woman's companions (8:13) – enough for quite an orgy. But this is also a queer orgy: apart from the ubiquitous plants and the odd gazelle and stag (8:14), there is childbirth and pregnant fucking (8:5), the sexuality of children (8:8), broached and then blocked (8:9) and incest (8:1). But everyone else is there, Sue, Beth, Sharon, Frank, Leb and Hermon, while the daughters of Jerusalem have their way with vineyard keepers, those who dwell in the gardens and the companions (8:13). Although there is no mass money shot, this final sequence is very disjointed, but only because the camera passes continually from one sexual combination to another, as with many a porn film. It is no longer possible to encompass the whole. And so the film closes with an urging to come, to 'make haste' like 'a gazelle or a young stag on the mountains of spices' (8:14).

(I stretched, clicked the rewind button on the VCR, and felt slightly disappointed. I had been hoping for at least one rainbow shower. Yet, now I at least knew what they looked like 'live'. I found Sue and Solomon in the office, talking business. 'Do you know where they used to meet?' I asked.

'Over at Madame Hokhma's', Sue replied.)

4

STOLEN WATER IS SWEETER, STOLEN BREAD TASTES BETTER

On representing sex workers

Meretrix: one who earns money

Prostitutes are people. Treat them with the same respect you'd want back plus some. Take a good shower, and wash everywhere. ... Try not to attract too much attention to yourself and beware of undercover cops posing as hookers. ... Leave your checkbook at home. Pay in cash. Don't try to bargain whores down. They're not at all rolling in the dough and they have just as many, if not more, expenses than you. For most of them, this is their living. On the other hand don't try and bribe someone into doing something they don't want to do, especially sex without condoms. ... It's an adventure; keep an open mind. Don't look for only the 'perfect one'. ... If the person isn't quite what you expected, have an excuse ready ... and give them money for their time ... . Tips are appreciated.

(John, J. 'What they don't teach in school', *Whorezine*
April 1993: 3–4, quoted in Chapkis 1997: 188)

(Madame Hokhma's was just across the Parramatta River on Sorrell Street. I left Sue's place in the old church as the new day began a second past midnight, made my way through the alleys and lanes to the bike bridge, my boots clicking on the deserted wet cement. A solitary cyclist warily passed me, tyres hissing in the water, face hidden under the shadow of the lamps that had somehow avoided being smashed. The path twisted its way up the northern bank, although I opted for the stairs. More rain came with the wind, soaking my neck left bare by the woollen cap. One hundred meters past the top of the bank an old work-er's cottage came up on the left. A small gate on the footpath opened onto a low verandah; one step later I was inside the convict brick walls. A tall handsome woman in her fifties greeted me with a faint Ameri-can accent. A narrow corridor passed by two doors on each side before it gave way to a small parlour: in one of the chairs at the undersize table sat a quizzical Frenchman. He looked a little pale. 'This is Alex,' said Madame Hokhma.)

71

Like pornography, the Censor is central to sex work, particularly with regard to the whore stigma. And it is this stigma that is crucial for the biblical text of Proverbs 1–9. I will argue in this chapter that contemporary work on the whore stigma enables a 'stigmatic' reading of this stretch of the Bible, and that Proverbs 1–9 provides one possibility for overcoming the stigma.

But let me flush out the Censor first. For the contemporary study of sex work has its moment of origin and continuing existence, like popular culture itself and the Bible, under the sign of the Censor. And, like Nisard with popular culture, that moment took place in France, with the work by Dr. Alexandre Parent-Duchâtelet, *De la Prostitution dans la Ville de Paris*, published first in 1836, the year he died from exhaustion at the age of forty-six. (*No wonder he was pale; I had thought he was ill.*) This was in the time of the Third Republic, before the 1848 revolutions and the restoration of order that followed.[1] Parent-Duchâtelet's two volume work, compiled with the same thoroughness and groundwork as his work on Paris's sewage and drainage system,[2] provided the data and the arguments for the regulationist approach to prostitution that followed (see further Bell 1994b: 45–51; Bernheimer 1989: 8–33; Corbin, 1990; Walkowitz 1980: 36–38). He saw prostitution as a necessary evil, to be tolerated and supervised, a safety valve similar to the sewers of Paris, as undesirable as they were fundamental to the health of the city.

> Prostitutes are as inevitable in an agglomeration of men as sewers, cesspits, and garbage dumps; civil authority should conduct itself in the same manner in regard to the one as to the other: its duty is to survey them, to attenuate by every possible means the detriments inherent to them, and for that purpose to hide them, to relegate them to the most obscure corners, in a word to render their presence as inconspicuous as possible.
>
> (Parent-Duchâtelet 1836, II: 513–14;
> quoted in Bernheimer 1989: 16)

The important point in all of this is that Parent-Duchâtelet based his study of 12,600 prostitutes who had been inscribed for fifteen years between 1816 and 1831 on police, prison and hospital records.[3] His data came, in other words, from the records of repression, coupled with his own observation. In his characteristically thorough manner (what was to become standard social scientific practice), he traced their former occupation, place of birth, age, father's and mother's profession, place of residence, arrest record, education, number of children, social origins, marital status and the physiology of prostitutes (including quality of voice, colour of hair and eyes, physical abnormalities, nature of the vagina with a specific focus on the clitoris).

Parent-Duchâtelet's findings were ambiguous. On the one hand, he found that many prostitutes moved in and out of the occupation, depending on social and economic circumstances, and that they were primarily young working class women, engaged as domestic and factory workers before and after working as prostitutes. Prostitutes were more resistant to general disease than other working class girls (a finding in line with his rejection of the ill-effects of working in the sewers). On the other hand, there were the evils of prostitution – bad habits, physical degeneration and a propensity to genital diseases and abscesses. What alarmed him was the conjunction between these two: the fluidity of prostitution and everyday family and social life over against the social and physical dangers they posed. Thus, as Bell argues, underlying Parent-Duchâtelet's study is a duplicity, a binary opposition of sameness and difference – 'that prostitutes are different from ordinary women and that prostitutes are the same as ordinary women' (1994b: 50) – that is replicated in the many studies that follow his model.[4] In other words, here in the founding document of the modern sociological study of prostitution – itself based upon the material thrown up by the repression of sex work – is the contradiction of the whore stigma.

Yet, this moment of censorship was the culmination of a build-up that waxed and waned from the beginning of capitalism in the early sixteenth century, when the first voices saw prostitution as a problem and argued for its suppression (see Nash, 1994: xiii–xiv).[5] Religious revival, the Reformation and the arrival of a virulent form of STD all had a part to play, but the net effect was not only the repression of prostitution but the production of literature on the topic. Such writing – police and judicial records, pieces outlining its deleterious effects on society and fiction – relied on the effort of censorship and repression, all of which was to culminate in the explosion of censorship and study in the mid-nineteenth century.[6]

('But Alex', I said, 'this is all very interesting, I'm sure, but I am investigating some bizarre murders, mutilated corpses. Each of the male bodies was castrated and each had a blood-stained note pinned to their left breasts with a yellow "M" drawn on it.'
'What brings you here?' he asked.
'Sue Lammith suggested I call in.')

SITUATING STIGMA(TA)

Prostitutes stand at the flash points of marriage and market, taking sex into the streets and money into the bedroom. Flagrantly and publicly demanding money for sexual services that men expect for free, prostitutes insist on exhibiting their sexwork as having economic *value*. The whore stigma reflects deeply felt anxieties about women trespassing the dangerous boundaries between private and public. Streetwalkers display their sexual and economic values in

the crowd – that social element permanently on the edge of breakdown – and thereby give the lie to the rational control of 'deviance'
and disorder. Hence the fetishistic investment of the law in violently policing the prostitute's body.

(McClintock 1992: 72–3)

Not only is the whore stigma structurally critical, through the Censor, to the
study of sex work, but it also works in tandem with the ideological construction of 'woman'. Thus, sex work is directly tied up with a series of related
bifurcations – whore/virgin, mother/slut, good girl/bad girl, goddess/harpie,
temptress/seducer, but also lesbian/heterosexual, reproductive/nonreproduc-
tive, white/nonwhite – in the representational presence of women in many
societies.[7] For Jill Nagle, the strength of such binaries forces 'females to choose,
or at least negotiate between them' (Nagle 1997: 5), in the construction of
identity. Nagle argues that just as bisexuals trouble the distinction between
gays/lesbians and heterosexuals, so also feminist whores, producing a 'prostitute discourse' (Bell 1994b: 2), undermine the good girl/bad girl trope, one
that now includes sex-negative/sex-positive feminists, or pro-prostitution/anti-
prostitution feminists. By 'feminist whores' are meant those who do not see
their experience in the sex industry as overwhelmingly negative/in the past/
coerced/victimizing, but rather as positive/present/consciously chosen/in control.
Part of such a discourse includes gay, lesbian, bisexual, transvestite and transgender
sex work, an inclusion that leaves such oppositions on shaky ground and
provides, given the more integrated role of sex work within these communi-
ties, a possible vision of a shift in stigma (see Boyer 1989; Mathews 1988;
Salamon 1989; Shrage 1989).

What I am interested in are the myriad tactics, to invoke Michel de Certeau's
distinction between strategies and tactics, of destigmatization and of trou-
bling the binaries on which the whore stigma trades. It will then be these
tactics of destigmatization that lead into a rereading of Proverbs 1–9.

Since stigma functions as something of a peg onto which are attached a
variety of moral, criminal, social and medical assumptions and arguments,[8]
the tactics of destigmatization tend to follow similar lines. The problem seems
to lie with the assumption of causal connections between these factors, rather
than the awareness that any activity will attract criminal factors if legally
proscribed.

*(Alex noticed the strained look on Madame Hokhma's face. 'It's all right',
he said, 'I'm past working for the Law. But I must be off'.*

*Brief relief was replaced by fear when he had gone; 'yes, I heard about
the deaths', she said in her deep voice.*

*'I thought you might have', I said, 'Sue mentioned that they met here
for a while.'*

74

'They used to arrive one at a time on different evenings, coming here under the cover of stigmatized sex.')

The codification of stigma in the Law – although of course, as Žižek would argue, it is also the Law that in its turn generates stigma (so also Daniels 1984: 12) – has produced tactics to have sex work decriminalized (Chapkis 1997: 155–164; Shrage 1996).[9] For some, the laws themselves make sex work dangerous – included in this is police harassment – so decriminilization will assist in the process of reducing the problem of violence against sex workers (Bell 1994b: 9). For others, however, the institutional, political and economic nature of stigma needs to be overcome as a whole in order to address the violence and exploitation that are so much part of sex work for many (McKeganey and Barnard 1996: 79–80; Davis 1993: xii; Ericsson 1980).

Medically, the rapid spread of HIV/AIDS, comparable to the role of earlier STDs, has seen sex work the focus of intense scrutiny, since this is felt (along with intravenous drug use) to be an entry point in western societies for HIV into the heterosexual community – incorrectly, it seems.[10] Sometimes stigma itself is used as a tactic, as with PROS, the Prostitute's Rights Organization in New South Wales, Australia, which was able to obtain $120,000 from the state government to address STDs and AIDS among working women (Chapkis 1997: 175–6).

PROS is one of a number of sex worker advocacy organizations that have campaigned against stigma, a tactic often borne in the very names of these organizations, such as COYOTE, 'Call Off Your Old Tired Ethics', (see Jenness 1990) which has battled to shift the associations of sex work with sin, crime, and illicit sex to questions of work, choice and civil rights. Yet even here the binaries I have noted above resurface, with a discursive battle waged between WHISPER, 'Women Hurt in Systems of Prostitution Engaged in Revolt', COYOTE, PONY (Prostitutes of New York) and others.[11]

(Madame Hokhma continued, 'Although they had close links with PROS and POP, the Prostitutes of Parramatta, they had their own agenda. They drank and smoked and talked into the early morning, planning, writing, checking the web, hacking into police "intelligence". They never made any bombs here, but there was a lot of talk of bomb devices, timing, location, minimization of casualties. Most recently they were working on a foolproof warning system to get people out in a hurry.')

Another angle of attack on stigma is the sort of historical work done by Judith Walkowitz and others. In her study of the Contagious Diseases Acts in England (1864, 1866, 1869), Walkowitz reconstructs sex workers as 'important historical actors, as women who made their own history, albeit under very restrictive conditions'. The decision of these poor working women with few employment opportunities to enter sex work 'was in many ways a rational choice, given the limited alternatives open to them' (Walkowitz 1980: 9). A number of studies, such as Mahood on Scotland (1990), Oldenburg on India (1990) and Perkins on Australia (1994), have followed Walkowitz's stress on prostitute agency and use of the system for their own benefit.

Indeed, the working class emphasis of these studies is part of the drive to have sex work recast as work. My terminology of 'sex work', coined by Scarlot Harlot (Leigh 1997; see also 1996) is chosen for political reasons, since it foregrounds sex work as part of the structure of contemporary capitalism, with its sale of labour power and class conflicts.[12] The problems for sex workers then become particular, often exacerbated, examples of working class problems, such as exploitation and gender inequality,[13] so that the battles become ones of working conditions and class struggle (so Shrage 1996; Chapkis 1997: 131). Sex workers, rather than being cast as degraded or as heroines, become workers, with all the ambiguity that entails.[14]

But there is a more technical indicator of sex work: following Žižek's comments on psychoanalysis, my suggestion is that the transfer of money is crucial for sex work to take place.[15] The transfer of the fee, as is the case with an analyst, signals the negation of emotional attachment: in the very act of giving over the fee the client foregoes any affection or lingering connection. Where emotional attachment creeps in, as with commitment at work (the absence of which is a perpetual perplexity for employers), the nature of sex work is thereby compromised. This distinguishes sex work from sexual acts that take place for a host of other reasons and expectations that may exist in a social formation.[16] The distinctly capitalist dimension to this is to commodify the transfer of money for sexual services.[17]

> ('But I heard there were four bodies; seven used to meet ...'
>
> 'Isaac Moses from the baseball club', I cut in, 'old Aaron Murphy from the garage on Windsor Road, Melekh Agag and a woman whose name we think is Merab, but we aren't sure yet. She had some connection with Agag.'
>
> 'Do you think the scraps of paper on their nipples have anything to do with their names?' she asked.
>
> 'I've been thinking,' I said, 'but then we have a psychopath.' I paused, 'You said there were seven ...'. The phone rang, and she got up to answer it.)

In the end, there seem to be two ways by which stigma has been approached, one seeking to abolish prostitution as such (Barry 1979; 1991; 1995; Pateman 1983), the other wanting to recast sex work as work. Few have taken the more risky homeopathic option of not so much attempting to sidestep or avoid stigma, but of claiming stigma itself as a positive.[18] I am thinking here of Annie Sprinkle's *Sluts and Goddesses Video Workshop* as a lead-in to Proverbs 1–9. Both video and the workshop on which it is based trade on a dual opposition (see also Sprinkle 1998: 118–25, 183, 186–7; Bell 1994b: 148–51; Bell 1995: 35–6; Thomas 1996: chapter 4). First, 'regular people' are reconstructed, with makeup, clothing and lighting, into 'sex stars'.[19] And then the porn stars are reconstructed as goddesses. With a studied naivety characteristic of Sprinkle's work, the workshop celebrates each of the identities constructed: each woman is regular, slut and goddess. 'Through slut, through the animal, through the body you can go into the goddess or spiritual, or you can go through the goddess into the intensely physical' (Sprinkle, quoted in Bell 1995: 37). Annie likes it any way possible, for the crucial point here is precisely the refusal of any divide or split, any moral approval or approbation.[20] Is it possible, then, to find a logic comparable to Annie Sprinkle's *Sluts and Goddesses Video Workshop* in the Bible?

SOLICITING WISDOM

... the fine line between being a celebrity and a slut ...
(Bell 1994b: 147, reporting on the film *Deep Inside Porn Stars*)

(For some years Madame Hokhma had been in competition with Madame Zara's house, a few doors up on the other side of the road. They were two of the eighteen licensed brothels in the Parramatta area, part of the city planning to turn Parramatta into an international city. Each had felt that they had an appeal and a service that was distinct from one another, advertising in the local papers. Madame Hokhma tried to cater for a sophisticated clientele, providing intellectual and physical stimulation, a kind of asceticism that promised sexual ecstasy; Madame Zara, however, worked hard at producing phantasies for her clients, guiding them to let their inhibitions go.)

The work I have traced above on the whore stigma enables a reading of the Bible with this in mind. Thus, the story of Gomer and Hosea (chapters 1–3) seeps with stigma, connected as it is with the image of Israel's apostasy (for instance, Ezekiel 16 and 23). The image of the whore of Babylon is similar (Revelations 17–18). Other texts, however, carry little ethical loading at all, the sex worker playing a crucial role in the narrative. Thus, Rahab's house is a place of refuge in the siege of Jericho (Joshua 2:1–24; 6:25), Tamar gains revenge on Judah and then becomes the ancestor of David via Perez (Genesis 38:12–30), both in turn appearing in Matthew's genealogy of Jesus (Matthew 1:3, 5). Yet, Proverbs 1–9 has not entered the discussions of such texts.[21]

However, it seems to me that the best example of both stigma and the glorification of sex work – and the simultaneous refusal of this bifurcation – in the Bible may be found in Proverbs 1–9. To begin with, the assumed reader, the absent client, is constructed as male (or lesbian), since the opposition seems to be between two females, two women, one the figure of 'wisdom', *ḥokhmah*, and the other the 'strange woman', *'iššah zarah* (Proverbs 2:16). What entices me here is the way these two women beckon their clients to come into their embrace, call to them on the street so that they will come into their houses. Indeed, it seems to me that the whole of Proverbs 1–9 may be understood as a display of the erotics of knowledge.[22] It is not so much that knowledge is sexualized, that sexual associations are insinuated into knowledge in the text; rather, knowledge always already has a sexual charge, already bears a libidinal investment. The enticement of Proverbs 1–9 is that it makes such an investment stand out, it seduces and penetrates the reader.[23] In this light it is interesting to note that the more overt female characterization begins slowly, with an introduction to wisdom crying out in the street in 1:20–1 and her words in vv 22–33. In terms of direct sexual content, up until 6:23 the explicit sexual references are less direct, interspersed with other material and appearing only in 2:16–19, 3:13–18, 4:4–9, 5:3–14, 18–23. With 6:24, however, the content remains sexual in some way or another until the close of the first nine chapters, where a new unit, 'The Proverbs of Solomon', begins. Thus, 6:24–9:18 may be regarded as the climax of these first nine chapters.

(Whereas Madame Hokhma targeted a more intellectual clientele, from the universities, schools and colleges about Parramatta, Madame Zara catered for the trades people, workers and those who relied on their bodies for their money. Yet, curiously, their clientele did not differ too much.)

However, like many critics, I have assumed too quickly that there is a simple opposition between Wisdom and the Strange Woman.[24] In fact, a range of characters appear, although there seems to be significant elision between them by the end. Wisdom herself emerges as a composite in 1:20–33, 3:13–18, 4:4–9, 8:1–36 and 9:1–12 (see Camp 1997: 87–9). There is the 'strange woman' in 2:16, 5:3, 20 and 7:5, as well as the 'alien woman' (*nokhriyya*) in 2:16, 5:20, 6:24 and 7:5 (see also 23:27). But there also appear other women, notably the 'wife of your youth' in 5:18, the 'evil woman' (*'ešet ra'*) in 6:24, the 'prostitute' (*'iššah zonah*) in 6:26 and 7:10 (see 23:27), the 'wife of another' (*'ešet 'iš*) in 6:26, 'neighbour's wife' in 6:29, and finally the 'foolish woman' (*'ešet kesilut*) in 9:13.[25]

(Madame Zara had managed to attract a number of workers with good reputations in the sex trade. There was the Alien, who provided phantasies of alien worlds and creatures, the Evil One, whose room allowed clients to live out satanic desires, the Woman Next Door, who generated phantasies of sex with one's neighbour's wife, and the Young Wife, for those who dreamed about teenage partners. The Dumb Blonde and the Sleazy Hooker completed the group of six.)

The 'wife of your youth' (5:18) is a little the odd one out here, although the potential client will stay with her if wisdom is followed. Yet the description has echoes of the fetishistic Song of Songs:

Let your fountain be blessed,[26]
and rejoice in the wife of your youth,
a lovely deer, a graceful doe.
May her breasts satisfy you at all times;
may you be intoxicated always by her love.

(5:18–19)

The contrast is with the 'strange woman' and the 'alien woman' of 5:20 and it is this group I want to interrogate. Initially, Wisdom and the 'wife of your youth' would seem to slide into one another, given that the call to the young man is to follow Wisdom and not be misled in the passions of youth. Yet, in the context of the shifting female identities in these chapters, Wisdom also has a persona that is more than the 'wife of your youth', a seduction leading either to conflict (mistress) or reinforcement (polygamy) of this wife (note the sexual appeal of Wisdom in 4:6–9). And does not 'wife of your youth' imply an older reader/client. In fact, are there not more than one of these readers? As with the various figures of this passage, it is hardly to be assumed that the reader/listener constructed by the text is unitary.

The great opposition in Proverbs 1–9 is, however, not between the 'wife of your youth' and the strange or alien woman but between Wisdom and the 'strange woman', the 'alien woman', the 'evil woman', the 'wife of another', the 'neighbour's wife', the 'foolish woman' and the 'prostitute'.[27] It is of course more conventional to treat these designators as variations on the same motif (so Yee 1995: 111), but it seems to me that an approach that treats them as somewhat distinct, as semi-autonomous, may discover some aspects that may be elided with too rapid an identification.

(As Hokhma ducked her tall frame through the low doorway, I caught a glance of lust directed at my breasts. 'Care for a drink?' she asked.
'Thanks', I said, 'I could handle a Toohey's Old.' The rain beat down upon the low tin roof of the back of the house while I wondered about finding out who the other three of the M-group were. She pulled a couple of bottles from the small fridge, opened them silently and began sucking sensuously on hers.)

To start with, there is the great depiction of the 'strange woman', the text's 'primary image of otherness' (Newsom 1989: 148). On three occasions there is parallelism with 'alien woman' (2:16; 5:20; 7:5), although once she appears on her own (5:3). In opposition to Wisdom, this woman is a trap, she has been unable to repress her lust and remain faithful to the 'partner of her youth', offering a house that 'leads down to death' (2:18), 'paths to the shades' (2:18). It is a road of no return, an option for which there is no second chance. The association between death, the world of shades and shadows and bodily orifices such as the anus and the vagina makes this simultaneously a more powerful threat and an appeal. The Strange Woman reappears in 5:3–14, 15–20 and 7:5. In the first passage she appears much more enticing: her lips drip 'honey' and 'her mouth is smoother than oil' (5:3). Yet, once again the images of destruction, death and Sheol appear, helped by a 'two-edged sword' (5:4).

A number of items open up, or, if you like, stick out, here: one is the association with crime and worthless people that such a woman entails, another the intertwining of wanton sex with the absence of discipline and instruction, a third the connections between sex, knowledge and death. In the first, sex with/wisdom from such a woman means giving one's 'years to the merciless' (5:9), strangers will 'take their fill of your wealth' and one's labours will 'go to the house of an alien' (5:10). All that is left is 'utter ruin' (5:14). The second item appears in 5:12–14, the putative words of the wayward person who gives himself over to the Strange Woman – 'I did not listen to the voice of my teachers, nor incline my ear to my instructors' (5:13). Third, transference from the lips and mouth of 5:3 to anus and vagina ensures that the three major orifices used for sexual activity appear: as I suggested in the preceding chapter, liquids like honey and oil may also have a sexual register. These orifices link in with death and Sheol in 5:4, as though a bodily orifice was an existential one at the same time; once again what is potentially more destructive is eminently more appealing.[28] A picture of stigma is beginning to make its presence felt in this depiction of the Strange Woman, a depiction that slides into the 'alien woman' with whom she is paralleled and then with the prostitute of 7:10.

Of course, commentators are only too eager to pile up more stigma, although one can detect a little desire as well. For McKane:

> *nokriya* and *'iššā zarā* are synonymous terms and denote one who is beyond the pale and who, because she is beyond the pale, is both desperate and uninhibited – desperate because she suffers ostracism and insecurity, and uninhibited because she defies religious and social sanctions and conventions and is a law to herself. As such she is particularly deadly to young men who become embroiled with her.
>
> (McKane 1970: 285)

In the passage of 6:20–35 another group appears: an 'evil woman', (6:24) a 'prostitute' (6:26), a 'wife of another', (6:26) and a 'neighbour's wife' (6:29). These four 'shady ladies' (Yee 1995: 111) are connected with the 'alien woman' in 6:24 (who, as I have indicated, is herself paralleled with the 'strange woman' in 2:16; 5:20 and 7:5). All of these women appear in a passage that warns the hearer to keep one's father's commandment and not forget one's mother's teaching (6:20). Over against such discipline are the lures of these women, who appear one after another so that they blend into one. The first two – 'evil woman' and 'alien woman' – have a 'smooth tongue' (6:24), desirable 'beauty' (6:25), and eyelashes that may capture one (6:25). The 'neighbour's wife' (6:29) turns up in a moment, via the 'wife of another' (6:26), now depicted as a trap fraught with danger, as fire in the bosom (6:27), leading to wounds, dishonour, disgrace, and destruction, all apparently at the hands of a jealous husband (6:34–5). Here stigma attaches not to the alluring woman but to the man who gives in to her wiles – a distinct contrast to the patterns of stigma in other social formations except that the women/woman here seems to be irreparably evil. This passage (6:24–35) also provides a good argument for the fluidity of the differences between the various women. Yet such a fluidity takes place in a very interesting contrast that has its own textual problems. In 6:26 it seems as though the 'wife of another', who threatens the very life of a man, is set over against the prostitute, who merely demands payment (a loaf or a piece of bread) rather than one's life. If the parallelism here operates for the purpose of contrast rather than reinforcement, then there is a remarkable consonance with the understanding of the function of the sex worker I outlined earlier: with the passing over of the fee – here a loaf/piece of bread – all emotional attachment is also passed over. The fee transfers any emotional connection that may attach to the sex act itself: hence there is no consequence from sex with a sex worker, in contrast to adultery with another's wife, since here a whole set of unresolved emotional dimensions remain unresolved. Thus, 'the wife of another stalks a man's very life' (6:26). The other issue is that the prostitute is set over against the other women/woman of this passage; the contrast in these verses seems to be not between Wisdom and the sex worker/strange woman/adulteress etc. Later this opposition will disappear, indicating a series of sliding identifications and associations.

(A few minutes and sucks on the bottle later, Hokhma leant over the small table and planted a kiss on my forehead. It had been a while, and I needed a cooperative informant, so I grasped her head under the ears and played some tongue hockey with her. She had the smoothest tongue, almost like honey, that I had tasted for a long time. I broke, saying, 'Who were the other three?' She responded by pushing the table aside and drawing me to her. Breast pressed up against breast.)

Indeed, in the very next verses (7:1–5) the 'strange woman' and the 'alien woman' return, but now in direct contrast with Wisdom:

Say to wisdom, 'You are my sister',
and call insight your intimate friend,
that they may keep you from the strange woman,
from the alien woman with her smooth words.

In opposition to the parallels in 2:16 and 5:20, the connection is made with the prostitute, and what follows in the rest of 7:6–27 is the most detailed description of both the allures and the stigma of the prostitute. By this time, the sexual crescendo of Proverbs 1–9 is in full swing, having begun in 6:24: now everything has a direct sexual reference. And the various women who have appeared thus far, the ones that may tempt the diverse readers and listeners away from Wisdom, are wrapped up in the depiction of the prostitute. She seems to envelop or swallow up the material that has gone before.[29] I want to pay particular attention to this description, since the echoes of the characterization of Wisdom in the verses that follow are very close.[30] For the composite stigmatized woman, culminating in the whore of 7:6–27, that has been constructed until this point starts to take on a new guise.

> (*After some years in fierce competition, Madame Hokhma and Madame Zara realized that they would do better if they combined their operations, rather than fighting each other for clients. They kept their two houses, one across the street from the other, and they still tried to attract different clients, but their administration, management and finance took place at Zara's larger place.*)

To begin with, the prostitute is out in the street. She walks the streets and squares, seeking to entice potential clients with her lures. She calls out with her loud voice, 'now in the streets, now in the squares, and at every corner she lies in wait' (7:12; see 7:8). Similarly, Wisdom cries out 'in the streets', 'in the squares', 'at the busiest corner', 'at the entrance of the city gates' (1:20–21), 'on the heights, beside the way, at the crossroads' (8:2), 'beside the gates' and 'at the entrance to the portals' (8:3). At her gates and doors one should wait and watch (8:34). Both, it seems, walk the streets, calling out at the gates, squares, corners, roads and crossroads, offering their wares to those who pass by, to anyone who will look and listen.[31] One has the impression of two figures out in the city, crossing paths, competing for customers, trying to avoid the other getting her clients. The difference between the two is only in the content of their words, for they both rely on speech to entice the client.[32] For the first sex worker, those words speak of availability (7:19–20), eagerness (7:15), an expensive bed (7:16), perfumes (7:17) and desire (7:18).[33] The second – Wisdom – is more garrulous, speaking in her turn of reproof for ignoring her (1:22–5), warning of the dangers of doing so (1:26–33), offering prudence and intelligence (8:5, 12; see 3:21), fear of the Lord (8:13; see 3:7), happiness (8:32–34; see 3:13, 18), life (8:35; 9:6), maturity (9:6), but primarily Wisdom herself (8:11–31; see also 3:19–26).

I have already moved on to the words of both, which attempt to influence, beguile, and persuade those around them to sample their own particular wares (see 8:6–7 and 5:3–4; 8:8 and 7:21). Although the content differs – come with me and you'll have the best time of your life, or, come with me and you will acquire the wisdom of a lifetime – the means are the same. Thus, vocabulary moves from one figure to the other (so Camp 1995: 136–7; 1997: 94, who follows Alleti 1977: 132–4): both Wisdom and the Strange Woman may be embraced (4:8; 5:20); they are to be grasped or they grasp one (3:18; 4:13; 7:13); they offer food and drink in their houses (9:4–6, 16–17); and the same term is used for the instruction of the wise one and for the Strange Woman, 'wily of heart' (*lqḥ*, 1:5; 4:2; 9:9; 7:21). Each uses various rhetorical skills in order to entice the man who pauses for a moment, looks up and glances into her eyes, for the choice is one or the other for the night. But is there the possibility of a threesome, both Wisdom and the Strange Woman at a reasonable rate?

> (*'Is Zara about?' I asked, for I was starting to feel like a threesome.*
> *'I'll call her if you like', she said. We broke for a moment while she made to page Zara. 'She should be here in a moment', she said, as we resumed, she sitting on the table, me standing.*)

A third overlap is with the reference to a husband or partner, or, perhaps pimp. Maligned and praised, as one who exploits and protects, in nearly all places anyone who lives from or is a beneficiary of 'immoral earnings' – partner, husband, brothel director, accountant, or even wider family – is subject to exorbitant tax rates and other penalties. The stigma of sex work falls very heavily on these people. However, the depiction of the Strange Woman is at some points one of a woman who trades in sex while her husband, or man, is away (7:19–20); or, since an independent woman who is not dependent on any male is an impossible category for this text, the reference to the absent husband/man is a necessary assurance to would-be customers that they will not be caught in the act by an irate husband (although this is precisely the threat of 6:34–5). In this case 'absent man' means 'no man', although most pimps will stay clear of the action unless needed. Wisdom also has a 'man', but in this case it is Yahweh. Here it would seem that Yahweh is the business director, the pimp, for Wisdom's trade. She has, after all, been working for Yahweh, indeed has been his consort, since the beginning of the world (8:22–31). Is it possible that the 'absent man' of the Strange Woman, the prostitute, is also Yahweh, the pimp?

Further, Wisdom and the other women both have houses, their other area of work apart from the street.[34] Whereas only some sex workers are out working the streets, walking their beat, looking for clients, all sex workers require some place to get down to business, to do their work, of whatever form. This may be a quiet corner, an alley, a car, a toilet, or it may be a hotel, a room, an apartment, a brothel, a house. Ultimately the street, the newspaper advertisements, the listings in the telephone directory are designed to attract clients to this place of work. And so it is appropriate that both Wisdom and the other women describe their places of work. In 7:10–11 the sex worker says 'I have decked my couch with coverings, coloured spreads of Egyptian linen, I have perfumed my bed with myrrh, aloes, and cinnamon'; whereas in 9:1 Wisdom 'has built her house, she has hewn her seven pillars'. And then, the 'foolish woman', the last of the list to appear, 'sits at the door of her house' (9:14). By this time, the opposition is firmly lodged in place and the 'foolish woman' slides into the prostitute.

It is precisely in the comparison between Wisdom and the foolish woman that a complete breakdown of the opposition begins, for here both have houses (9:1, 14), call from or sit at the high places of the town (9:3, 14), call out to passersby (9:3, 15), speaking the same words, offering food, where eating is of course a signifier of both sex and knowledge:

> 'You that are simple, turn in here!'
> To those without sense she says,
> 'Come, eat of my bread and drink of the wine I have mixed.
> Lay aside immaturity and live, and walk in the way of insight'
> (Proverbs 9:4–6)
> 'You who are simple, turn in here!'
> And to those without sense she says,
> 'Stolen water is sweeter (compare 5:15), stolen bread tastes better'.[35]
> (Proverbs 9:16–17)

All that is left upon entering the house is the line-up. Apart from the omniscient poet's comments in 9:18, the foolish woman in fact speaks the last words, rather than Wisdom. It is not so much that the two are one, but that both Wisdom and the composite Strange Woman function as sex workers in these chapters, thereby simultaneously transferring stigma and honour from one to the other. What is delectable about these chapters is this final interweaving, especially on a formal level. Here the negative and the positive begin to coalesce at the very point at which the content attempts to make the sharpest separation: the choice, it seems, is between life and death. Yet the very effort to sharpen the difference between stigma and honour seems to produce their interaction. The one does not seem to be able to operate without the other. So it is not so much the allocation of positive and negative moral qualities to different people but the presence of both in the same figure that is at issue here. In other words, as with the glorification and condemnation of the sex worker noted in my earlier discussion, in Proverbs 1–9 the sex worker is depicted as a force of life and death. The very ambivalence of sex work *and* of wisdom itself is then embodied in the two figures of Proverbs 1–9. Both are slut and goddess, whore and teacher of wisdom, like Sade's Juliette (see Norberg 1993: 248–9).[36]

(Hokhma removed my cap and jacket; I started undoing her blouse. Large, dark areoli surrounded huge nipples on her breasts. My woollen shirt

*came away, my slightly smaller breasts falling out into her hands. But
her hands didn't stay there, for they moved down my back, undoing my
belt and loosening my pants. When she felt my cock, she laughed in anticipation. 'This will be fun', she said.*
    'What about those other three?' I repeated.)

CONCLUSION

Not only does the melding of Wisdom and the Strange Woman in the
figure of the prostitute question the bifurcation I have traced in this chapter,
it also brings forth the image of the prostitute teacher. She appears already in
the *Epic of Gilgamesh*, in which the wild man created by the goddess Aruru as
a foil to the rampaging Gilgamesh gains wisdom and civilization through the
prostitute Shamhat. After six days and seven nights, Enkidu can no longer
return to his former animal companions. Having been taught about the attractions of the city, Shamhat shows Enkidu how to shave and dress and then
leads him to the city, where he becomes Gilgamesh's beloved companion.

Further, the ancient tradition of the holy whore, the *hetaira* of ancient
Greece, in which the binary I have traced earlier is broken down, has been
reappropriated by sex-worker artists and writers such as Annie Sprinkle, Cosi
Fabian (1997) and Shannon Bell (1994b: 19–39).[37] Here the discursive battle
is to break out of the modern construction of the prostitute (as diseased body,
suffering victim, working class, sexual deviant, urban blight, mother body,
criminal, physically abnormal, and desublimated sexual woman (Bell 1994b:
71)). Chapkis (1997: 194–5) suggests that the recovery of the sacred prostitute is a strategic response to stigmatization. Does Wisdom, as erotic teacher,
have a role to play here, particularly in light of the connection with ancient
Near Eastern mythological and cultic elements in some criticism of Proverbs
1–9?[38] At a discursive level, it may be possible, but with any ideological conflict it is necessary to ask who is producing these discourses, and for whom.
And in the end, they are the clients, nervously hidden under the expensive
Egyptian linen (7:16) or behind the perfumed bed, smelling of myrrh, aloes
and cinnamon (7:17).

In fact, I have not said too much about the client, the item in sex work that
is both ubiquitous and largely invisible. Both older (British Social Biology
Council 1955: 76) and newer studies (McKeganey and Barnard 1996) perpetually reiterate the absence of the client in research.[39] Curiously, the dominant
gender of clients for the two largest areas – heterosexual female and homosexual male – is as absent from writing on sex work as are the clients themselves
from such studies. Indeed, the hidden client is what seems to me to character-
ize work on Proverbs 1–9 as well, although that assumes what I want to argue
about those chapters. Yet, even here, as Ecstavasia suggests in a reading indebted to Deleuze and Guatarri, both client and sex worker are constructed as

85

fantasies, as 'cyborg assemblages ... and subject-positions'. 'The client is paying to interact with his "fantasy girl," his object of desire; he is paying to construct his cyborg (BwO)' (1993: 181). So also with client, Wisdom and the Strange Women of Proverbs 1–9.

For what I have been doing is tracing the efforts to overcome an ideological contradiction, in which the texts become efforts at providing imaginary solutions to social and economic contradictions. For, as Newsom notes, the oppositions in Proverbs 1–9 both coalesce and hold apart: '[o]ne is the gate of Sheol, the other the gate of Heaven. Together they define and secure the boundaries of the symbolic order of patriarchal wisdom' (1989: 157).[40] The text attempts a resolution which simultaneously has all the marks of the contradiction it tries to resolve. A proper resolution, even for the homeopathic option I favour so much, requires a concommittent socio-economic resolution.

But perhaps there is one final secret, also hidden under the covers, as it were, which must be uncovered for such a resolution to take place. Is not Wisdom, who is also the Strange/Evil/Alien/Foolish Woman and sex worker, in fact a man in drag? Is Wisdom, after all this, a she-male? And of course the only one in drag here, the only she-male, with his smooth tongue (6:24) that drips honey (5:3), large eyelashes (6:15) and sex worker's clothes (7:10) – six-inch heels, big hair, miniskirt – is Yahweh himself.

(My left hand slipped up her skirt, pulling it up as I eased beneath her panties. The skirt unclipped and fell away and I slid the panties down. Beneath was a rapidly rising penis supported by the hairiest balls I have ever seen. My dream lover, I thought: I could take my preferred role and live out my passive phantasies. 'What about Zara?' I said.

'She would normally be here by now', said Hokhma. I had my suspicions that they were one and the same.

'You were in the cell, weren't you?' I said, caressing her balls. She nodded, as she pulled on a condom and we locked together, dressed only in our boots and stilettos.)

5

EZEKIEL'S AXL, OR,
ANARCHISM AND ECSTASY

Music is prophecy. Its styles and economic organization are ahead of the rest of society because it explores, much faster than material reality can, the entire range of possibilities in a given code. It makes audible the new world that will gradually become visible, that will impose itself and regulate the order of things; it is not only the image of things, but the transcending of the everyday, the herald of the future. For this reason musicians, even when officially recognized, are dangerous, disturbing, and subversive; for this reason it is impossible to separate their history from that of repression and surveillance.

(Attali 1985: 11)

… and heavy metal had emerged as one of the coolest, most critically respectable and most diverse of musical forms.

(Straw 1993: 381)

What if Axl Rose, temperamental singer from the heavy metal band Guns 'n' Roses, and Ezekiel, eccentric prophet from the Hebrew Bible, were to be compared with each other? The exploration of this rather far-fetched proposal – that is, a comparison between Axl Rose and Ezekiel, and the phenomena they represent (heavy metal and prophecy) – is the burden of this chapter, in which I want to make use of a number of theoretical currents, in particular the long tradition of political anarchism, Bakhtin's notion of the carnivalesque, the study of ecstatic or possession behaviour among prophetic and shamanistic figures, the Gramscian concept of hegemony, and Jacques Attali's study of the possible revolutionary, utopian, functions of music. In what follows I will focus on heavy metal in the first two sections, with a shift to prophecy in the third.

Heavy metal, of course, has a symbiotic relationship with the Censor (see Weinstein 1991: 245–75). The inaugural moment was the so-called PMRC (Parents Music Resource Center) hearing – or, more properly, Record labelling, Senate Hearing 99–259 – held in Washington DC during September 1985. Conservative social and religious forces, including Tipper Gore's infamous contribution, attacked heavy metal for its focus – typically via the lyrics – on suicide and aggression, sexual perversion and satanism. This merely reinforced heavy metal's pariah status, Tipper Gore's name being ubiquitously invoked at metal concerts for ridicule, and the (voluntary) labels becoming markers of desirable metal albums. The drive for censorship and restriction, and the oppositional status of the genre, remain defining features of heavy metal itself.

(I didn't have time for a wash, even though Hokhma was a quick lover. I had already talked and stayed too long; it would be dawn in another hour. I pulled on woollen underwear, pants and shirt, saying to her, 'You'll have to come with me. There's still three more, and you haven't told me who.'

Out on the street an engine was cut, footsteps rushed. 'Quick', she said, 'it's dangerous for me, and you're with me now.' A hatch in the toilet opened up, and we crawled through a low tunnel out to a storm-water drain that had once been Brickfield Creek.)

AXL AND ANARCHISM

This fire is burnin' and it's out of control,
It's not a problem you can stop
It's rock and roll
I read it on a wall
it went straight to my head
it said 'dance to the tension
of a world on edge'

('Garden of Eden', Guns 'n' Roses 1991)

I'm such a Victory or Death type of person.

(Axl Rose, in Flanagan 1992)

It seems to me that a good deal of sense may be made by considering heavy metal (and then later prophecy) from the perspective of the long political tradition of anarchism. Etymologically, anarchism refers to the absence of any form of organized governance. A distinction may be made that follows the historical development of anarchism itself – between plans for the uto-pian state beyond the necessary revolution and the increasingly violent process of destroying the old before the new may be inaugurated – a distinction that is succinctly expressed in the terms utopia and violence. Earlier writers and activists devoted more attention to the political, economic and social forms of an anarchist state of existence. For example, William Godwin (1756–1826), credited with the first full statement of anarchist thought in his *Enquiry Concerning Political Justice* of 1793 (Joll 1979: 16), argued for the indissoluble connection between justice and happiness in social formation, for the aboli-tion of property, the eradication of evil and crime through education. In

Charles Fourier's[1] ideal anarchist society, 'Harmony,' social forms and the natural world were adapted to human needs and reason was to dominate. The 'phalansteries', autonomous social and political units without an over-arching state, operated on the principle of selfless cooperation, following the deeper patterns of universal harmony (see further Fourier 1971). And then Proudhon[2] proposed the complete abolition of capitalism and the establishment of direct, negotiated exchange of produced goods, without property or government larger than the commune. Work lies at the heart of his system, being both a social necessity and moral virtue (see especially Proudhon 1970). Yet it is Kropotkin[3] who embodies all that is peaceful and generous about anarchism. He argued, especially in *Mutual Aid* (1902), for a scientific theory of anarchist development, in which the tendency of the natural world was towards greater cooperation, mutual aid and sympathy, all of which would be enabled by proper economic organization and a new system of morality, without obligation or sanction. Echoes of the prophetic utopia of the Hebrew Bible are everywhere in these visions.

(After passing southward under a couple of streets, the channel gave out near the river. This would be difficult, especially if we had to cross the river. A shape darted from behind a park bench. We locked still, and the shape halted in the lee of the channel a few metres in front of us. I went for the legs, Hokhma dove for the top, especially the arms and any potential weapons. Neither of us was armed. The struggle was short but vicious. 'Zara!', hissed Hokhma in surprise.
'Who the fuck do you think it is?' said Zara, very annoyed.
'One of the cops we just evaded', I said.
'I thought you were two of the cops I have just avoided', said Zara. 'They were all over the street at your place and mine.')

The second dimension is the role of the revolution itself, indelibly stamped by the experience of the French Revolution in 1789, but especially the period of the *sans-culottes* in the spring and summer of 1793. If Kropotkin is the epitome of gentle planning in anarchism, Mikhail Bakunin (1814–76), the great itinerant revolutionary intellectual, is most closely associated with the other great tradition of anarchism: the value of violence and terrorism in the revolutionary struggle. His reputation stands mainly on his continual revolutionary planning and activity throughout Europe, especially his final period in Switzerland (1867–76). Less energy was directed towards envisaging the nature of socio-economic life after the revolution, although freedom was predicated on a lawless, stateless society, and on the goodness and generosity of human beings. The principle of 'propaganda by the deed' was often enacted by anarchists through assassinations, bombs and symbolic acts of destruction against social institutions and people in positions of power, especially in the period 1880–1914. The names of Vaillant[4], Ravachol[5] (whose name gave us *ravacholiser*, to blow up), and Emile Henry[6] made anarchism synonymous with violence, while in Chicago there was the Haymarket bomb of 1886 and subsequent execution of four anarchists on slender evidence. (I will later return to the question of political violence.)

While the first strand of anarchism is reflected in contemporary literature such as that of Kim Stanley Robinson's *Mars* trilogy, it is the second strand that I want to associate with heavy metal groups such as Guns 'n' Roses. It may be argued that Guns 'n' Roses enact a long tradition of bohemian anarchism characteristic of artists and writers and going back at least to the great revolutionary painter Gustave Courbet (d. 1877), a contemporary of Proudhon.

> (*'Did you hear about the others?' asked Zara.*
>
> *'It was always a risk, although we never thought it would be so brutal', replied Hokhma. By this time I had figured that Zara was the sixth member of the cell. That left one.*
>
> *'Who's the wool man?' asked Zara.*
>
> *'He's trying to decipher what happened.'*
>
> *'A cop, then', said Zara.*
>
> *'Hardly', I replied.*)

Yet musicians have not been immune from such tendencies, whether members of orchestras and choirs or jazz musicians (Miles Davis comes to mind). In the realm of rock and roll proper the first great musical anarchist, if I may call him that, was Guitar Slim (born Eddie Jones), who rose to prominence in the early 1950s, but died in 1959 at 32 from bronchial pneumonia complicated by alcoholism and a chronic lack of adequate sleep and food (see Palmer 1991: 665–6). The greatest claimant to be Guitar Slim's successor in the 1960s is Jimi Hendrix who in a comparably short career epitomized all that was socially objectionable in rock music. The famous film clip of Hendrix performing 'Wild Thing' depicts the shock that even Hendrix's audience felt at the simulated sex with his guitar which is set alight, smashed in pieces and thrown at the audience. Numerous other examples might be given of socially transgressive behaviour from rock musicians – Elvis Presley (to begin with (Hill 1991: 681)), Jim Morrison and the Doors, the Rolling Stones, Johnny Rotten and the Sex Pistols (and then the whole punk thing), Joy Division, Kurt Cobain and Nirvana and an endless number of other grunge bands, are a few of the better known – but I have chosen Guitar Slim and Jimi Hendrix since, with their uses of the electric guitar, they may be identified as the forerunners of heavy metal, their techniques – such as playing the guitar behind one's neck, or with the teeth or while someone else is holding it – having become heavy metal mainstays. Indeed, the electric guitar provided the 'new sonic qualities' and a means of 'exploring the harmonics and overtones of noise-sound' that were to define rock in general (Gracyk 1996: 119 and 118; see also Weinstein 1991: 23). And this is true not only of the lead and rhythm guitars, but also the bass, which, with the amplification of bass enabled after 1960, provides the 'heavy' element of heavy metal (Weinstein 1991: 24–5).

> *('We need to find Zeke', said Hokhma as we walked along the storm water channel, keeping our heads low, 'he was always the hot-head of the group: heavy metal music, bombs, but he could look after himself.'*
> *'Where is he?' I asked.*
> *'That's the problem', she said, 'he is always on the move. Last I knew he was holed up in a cheap appartment on the Great Western Highway.'*
> *I groaned; that was at least a couple of kilometres away. As we paced it out, I rolled and lit another smoke, enjoying the bite on my throat.)*

Heavy metal[7] is agreed to have begun either with Led Zeppelin's album *Led Zeppelin I* in 1968, with its 'brash, raunchy and musically subversive arrangement' (Hinds 1992:151), or, if one is a critic from England, with Black Sabbath (Weinstein 1991: 14–15). The generic innovation, according to Weinstein, lay in the conjunction of psychedelic/acid-rock to traditional blues.[8] In this tradition Guns 'n' Roses appears as the peak metal band, at least in terms of popularity, at the turn of the decade from the 1980s to the 1990s, especially with the double album *Use Your Illusion* (1991).[9] *Appetite for Destruction* released only four years earlier was the best-selling debut album in the history of rock. At the same time the band has a frenzied and violent reputation, openly flaunting alcohol and drug consumption, sexual exploits, and the right to behave as they damn well please. This includes flying in the face of censorship moves (the Parents Music Resource Center (PMRC) objected to what they felt was the band's glorification of a degenerate lifestyle), so that their lyrics (typically the Censor's target) use graphic language, mention sexual bondage and discipline, psychological derangement and the effects of drugs. All of this is of course quite conventional for rock musicians, especially heavy metal (Weinstein (1991: 35–43) speaks of the themes of Dionysian revelry and chaos), but it also signifies the rejection of a cleaner 1980s in which mainstream bands seemed to eschew such practices, at least in public.

But there is also another dimension of the rock and roll persona that interests me here. Whether cultivated or not, the image of the temperamental rock musician is well played out by Axl Rose, long haired blond singer for Guns 'n' Roses and 'rock and roll's bad guy' (Rose 1992b). Noted for destructive rages, his fragility and 'hair-trigger temper' (Neely 1992), Rose's antics have both delighted and dismayed fans, especially his proverbial lateness to concerts and sheer unpredictability, and generally annoyed critics and the press. 'We're not afraid to go to excess with substances, sexually and everything … . When we started we wanted to be the coolest, sexiest, meanest, nastiest, loudest, funnest band. There was a group consciousness of rape, pillage, search, and destroy' (Axlbio.html). The drinking and drug use are flaunted with fans: … 'many times drugs and alcohol – there's a technical term that they're called, emotional suppressants

– are the only things that can help a person survive and get through and be able to deal with their pain' (Rose 1992a). There are the physical fights with Motley Crüe and David Bowie, the clash with Kurt Cobain at the 1992 MTV music awards, with Metallica on tour in August 1992, the two fans crushed at the Monsters of Rock Festival, the racial clash with Living Colour, and the riot at St. Louis on 2 July 1991. Axl has been arrested on over twenty occasions at his home in Indiana, was arrested after the St. Louis riot (17 July 1992, after returning from the European leg of the tour), in Los Angeles during the Motley Crüe tour, and has various arrests for attacking security guards in 1987, two arrests during the Aerosmith tour of 1988, and after an altercation with his neighbour in 1990. At least six law suits await resolution as well, from a former spouse, girl friends, St. Louis Riverport's Performing Arts Center, and by fans for a no show in Montreal. Like Jim Morrison, Rose is also a reflective, angst-ridden philosophical person, given to deeper thoughts about human existence or its end. 'Well, as you can see, being a fucking psycho basket-case like me does have its advantages' (Axlbio.html).

> (*'Tell me some more about Zeke'*, *I said after we felt safer and there was no sign of pursuit.*
>
> *'He's this old Jewish guy'*, *puffed Zara up the first part of Mays Hill,* *'been everywhere, World War 2, Korean War, Vietnam, Angola, Cuba, South Africa, Peru, the Gulf. He must be about 80, but he sure knows his bombs and his music. He and old Murphy used to get on.'*)

It is usual to focus on the lyrics, and eventually I too will need to do this, but it only a part of the total media presence. A significant marker of the nature of a rock band – and this applies just as much to heavy metal – is the graphical display on album covers. The Guns 'n' Roses coat of arms, if it may be called that, features two revolvers end to end, wrapped in roses, over the band's name in a gold circle. Outside the circle is a rich, red splash of blood that drips down the page. Variations include a snarling skull and a circle of barbed wire. Alternatively, the skulls, representing the five band members, appear superimposed on a cross, on the appropriately titled *Appetite for Destruction* album (1987). Indeed the band photographs on this album evoke more of the gritty street (as also *G 'n' R Lies* of 1988) and explicitly showcase their substance abuse. Yet it is the picture 'Appetite for Destruction' by Robert Williams, upon which the title of the album is based, that is the most significant graphic item. A semi-naked woman lies on the sidewalk, propped up against a fence and interrupted in peddling Mr Mini-Mites (small robots) by a larger, half dressed, robot. The robot is interrupted in the act of rape by a monstrous demon blood hound, bedecked with knives, armour and a host of parasite skulls and crossbones. The moment of recognition for the robot is already too late, although it is not clear whether the woman will be killed in the expected melée.

The graphics for Guns 'n' Roses albums are part of the broad expectations of heavy metal albums, as any visit to a heavy metal specialist store will soon reveal (although at the same time such visits open up the sub-generic variety of metal music itself), but in doing so they also signify the (gendered) violence of such music. Although there are some exceptions, the overbearing gender presence in metal music is male, even more so, apart from rap, than other types of contemporary music. There are some interesting exceptions, like Vixen and Cycle Sluts From Hell, or the postpunk homocore and riot grrrl bands like Pansy Division and C.W.A. (Cunts with Attitude). Here we find a homeopathic approach to the sexism of heavy metal, although it often serves to highlight the sexism itself. Simon Frith describes heavy metal bands as 'cock rockers writ large' (Frith 1990: 422; see also Frith and McRobbie 1990, with some essentialist misgivings). This is of course reflective of, and at the same time one of the constructive features of, the class/gender base of metal fans and bands, which is white, young, male and working class[10] (so Rubey 1991: 879, 884; Weinstein 1991: 98–117). I don't want to say too much about violence at this point, since such discussion moves too often into liberal hand-wringing, except to note the ubiquitous signals of violence in some features of the Guns 'n' Roses phenomenon: the band title, its coat of arms and graphics, and the copyright holder (Uzi Suicide).

('He can't be tied down', continued Hokhma. 'With his long grey hair, magnificent beard, stinking clothes, and continual arguments, he used to draw attention to himself. Then he moved into a Housing Commission apartment in North Parramatta, hacked off his beard, and sat all day in the bus shelter out the front of the building, like a senile old man waiting for the bus he used to catch to work.'

'Not the old guy at the top of Bourke Street, eternally waiting for his bus?' I asked.

'Same one', she said.

'I used to wave to him on my bike beats', I said.

'Well, now he's got a big job on his hands, so he's keeping low.'

'A big job?' I quizzed.)

However, what is interesting about the lyrics is that the violence that is foregrounded in the various symbols and graphical representations dissipates in the lyrics. Indeed, the subject matter ranges through life on the street, hopeless childhoods, persecution, life's a shit, alcohol and drugs, psychological disturbance, Oedipal longing, vanilla sex, bondage and discipline, jaded and often broken love, and then the sheer rejection of women and telling the world to get stuffed. At times the lyrics rise beyond the stage of Oedipal revolt (see Rubey 1991: 879) to a significant level of self-critical reflection, such as 'Bad Apples' (1991) and 'Don't Damn Me' (1991), and political comment, as in 'Paradise City' (1987), 'Garden of Eden' (1991), 'Civil War' (speaking of politics; 1991), and 'Knockin' on Heaven's Door' (1991, although this is a Bob Dylan cover).

In the last two violence itself is criticized. If anything, the violence becomes that which is experienced by the implied singer, and then by extension the implied listener – the covert violence of lived experience, of everyday life. The standard psychoanalytic move at this point is to suggest that this sort of violence, but more especially the introspective, self-inflicted violence, is internalized violence, turned in upon the self in the forms of alcohol, drug abuse, mental derangement, and troubled sexual relationships. At times this also takes the form of kicking against the traces, against the world.

It is, finally, the overall 'appetite for destruction' that connects Guns 'n' Roses with anarchism, particularly its violent, revolutionary form which has an extremely negative assessment of present, capitalist society, and a desire to see its end. The sort of anarchism that is pertinent here is that which focuses on the gleeful destruction of whatever existing, oppressive, socio-economic and cultural system is dominant. It is not for nothing that the fan club for Guns 'n' Roses is named 'Conspiracy Inc.'.

Similarly, much of the prophecy of Ezekiel focuses on the need for destruction, usually cast in terms of punishment for the wrongs of the people. Such destruction applies not only to those outside Judah (Ezekiel 25–32), but also to Judah itself, particularly in the prophecies of doom in chapters 1–24. For example, in chapters 6–7, there are prophecies on the devastation of Israel's mountains (6:1–14), and the oracle of the bitter day of the end of the land (7:1–27). Chapter 22, at the other end of this collection, has the three pieces on the city of blood (22:1–6), Israel in the smelting oven (22:17–22), and the depiction of the corruption of all classes in the land (22:23–31). The desire for destruction is coupled with an absolutely negative assessment of present society. In contrast to heavy metal, however, and closer to the anarchist tradition, Ezekiel has some notion of what the restored society may be like, although his vision of a new city and new temple is far from anarchist hopes.

(We passed by the Hammer House, Parramatta's specialist heavy metal shop, with its heavy bars and sombre graphics. 'The whole of Parramatta, hell, the whole of Sydney is wired to blow, or at least the points of power and knowledge – police stations, courts, prisons, churches, government, television, radio. He's even developed an internet "bomb".')

AXL AND HIS WORLD

Turned into my worst phobia, a crazy man's utopia.
('The Garden', Guns 'n' Roses 1991)

What I want to do, however, is thicken my discussion of anarchism and heavy metal by considering the work of Mikhail Bakhtin, particularly *Rabelais and*

His World, a study of the function of carnival in the feudal period and the way it informs Rabelais's work. At some length Bakhtin moves through Rabelais's novels *Pantagruel* and *Gargantua*, dealing not only with the novels themselves but also the immediate historical contexts (e.g. the drought of 1532 and its inscription in the novels (Bakhtin 1984: 439, see 340)). Bakhtin's work was produced in a period when the medieval practices of the carnival were beginning to fade before the steady and violent advance of capitalism. He traces in characteristic formalist fashion (something for which he was constantly under suspicion) the importance of laughter, the grotesque, the language of compliments and profane, scatological curses (drawn from the marketplace), and the integral relations between images of eating, drinking, defecation, urinating, beating, death, and birth – usually in absolute extremes of violence, gorging and bodily elimination (which also includes sneezing, sweating, blowing one's nose and so on). For example, Pantagruel's stomach trouble produces much urine, which then becomes a series of hot, therapeutic springs in France and Italy. He recovers when men armed with picks, shovels and baskets are lowered into his stomach in a copper globe which Pantagruel swallows like a pill. Their entry through his gaping jaws is connected both with swallowing and devouring, as well as stomach, womb and childbirth. Banqeting, death, destruction and hell also find echoes here, as do thirst, water, wine and urine. 'The grotesque body has no façade, no impenetrable surface, neither has it any expressive features. It represents either the fertile depths or the convexities of procreation and conception. It swallows and generates, gives and takes' (Bakhtin 1984: 339).

(I noticed that there was a larger than usual number of vehicles and people on the streets. It suited us, for it helped avoid detection, but the people were all heading out of the downtown area. A steady stream of sleepy people were disgorged from the apartment buildings, most in pyjamas, dressing-gowns and whatever they had slept in. Night-shift workers – cleaners, brothel workers, heavy-metal bands, and others, were getting out as they could. 'It looks like the pre-bomb warning has gone off', said Hokhma, 'the internet "bomb" will now be wreaking its havoc. I hope you didn't want to check any library catalogues today.')

Dan Rubey has suggested that rap music is close to Bakhtin's carnival, particularly as it is participatory, free and open, oriented to the future and not the past, and in its reversal of social hierarchy. But the real edge of carnival is found in the 'grotesque, the raucous laughter and abusive language of rap, the emphasis on lower bodily strata which is part of the carnival spirit' (1991: 889; on rap's social effrontery see Light (1991) and Garofalo (1993)). While rap arises from and appeals to black youth, heavy metal's appeal is, as I noted earlier, largely with young white males. Yet many of the features of carnival may be found in heavy metal music. Most obviously there is what Bakhtin calls the 'language of the market place', where the restrictions of polite, social speech give way before gleeful swearing, cursing and continual reference to bodily functions and sex. The most obvious Guns 'n' Roses piece is 'Get in the Ring' (1991), a track with a significant portion of the lyrics spoken so that they may be understood. It may best be described as a rich linguistic curse directed at critics, exploiters and unbelievers: 'You wanta antagonize me / Antagonize me motherfucker / Get in the ring motherfucker / And I'll kick your bitchy little ass / Punk'. The most memorable is that which attacks Bob Guccione Jr., of *Spin* magazine: 'What you pissed off cuz your Dad gets more pussy than you? / Fuck you / Suck my fuckin' dick'[11] (1991).

The whole idea of excess, which for Bakhtin is incorporated in the theme of the banquet, is embodied more in the publicly portrayed lifestyle of groups like Guns 'n' Roses. The enormous proportions of the food, drink, and swallowing that form part of the carnival scene – excess eating and drinking is 'one of the most significant manifestations of the grotesque body' (Bakhtin 1984: 281) – may be compared with the excess of substance abuse by Guns 'n' Roses. The alcohol and drugs that are very much part of their complex image function as a parallel to carnivalesque feasting (the alcohol of course has a one to one correspondence).[12] The key here is that is not so much an escape from the world but a celebratory consumption of and triumph over the world, sometimes through death. 'Fatally overdosing on drugs or alcohol, or dying while en route from one concert to another are great career moves' (Weinstein 1991: 89).

The body itself (and Bakhtin is an important contributor to the renewed interest in the body in postmodern criticism), especially as a grotesque form, plays a crucial role in both Bakhtin's work and in the imagery of Guns 'n' Roses (and other metal bands). Bodily parts are paraded forth in carnivalesque literature, often with a reference to genitals: bowels, genitals, buttocks, stomach, womb, mouth and nose are all interrelated (nose and mouth being standard transferred loci for penis and vagina). Much of the bodily imagery is in what Bakhtin calls the 'material bodily lower stratum' – all the imagery has a downward push, as it were, to what is below the diaphragm. The grotesque body is one that is incomplete, it is not closed off from the external world, but is open to it: what are important are its 'excrescences (sprouts, buds) and orifices, only that which leads beyond the body's limited space or into the body's depths' (Bakhtin 1984: 318). Not only are eating, drinking and elimination important, so also are copulation, pregnancy and dismemberment. Both the graphic display of Guns 'n' Roses and its lyrics are replete with this sort of representation of the body. Images of band members feature naked torsos (I counted 15 from four CDs), tattooed arms, and a variety of stills from frenzied public performances. When the bodies are adorned, it is with the characteristic flowing clothes of heavy metal bands, a variety of hats and heavy chains. The transgendered effect of the clothes such as spandex pants, as well as the long permed hair, has a distinctly homoerotic dimension to it. Especially on the *G 'n' R Lies* album, various members of the band strike orgasmic poses (mouths open, eyes shut), and Slash appears in a standard soft porn spread pose, substituting a beer bottle for his penis (on the videos his guitar has this function). The lyrics feature bodily parts, such as the tongue, lips, ears, face, knees, feet and asses, blood, shit, breasts, female genitals, usually as cunt or pussy, and also flaps, and male genitals, although only as dicks. And then there are skeletons, dead animal bodies, dismembered body parts, sex, death, and the grotesque body itself. The grotesque body features heavily in Ezekiel's text as well, particularly in the pornographic sections of chapters 16 and 23 and the grotesque image of the flesh returning to the bones in chapter 37.

(The internet bomb was set to trigger as soon as any virus warning or protection system engaged it. Otherwise, it gave a warning that acted as its own trigger. Its effect was neither hardware nor software destruction, but the freezing, or locking up of all information.)

What interests Bakhtin is the systematic inversion that the carnival provides: where misfortune is directed into celebration and the powerful abdicate for a period of time. This is particularly the case with the Church, its festivals and its clergy. Each of the Christian feasts had their carnivalesque parodies and the power hierarchy of the Church found itself debased and mocked. The king becomes a clown and the clown takes on the trappings of power. Debasement often moved beyond verbal abuse to beatings and other violence, but it is a violence that is beyond the ordinary, an extreme violence that is both destructive and regenerative (the connections with anarchism should not be missed). The mockery and laughter which was very much a part of this extended to the most sacred items of Christian belief and practice – death and resurrection, Eucharist, sin and salvation, the feasts of Christmas, Easter, corpus Christi and so on. The ultimate function of all of this was to reinforce the strong hierarchical structure of medieval society and the Church through the restoration of existing patterns after the carnival. That which was most sacrosanct was precisely open to the grossest parody amd mockery. While this may be read as a mark of respect, it also opens up the possibility, as in anarchism, of the destruction of those same structures and their transformation into something new. Thus battle becomes feast, slaughter turns into banquet, the stake becomes a hearth. 'Bloodshed, dismemberment, burning, death, beatings, blows, curses, and abuses – all these elements are steeped in "merry time," time which kills and gives birth, which allows nothing old to be perpetuated and never ceases to generate the new and the youthful' (Bakhtin 1984: 211). It is at this point that I need to move beyond Guns 'n' Roses for a few moments (although the positioning of Guns 'n' Roses at the tame edge of heavy metal is imporant for my later argument) to the core of heavy metal. For it is here, with the various subgenres of heavy metal itself – a process that began with the break into lite and speed/thrash metal (Weinstein 1991: 45–52) – that we find the extreme debasement of features of the dominant ideological structures of late capitalist society. For instance, hardcore metal parades incest, necrophilia, paedophilia, and excremental sex (see Hinds 1992 for the importance of explicit sexual reference in heavy metal), while death metal celebrates the myriad forms of death and its implications. Religion remains a dominant feature of much heavy metal, focused most often around Christianity or its traditional religious other, the occult. Indeed, the distinction between white metal and black metal is a religious one: white or Christian metal, with its evangelical drive (Weinstein (1991:54) notes more than 100 bands by 1987), opposes black, or satanic metal. Bands like Deicide and The Impaled Nazarene go to extreme lengths in their inversion of Christianity, while older bands like Black Sabbath, Led Zeppelin and The Cult travelled the worn road of Satanism (once again see Hinds 1992 on this, and the roots in blues). Indeed, many carnivalesque practices trace their origin to the pre-Christian paganism of Europe. On the other hand, Mortification, an Australian metal band, attempts a more positive assessment of Christianity.

Although the moment is not always clear in all forms of carnival practice or heavy metal – whose relations should now be clear – both provide a hint of another world, another side to the normal drudgery of life lived now. Less explicitly than fantasy, science fiction and utopian literature,[13] carnival, in its very overturning of social conventions and structures, provides a glimpse through its anarchic destruction of an alternative world. This is sometimes envisioned more explicitly, as in the image of Pantagruel's gaping jaws that I mentioned at the beginning of this section. At one stage in the story a certain Alcofribas journeys into Pantagruel's mouth, where he finds a completely unknown world, older than this one and replete with twenty five kingdoms. At the same time, it is a world that inverts this one, with people paid for sleeping rather than work (see Bakhtin 1984: 337–8). This is an appropriate image of the function of carnival in Bakhtin's assessment: the marketplace festivals, in distinction from the official feasts of the church, 'were the second life of the people, who for a time entered the utopian realm of community, freedom, equality, and abundance' (Bakhtin 1984: 9). The carnival is then a utopian event, something that foreshadows an alternative possibility in the face of the misfortune and disaster of present existence. Here it intersects most closely with anarchism, for both anarchism and carnival have distinct moments of destructive violence and the shape of a new world to come that is already enacted in the midst of the overturning of the old. Heavy metal works best when it tries to touch this liminal edge which then enables a glimpse of a better world.

(It was clear by now that Zeke wouldn't be home, and that if we did not move, we would be caught in the midst of whatever was coming. We veered westward, and then south to Parramatta Park, an old zone of Aboriginal back-burning and meeting as well as early colonial government. Open space and the sluggish river there seemed safer, even though

the huge government offices overlooked the park and the Returned Serv-
ices League was on its north-eastern edge. As we drew nearer, noises of a
band and drunken revelry came to our ears in snatches.)

EZEKIEL AND ECSTASY, OR THE PRONE POSITION

> Lost in the garden of Eden
> Said we're lost in the garden of Eden
> and there's no one's gonna believe this
> but we're lost in the garden of Eden.
>
> ('Garden of Eden', Guns 'n' Roses 1991)

The intersection of anarchism and Bakhtin's notion of the carnival provides, it seems to me, a usefully overlayed way to understand the social function of heavy metal (the primacy of the social being one of Marx's legacies for us). I now want to make a belated turn to the biblical text of Ezekiel, where anarchism and the carnival, violence and utopia, make their presence felt. This will be all the more treacherous in that there is a growing awareness that these texts project an implied author who is not only mentally disturbed, if not schizophrenic, but also distinctly misogynist. Yet it is here that some of the contacts between heavy metal and prophetic texts may be located.

Following David Shumway's suggestion that rock music should be understood as a cultural practice – comprising music, lyrics, scores, concerts, videos, performers, listeners, appearance, substance abuse and attitudes – I want to suggest that prophecy also is a cultural practice, that it is a combination of words, actions, attire, assumed experience, and social and political context that constitutes prophecy, rather than any one item alone. There is perhaps greater need to assert this about prophecy, since the great tendency is to equate the prophetic literary texts with prophecy. Of course, with the biblical text, it is always a mediated and literary construction of such a cultural practice.

But is it possible to read Ezekiel in terms of anarchism and carnival (something I have done spasmodically until now)? The link comes via the more conventional notion of ecstasy, possession, or trance, which has been for some time now an intermittent category in research on the prophets. From the anthropological study of shamans (a term interchangeable with medium, diviner, or intermediary; see Overholt 1989: 4) among indigenous peoples in various parts of the world, as well as from psychological studies of altered states of consciousness, it has been argued that the prophets of ancient Israel form part of this larger social phenomenon (for contrary positions see Westermann 1967: 62–3, and Parker 1978[14]). The textual representation of their activities – ranting, dancing, absence of fatigue, nakedness, catatonia, aphasia, visions, dialogue with the deity – show distinct signs of being ecstatic activity. The texts seem to describe individuals who 'stand outside' their normal selves, and it is at this moment that the divine is believed to make its presence felt. Perhaps the most important study is that of Robert Wilson, whose 1979 'Prophecy and Ecstasy: A Reexamination'[15] (see also the second chapter on 'prophecy in modern societies' in Wilson's *Prophecy and Society in Ancient Israel*, 1980) served not only to pick up the threads from earlier studies but also established Israelite prophecy firmly in the context of ecstatic experience. In moving away from the obfuscation of theological categories to those of anthropology and sociology, Wilson found that anthropology uses ecstasy, or trance, to describe a type of behaviour rather than divine–human communication, the claim to such communication taking the form of 'possession' and 'soul travel'. The great value of Wilson's work is the emphasis on stereotypical behaviour for those in states of ecstasy and possession. The complex interaction between individuals and their societies explains this behaviour, which is controlled by and conforms to these expectations. Thomas Overholt (1986; 1989) has since carried on Wilson's project, providing an extremely wide basis for comparison between contemporary prophecy in many different societies, emphasizing not so much what is said but the social dynamic of such intermediaries.

> (*A whump came through the air, and a small plume of smoke appeared over what I guessed was the former police station. No mixed feelings here, despite having worked there for many years. At the park gate, a large Tudor construction of red brick, we met a dishevelled old guy, balding on top with a week's growth on his chin. His pants and shirt smelt distinctly of gunpowder and he was dancing to the music. His wild, prophetic eyes gave him away.*
>
> '*Zeke*', *called Hokhma, and he stopped, looked at her for a moment, eyes flaring. A nod of recognition, and he beckoned us to follow him.*
> '*There's a safe spot over here*', *he said.*)

The usual exhibits of such stereotypical ecstatic or possession behaviour by prophets are texts like 1 Samuel 10:5–7, in which Samuel predicts that the newly annointed Saul will fall into a prophetic frenzy (the *Hitpa'el* of *nb'* is used here). The reporting of the narrative event in 1 Samuel 10:10–13 uses both the *Niph'al* and *Hithpa'el* of *nb'* with the very similar meanings of 'to speak prophetically', 'to be in prophetic ecstasy' or 'behave as a prophet'. Wilson argues that this is controlled, and thus acceptable, ecstatic behaviour. 1 Samuel 10:6 is perhaps one of the best descriptions: 'Then the spirit of the Lord will possess you, and you will be in a prophetic frenzy along with them and be turned into a different person.' By contrast, other appearances of the verb relating to Saul describe uncontrolled, and therefore socially unacceptable, behaviour. The first of these is in 1 Samuel 19:18–24, in which the uncontrollable spirit possesses three groups of messengers before Saul is himself possessed. In this story Saul strips off his clothes and lies naked for a day and a night, falling into a frenzy under Samuel. The same verb (*Hithpa'el*) is used in 1 Samuel 18:10 to describe Saul's activity when the 'evil spirit of God' came upon him. Even in this limited sample, prophetic activity and utterance is encapsulated in the same verb, although its precise nature seems to be unpredictable. Wilson has argued that the *Hithpa'el* of *nb'* was used 'to describe characteristic prophetic behaviour' (Wilson 1979: 336), although what was characteristic varied with time and place. It referred both to ecstatic or trance behaviour and, increasingly, particular forms of speech, eventually becoming synonymous with the *Niph'al* (thus 1 Kings 22:8, 10, 18, 20–3; Jeremiah 14:14; 23:13; 26:20–23; 29:24–28; Ezekiel 13:17; 37:10; 2 Chronicles 20:37).

It is then interesting to note where the verb is used in the prophetic literature, since it is most heavily used in Jeremiah and Ezekiel. In Ezekiel 4:7 (restricting my focus to those chapters that interest me here) the text reads (NRSV): 'You shall set your face toward the siege of Jerusalem, and with your arm bared you shall prophesy (*Niph'al* of *nb'*) against it.' The ecstatic dimension of the verb, or rather the ecstatic associations with the material concerning Saul, often fade away in the so-called writing prophets for all sorts of interesting ideological reasons (often expressed in the grammatical reasons I noted earlier), not least of which is the attribution of 'undesirable' elements to the rejected king (not to mention his queering as well) and more theologically desirable dimensions to the writing 'prophets'. Yet the *Niph'al* here would seem to convey a similar conjunction of ecstatic prophetic act along with the ecstatic word, especially when the context is considered. For here the narrative speaks of a distinctly ecstatic act or series of acts on the part of the prophet in the midst of which he is then commanded to prophecy. It is begging for interpretation in terms of ecstasy.

> (*Zeke led us past the gardens, around the back of the old government house along the park's rim to a disused concrete underpass beneath the railway line; people used it to pass from one part of the park to the other, but no vehicles could get through. Bottles, cans, chip packets and a few used needles lay about, but we had protection from flying debris. Indeed, the railway line itself functioned like a wall separating the north and south parts of downtown, in the same way that the freeways and major roads enclosed the city itself.*)

The episode in which the verb is used (4:1–15) is the one in which Ezekiel is instructed by Yahweh to make a model of Jerusalem: on a brick Jerusalem is to be portrayed, siegeworks (wall, ramp, camps, and battering rams) are then to be arrayed against the brick-as-Jerusalem, as well as an iron plate that is to be between the prophet and the model. This war game is then made more extreme by the command to Ezekiel to lie on his left side for three hundred and ninety days (Septuagint has 190), in some sort of symbolism for the period in years of the punishment of Israel. On behalf of

Judah, the prophet is instructed to lie on his right side for forty days. It is not clear whether he is to gather his starvation rations of multigrain bread and water before taking up the prone position or whether daily relief will be permitted in order to do so. The issue of bodily elimination is not dealt with, although the implications of a little over one year and two months of defecation are rather alarming.[16] The sheer discipline, discomfort, and endurance required for this sort of act is one that suggests the sustained trance of an ascetic (so Cooke 1936: 50).[17] In 5:1–4 the instructions continue. In this case, Ezekiel is to shave his head and beard, weigh the results and divide them in three. One part is to be burnt (inside the city when the siege is over), another struck with the sword around the city, and the last scattered in the wind. Yet not all is to be dispersed: from a small reserved portion, Ezekiel will take a few strands and burn them in 'the fire'. In chapter 5 the text falls over itself to get to the 'application' (5:5–17, compare 4:16–17). Yet it is important to note a feature of both these narratives that is all too often neglected: they remain at the level of Yahweh's command; there is no point where Ezekiel is reported to have carried out the instructions. Through being frozen on the divine tongue, as it were, these words, as well as the dialogue over the dung between prophet and God (4:13–15), are formally analogous with the Merkebah vision – they are various modes (visual, oral and aural) of communication with the divine, a central feature of ecstatic experience. It is thus as instructions that they are ecstatic, as well as any enactment itself.

Both of these acts are closely related to each other through their status as instructions without narrative execution. If enacted, they would constitute controlled, and thus acceptable, ecstatic behaviour.[18] Some other ecstatic acts appear in the vicinity of these chapters. Catatonia or aphasia, a common aspect of an ecstatic period, is mentioned in both Ezekiel 3:15 and 3:26. In the first case, the prophet sits 'stunned',[19] after the story of what has the marks of an ecstatic visit to the gods or the spirits and divinely powered air transport (3:12–15) – he is lifted up by the spirit 'in bitterness[20] in the heat of my spirit, the hand of the Lord being strong upon me' (3:14; Blenkinsopp reads this as a description of ecstasy (1990: 28)). This is the only incident in the texts I am considering that is reported directly, for when we encounter the second incident of catatonia it is once again in the form of instructions, given by the 'spirit', which had 'entered into' him (3:24). Here he is told to lock himself in his house, be bound with cords, and his tongue will cleave to the roof of his mouth so that he is speechless (3:25–26). Only when Yahweh opens his mouth will he be able to speak to the people, although when this is to happen has been a cause of some exegetical consternation (see 24:25–27; 33:21–22; see Wilson 1972). Indeed, this material in chapter 3 has the strongest claim to ecstatic activity (thus the ancient Cooke 1936: 47), including the story of the eating of the scroll in 3:1–3[21] (so Eichrodt 1970: 64). Now that I have regressed to the beginning of the stretch of texts that interest me (Ezekiel 3–5), it is possible to situate the instructions of chapters 4 and 5, and this is none other than as the words of the 'spirit' responsible for the ecstatic events in chapter 3, the same one that enters the prophet in 3:24 and begins giving instructions that do not cease until 5:4.

(Wave after wave of explosions rocked the city, and occasionally clumps of masonry thumped on the roof of the underpass. Zeke, humming along with the snatches of music that came from over the hill, had a look of ecstatic satisfaction on his face. 'Four hundred and thirty days I spent preparing for this', he said.

'How did you avoid being taken out?' I asked, in between explosions.

'I booby-trapped my last place and then moved on. I didn't get to be this old by accident, you know.')

All of this suggests that Ezekiel 3–5 may be understood in terms of ecstatic, or possession, activity. Indeed, Cooke (1936: 42) reads the effect of the 'hand of Yahweh' (*yd yhwh*) in Ezekiel 1:3; 3:14; 8:1, Isaiah 8:11 and 2 Kings 3:15 as that of ecstasy. If I add, without elaboration, the Merkebah visions in Ezekiel 1 and 10 and the vision of its movement in 3:12–13, then a narrative character who is subject to ecstatic states and perhaps madness (the two are often closely related in the shamans of various societies, as also with rock musicians[22]) comes through with reasonable clarity (see Cooke 1936: 48).

Yet I want not only to add the category of ecstasy to anarchy and carnival to provide a much thicker way of analysing both prophetic actvity and heavy metal, but also to use the whole practice of ecstatic prophecy to move onto the next phase of my argument. Before doing so, I need to attach the ecstatic label to Axl Rose and the practice of heavy metal music itself. And of course the obvious way to do this is via the word 'Ecstasy', which denotes not only a state of altered consciousness and behaviour, but also a designer drug very popular in the 1990s, so named for obvious reasons. Ecstatic states were and are most often induced through changes in bodily chemistry, either through certain types of deprivation – food and sleep are the most common – or through additional stimuli, most commonly in herbs, drugs or alcohol, but also as music and noise. I have already stressed the importance of alcohol and drugs in heavy metal subculture, although with a focus on anarchism and carnival. As a category, ecstasy joins this group with very little effort. Indeed, Weinstein (1991: 213–7) argues that ecstasy is the desired effect of a heavy metal concert, induced by alcohol, dope, the music and the whole show itself. Although all three – anarchism, carnival and ecstatsy – share in the wild breach of conventional patterns of behaviour, ecstasy and carnival draw more closely together in that ecstasy is often induced in carnivalesque moments: the shaman or prophet was expected to rave at the carnival. Finally, the ecstatic is also anarchistic and carnivalesque in its ability to give some glimpse of a better world, an alternative world to this one.

(The large government offices building, all plexiglass and metal frame, disappeared in the next explosion. About a kilometre away, we could see it clearly from where we were, and a rain of plexiglass pieces washed down on the underpass. My ears were ringing and I could barely hear what the others were saying; they seemed to be having the same problem. I wondered about ear damage, watching the last plumes ascend skyward over the city while the highrises crumbled and fell.)

HEGEMONY AND NOISE

I've been draggin' my heels
with a bitch called hope,
let the undercurrent drag me along.

('Garden of Eden', Guns 'n' Roses 1991)

I have already moved into the realm of what, following Antonio Gramsci (1971: 268, 328, 348, 365, 370, 376), is now called hegemony. To begin with, the problem may be set up as an opposition between subversive forces and the efforts by the ruling classes to maintain social control. This is of course the basis of the classic Marxist understanding of class structure and class conflict (not surprisingly, given Gramsci's central role in the Italian Communist Party). Yet, the further such a relation is pursued the more complex it becomes. One may see an echo in discussions of rock music that return time and again to the issue of the subversiveness of rock (for example, Born 1993; Buxton 1990; Davies 1993; DeCurtis 1991; Grossberg 1984, 1990, 1993; Hill 1991; Sturma 1992; Ullestad 1987; and Chow 1993 for a Chinese perspective on the same theme[23]), although Regev (1994) has argued that this is but a step on the way to the traditional (Romantic) claim for the autonomy of rock music as an art form (see also Stratton 1983: 153). Gracyk agrees: suggesting that '[d]espite its power to disrupt, rock has always been a reactionary art', a judgement based on the traditional, which here means 'liberal', 'modernist', or 'bourgeois', artistic goals espoused by rock: the expression of emotion, intensity of feeling, the claims for authenticity and truth (Gracyk 1996: 124, 218–26). 'As a cultural space in which the concept of "art" burrows into popular culture, rock seems to be a bastion of Enlightenment assumptions about the self' (226; this is epitomized in Weinstein's study (1991)).

How may rock undermine social norms? This chapter, coming as it does from a perspective similar to that of Gramsci, trades on this question, extending it to the role of prophets in the biblical text and in ancient Israel. And so, in a further turn of the original opposition, the question becomes how the anti-social and subversive behaviour of the prophets, and so also of metal groups such as Guns 'n' Roses, is in tension with the effort, by the very social

104

forces they wish to undermine, to contain them. This might also be phrased in terms of the continual attempt to harness and redirect the disruptive dimensions of anarchism, carnival and ecstasy.

(Zeke was beside himself. 'It worked! It worked!' he sang, leaping about. 'After all these years, it finally worked! Now, wait for the grand finale!' A series of plumes started to appear in all directions, the sounds faint and strong, coming from far and near. And then a mushroom cloud rose over central Parramatta.)

Hegemony is then the dominant ideological structure in a given society, the exercise of power without direct violence. The study of hegemony is concerned with the struggle of the ruling classes to set the ideological agenda for all social classes, attempting to structure desires, feelings, practices, expectations and thoughts. Yet this ideological control is never secure, never complete, and so there is a contradictory move both to allow discontent and a certain level of rebellion – in order to allow people to vent their feelings – and a continual effort at encirclement of those elements that are too subversive. At first sight there would seem to be little hope, as my closer look at the notion of ecstasy above suggests. The possibility and nature of ecstatic behaviour is controlled by a whole range of unexpressed social expectations which serve to (de)legitimate the prophet or shaman in question, as emphasized repeatedly by Overholt. Similarly, the behavioural patterns of Guns 'n' Roses and other heavy metal groups fall into expected anti-social patterns so that they may then be identified as precisely what they wish to be, a heavy metal group. This type of ideological control works at a couple of levels: first, there are the norms of marginal social groups or so-called 'sub-cultures' which normally have strict codes of behaviour.[24] Thus, Guns 'n' Roses conform in many respects to the codes of what may described as the heavy metal subculture – type of music, 'lifestyle', substance abuse, in short, being repulsive to dominant middle class culture. What is significant about Guns 'n' Roses is that their edge is not as sharp as groups like Ministry, Deicide and the Impaled Nazarene, yet even these groups conform to the expectations of metal subculture. In a similar way prophetic texts such as Ezekiel operate on the basis of shock value: the sheer negativity of the judgement passages, the violence continually evoked as a divine prerogative, and the misogyny of many sections to name a few.

The second level of hegemony over heavy metal and prophecy is in the wider social expectations of the behaviour of such sub-cultures. It is as though, in a perverse way, a group like Guns 'n' Roses is expected to be involved in precisely the sorts of things in which they are involved. Yet, whenever these expectations are transgressed a little too far, the machinery of censorship is brought to bear. Similarly, there seems to be in the Hebrew Bible a symbiotic, although not exclusive, relation between prophecy and kingship: prophets played a political role that was either appreciated, tolerated, or repressed. Yet there was an expected way in which the cultural phenomenon of prophecy ought to operate.

> ('What was that?' I asked.
> 'Every single fast food outlet in Sydney is now rubble', said Zeke, 'and that' – he pointed to the cloud – 'was McDonald's southern hemisphere headquarters. Worst bunch of terrorists around!' he chanted.)

There is, finally, a more comprehensive level of control in operation, for the controlling ideologies of a particular social formation are adept at incorporating and using for their own ends the strongest oppositional forces, either as neutralized forms of critical thinking or as negative examples to avoid. Thus prophets such as Ezekiel had their words recorded (assuming for a moment the existence of an Ezekiel) and eventually collected in a religious canon, and rock groups such as Guns 'n' Roses become what may be termed a 'research arm' of multinational capitalism, setting patterns for clothing fashion (jeans, T-shirts with logos and jackets), hair (long), physique (muscled mesomorph), food (beer and hamburgers) and so on. Guns 'n' Roses is crucially positioned between the subversive core of heavy metal and its softened, commercial side, but the group also signals the always-already commodified nature of the most extreme forms of metal music. The most pervasive way rock music as a whole is incorporated into mainstream commercial culture is through advertising (the continual reuse of certain riffs and words on television advertisements), sports programmes (here heavy metal functions as a background to masculine events) and in the very video clips themselves, which may be understood as advertisements to buy the recording (see Herman 1993: 14). Similarly, the Hebrew prophets, even those like Ezekiel, who were the ideological heroes of the reformers, have become the texts of largely middle-class, elderly and conservative churches, who practise a liberal, hand-wringing, approach to social justice that incorporates the prophets among their central texts.

But to speak of 'incorporation' is to grant some external existence to a subversive current in prophecy and heavy metal, something that Grossberg terms 'excorporation' (1984). Yet, as David Buxton has suggested, countercultural values are not always in conflict with commercial processes: 'it is important not to see rock music as a perpetual conflict between two pure entities, counterculture and corporate capitalism, in which the latter always unfortunately appropriates the former to its own ends' (1990: 434). Buxton backs this up with an argument for the integral role of the star system, the burgeoning of the record industry, and the suggestion that recorded music has 'become one of the key elements in the constitution of the modern self, increasingly defined in terms of lifestyle' (1990: 434). These arguments are in themselves elaborations of Adorno's classic argument in 'On Popular Music', which, using the model of Tin Pan Alley music production, suggested that popular music is riven with the marks of capitalist production – standardization and pseudo-individualization. There is no chance here for any viable opposition from a mode of cultural production that is capitalist through and through, although Gendron has argued that Adorno's homologous connection between the production line and popular music is a little too simplistic.[25] Indeed, Guns 'n' Roses is itself now a corporation, with Axl and Duff the sole owners.

This is in the end a rather bleak prospect for any subversive and marginal practice, whether in prophecy or metal music, unless an alternative culture can be established in which these patterns of existence are nourished. While I am not in the habit of turning too quickly to the possibility of subversive practice, Gramsci's notion of hegemony has a second dimension, which is that the efforts at encirclement and control by the dominant ideological structures are never complete, hence the frenzy of such efforts and their sheer crassness (such as the national anthem at all major sports events). There are, it seems, shards of opposition that remain, or, to avoid the modernist perception of resistant enclaves, modes of opposition that have not yet been explored with sufficient vigour, at times generated out of capitalism itself, as Dyer argues regarding disco (1990: 412). I also want to avoid Grossberg's twist on the 'enclave' argument, in which the edge of rock and roll lies in its ability to create a 'rupture between the rock and roll audience (in their everyday lives) and the larger hegemonic context within which it necessarily exists' (Grossberg 1990: 116).[26]

(The music we had heard earlier returned now that the bombs were over. 'There's a small party over in the amphitheatre', said Zeke, 'let's go and see.' Over the hill to the north, past the still standing old government house, now a restaurant, and down to the river we went. A natural amphitheatre had been complemented with a stage at some time in the past. A ragged crowd was picking itself up from the ground, and the band had returned to its instruments, celebrating I knew not what. They started playing the old Bob Dylan number, later retooled by Guns 'n' Roses – 'Knockin' on Heaven's Door'.)

In order to locate the possibility of viable opposition, and also to move onto my conclusion, I turn to the remarkable work by Jacques Attali, *Bruits* (Noises). For Attali (once economic advisor to Mitterrand in the early days of France's socialist experiment), music is the 'organisation du bruit' (1977: 9), a remarkably prescient description, perhaps even a definition, of heavy metal itself. Indeed, for Weinstein (1991: 23) and Gracyk (1996: 99–124), noise, especially in terms of volume, is a crucial feature of heavy metal. Working with the conventional Marxist model of base and superstructure, Attali does not take a restrospective approach, seeing the superstructure as lagging behind and thereby dependent on, or determined by, the base; rather, he investigates the possibility that the superstructure may anticipate new social formations with which the base may in time catch up. It is music that plays this annunciatory role for Attali, foreshadowing in its own peculiar way the potential of another, better mode of production, but also the possibility of a much worse state of affairs, which is itself the underside of the promised improvement. What is attractive about Attali's proposal is this ambiguity that he traces in the promise of music. The very chance of a new social and economic formation depends upon Attali's perception that the new forms of social relations may be seen developing all around us, in the cracks of the old as it begins to break up, and that the new economic order that is part of these social relations is foreshadowed in cultural production such as music, especially popular music. It takes little extension to suggest that it is precisely those forms that operate on the extreme edge of mainstream culture, such as heavy metal, that may be said to provide, in their very anarchism and carnivalesque practices, a taste of radically new social, political and economic formations. Cultural forms such as music or prophecy may therefore have profoundly utopian functions.

That this provides a Marxist model for understanding prophecy hardly needs to be mentioned. Prophecy, then, like music (especially heavy metal), provides glimpses as an item of the superstructure of an alternative world that the economic base may one day realize. In this thoroughly materialist way of approaching prophecy, what will then be interesting is whether the modes of production that follow that of the Hebrew Bible may be traced in the prophetic texts themselves.

However, I do not want to close without offering some comments on the role of violence in the utopian vision. My earlier discussions of anarchy and carnival indicate the crucial role of violence in both of those cultural and political practices, particularly in the need for the destruction of a present corrupt order before the new may be inaugurated. The problem of course is that in both heavy metal and so much of Ezekiel the violence is gendered violence, something that is of course as undesirable as racial or sexual violence. Yet, I want to suggest that these are examples of misdirected violence, of an explosion into unacceptable realms of what should be political violence, for the primal impulse of anarchism and carnival is precisely political violence. And this may, unfortunately, be required in the light of the implications of hegemony with violence; hegemony, as I argued in chapter 2, being the originary and usurping violence of a social structure whose violent character has been effaced. Such a structure then simultaneously conceals its foundational violence while designating that which disrupts as violence. This of course means that hegemony, in its very concealment, is the location of supreme violence: any act of violence that disrupts and makes explicit *this* violence is what may be termed political violence. It is then a sad reflection on our own situation – and it seems of Ezekiel's texts – that the strength of the originary, hegemonic, violence requires something like Ezekiel or Axl Rose to offer the possibility that it may be broken.

(We didn't stay long at the party, although the music was good, if a little unexpected. 'I want to survey my handiwork', said Zeke. Hokhma, Zara and I were now without any immediate jobs, so we had little choice.)

6

PAWING THROUGH GARBAGE

On the dialectics of dystopia in Lamentations and the Strugatsky brothers

In other words, utopias are 'utopian' not because they depict an 'impossible Ideal', a dream not for this world, but because they misrecognize the way their ideal state is already realized in its basic content ('in its notion', as Hegel would say).

(Žižek 1991b: 184)

(We followed the river's bend, turning from southbound to east, past the waterhole where aboriginal children used to swim less than two centuries ago. The Tudor Gates on the eastern edge of the park were a pile of red rubble, a casualty of the utter destruction of the government offices building across the road. Both court-houses, next door to the offices, were craters of twisted metal and concrete rubble. Zeke was still ecstatic, although he seemed to be on the way out, sliding down into depression. The human casualties were sobering. At what was left of the gates, someone was slumped against the sandstone gate-post, a Gothic 'C' on her helmet.)

The Strugatsky brothers, Arkady (1925–91) and Boris (1933–), Russia's foremost science fiction writers, have found the Censor difficult to avoid, both before and after the 1987–9 shake-up in communist rule. Before 1987, especially in the 1960s and 1970s, they faced continual intervention and criticism of their works; it was, as Arkady notes, 'a very difficult time, as if you were living under a woollen quilt' (Gopman 1991: 3). Even before this, in 1964 with the Russian release of *Hard to Be a God* (1973), which explores the tension and ambiguity between allowing a people's history to take its course or benevolently intervening, they were attacked in articles that exposed the 'reactionary essence of the Strugatskys' SF'; their work, it was argued, 'libels Soviet life' (Gopman 1991: 2). Subsequently *The Second Invasion from Mars* (Russian 1968; English 1979a), *Predatory Things of Our Times* (Russian 1965; English as *The Final Circle of Paradise* 1976), *The Tale of the Troika* (Russian 1968; English 1977b), and *The Snail on the Slope* (Russian 1966 and 1968; English 1980) were also criticized (see further Greene 1986: 98–9; Suvin 1972). But it was after someone sent *The Ugly Swans* (1979b) to West Germany and its unauthorized publication in 1972 by the Possev publishing house in Frankfurt am Main that the Strugatskys were blacklisted, despite an official protest by the authors themselves as to the circumstances of the publication. After this, notes Arkady, 'for many publishers, our name became an object of fear' (Gopman 1991: 2). It was only with perestroika that *The Ugly Swans* could be published in the USSR in 1987, along with a full text of *Tale of the Troika*. Yet, it would be a mistake to see the Strugatskys as dissidents in the Soviet era, a view that led in part to the flood of translations and publications of their works in the 1970s (see Potts 1991: 13–17).

However, at a deeper level it seems that it was the context of censorship that provided the generic possibilities and contradictions of the Strugatskys' work. For, as Gomel argues (1995), their work operates on a tension between allegory and science fiction. Allegory is the distinct signal of censorship in Russian writing, having a long tradition that goes back before the Revolution of 1917. Most of their works involve elements of both (e.g. *Hard to Be a God* and *Escape Attempt* (Russian 1962; English 1982)), although some are more clearly science fiction (*Space Mowgli* (Russian 1973; English 1982); *Roadside Picnic* (Russian 1974; English 1977b)), while others are allegory, especially political satire. It is precisely the allegorical tales that have caused the problems with the Censor, attuned as it has been to precisely such a tactic. Gomel argues that the purer science fiction is better, but it seems to me that this misses one of the main features of science fiction itself, namely, its perpetual reference to and critique of the contemporary world of the writers (see Boer 1997: 118–20). However, the function of such reference is not so much to criticize, but to generate a space in which the alternative worlds of science fiction may be thought – a feature signalled by the oblique and overdetermined referential patterns of science fiction (see McGuire 1982: 116–17). The allegorical tales thereby make more explicit a feature of science fiction. In his own way, Suvin (1988: 151–71), finds the allegorical, or, as he prefers, parabolic, nature of works like *Hard to Be a God*, *The Second Invasion from Mars* and *The Tale of the Troika* among their best.

It is interesting, of course, that science fiction has, in the case of the Strugatskys, been more successful in outsmarting the Censor. In this light *Roadside Picnic* is unanimously regarded as the crowning achievement in the Strugatsky corpus (hence its presence in this chapter). The removal, or rather shifting, of the Censor after 1987–9, has seen what Gomel regards as a floundering of the Strugatskys' work, notably in the increasing religious allegory of the as yet untranslated *The Doomed City* (1987), *Crooked Destiny* (1989) and *Burdened by Evil* (1989).

One of the major features of the transformation of the Censor under the globally rampant world of late capitalism is the extraordinary difficulty of obtaining any of the Strugatskys' works at the end of the 1990s. Despite the efforts of journals like *Science Fiction Studies* and Macmillan's 'Best of Soviet Science Fiction' series, the Strugatskys remain largely unknown outside their own country. Here in Australia – a place where books are thinner on the ground – specialist science fiction bookstores hardly know of them, and the effort to purchase or borrow one of their books impossible without international searches. The holdings in public libraries – even the State Library of New South Wales and the National Library in Canberra – are virtually non-existent and only spasmodic volumes appear in the university libraries or in the stacks of obscure public branch libraries. Is this a legacy of the Cold War, or perhaps a more forthright manifestation of Jameson's charge that the utopian imagination under capitalism has atrophied? It is as though the effort at obliterating 'actually existing socialism' is now devoted to the legacy of its popular culture.

(There was little left of certain streets, Zeke having taken a special delight in mining those with names like George, Macquarie, Phillip or Marsden, named after English kings or governors or clergy of the early colony. So we picked our way as best we could, over piles of asphalt and masonry, skirting craters and pits. Close by what had been the local government headquarters, Zeke slipped on some blood and a broken piece of footpath gave way to the sewers beneath. He managed to hold on long enough for us to pull him out of the effluential slime.)

ON (E)UTOPIA, AGAIN

The initial trigger for this chapter comes from the work of Fredric Jameson, who continues to influence my thinking in so many ways. For it is Jameson who almost single-handedly in western literary and cultural circles at least has made utopia a central rather than peripheral concern. Of course, utopia, particularly in the present historical conjuncture of late capitalism, designates socialism or communism, however one wants to describe such social and economic formations. And this is one of the major reasons for my own pressing of the question of utopia, particularly in a religious and biblical context, for there is a significant overlap between religion and socialism in the desire for a world radically different from this one, even though the contours of that world may only faintly be discerned. Yet, the negative, impractical, dreamy feel of the term 'utopia' tenaciously hangs on, one of the more signal victories of late capitalist hegemony (understood as a perpetually contested zone of class conflict and its attendant discourses).

Yet I want to argue that utopia remains not just a category of literary and cultural study but a political slogan that bears with it an urgency brought about by the events in Eastern Europe in 1989. In this light, Fredric Jameson's arguments (1982; 1988: 75–101) about utopian literature and science fiction gain a new dimension. Jameson's line is that those science fiction works produced under capitalism that seek to create an alternative world, that seek to construct a literary utopia, inevitably fail the moment the effort is made. Some mark, some signal emanates from the novel (or film) itself that brings the whole project crashing down – there is, in other words, an absence of the utopian imagination that appears most strongly in the very act of attempting to imagine one in literature. Such a signal may be the woodenness characteristic of utopian writing, the absence of some means to achieve the utopian state or, conversely, too close a connection to this world with the result that it readily coalesces, the descriptive paucity or incoherence of the new world, or the assumption that constructed items of contemporary existence (such as commodity relations, competition, gender constructions, or perceptions of the body) are 'natural' and thereby would persist in any future or alternative world.

But such an inability to imagine utopia – what Jameson terms the atrophied utopian imagination – is not merely some flaw in writers of utopian works or of science fiction, some shortcoming that awaits a supremely skilled master to produce a utopia that succeeds where the others have failed. It is, rather, something that runs in the fabric of capitalism and its associated cultural forms. It is, in other words, the impossibility of imagining socialism in the context of capitalism. (Here I make explicit some of the underlying patterns of Jameson's own arguments.) And this should come as no surprise, for how is it possible to imagine a world without advertising when advertising is all around us, indeed, is a structural feature of capitalist political, social and economic existence? How might the patterns of clothing, art, literature, film, scholarship, biblical studies – to name but a few items – look without the fundamentally capitalist need for fashion and its change? How might non-reified relations work when all we know are precisely such relations, when our psyches are so deeply reified it appears natural? And what might a society look like without competition at the cost of the other? In the very asking of such questions it seems that the only way even to begin considering utopia is through a sort of *via negativa*, an apophatic theology of utopia and science fiction itself.

> (*The financial heart of the city looked as though it had been ripped out: highrises flattened, banks blown open, safes cracked, an odd teetering wall left here and there. 'We shouldn't have come in', said Zeke.*
> *'Why not?' asked Hokhma.*
> *'It's too lethal', he said. 'Unexploded devices, unstable surfaces, collapsing buildings …'*)

In a characteristic dialectical move, Jameson argues that, since the intentional construction of utopias fails at the moment building begins, the possibility of utopia may be glimpsed in the opposite situation, namely, in the very effort to show that utopias cannot be written or constructed. The sorts of works meant here are not only dystopias, of which there are many, but anti-utopian texts – those works in which the reasons for the impossibility of utopia are explored, or in which the advocacy of anti-utopianism is strongest, or in which despair of ever achieving utopia is foremost. That there is a distinctly reactionary strain to much of this writing makes it all the more attractive for Jameson, not because of the explicit politics, but because of the unwitting glimpses that this material gives of the possibility of utopia itself.

I will explore what this might mean in a moment or two, but the crucial term for Jameson here is figuration (see Boer 1996a: 80–4), the process by which cultural products signify things entirely other than their overt structure and content would indicate. Thus, it is possible to glimpse a revolutionary moment in a reactionary text if one is prepared to look slightly askance and seek such figures in less well-trodden areas of the text. These might be features of form, odd linguistic turns, curious and unexplainable ideological features of the text. Indeed, the whole idea of figuration (with its relation to the Derridean trace and the symptom) owes its formulation to Freud and his discussion of parapraxes, of slips, of the glimpses whereby the unconscious makes its presence felt. For Jameson of course this is always already politicized rather than personalized – hence the 'political unconscious' of his most well-known book (1981).

Another important idea in my pursuit of the utopian is drawn from Louis Marin, specifically his *Utopiques: Jeux d'Espaces* (1973; see Boer 1997: 112–22), in which he argues that it is not so much the blueprint of utopia that is important, not the (almost necessarily dull) narrative describing the new society – in fact these items stall the utopian drive – but rather the very act of writing a utopia in the first place. It is the language itself, in all its uncertainties and instabilities that gives a glimpse of what it might be like to speak of something about which it is impossible to speak because the tools and terms are not available to us. The key term for Marin is neutralization: (e)utopia – a good place and no place – is the intersection of *le neutre* (the indefinite) and the *le pluriel* (the dispersal of utopian discourse). Utopia is 'the double figure, the ambiguous representation, the equivocal picture of possible synthesis and of productive differentiation' (Marin 1973: 24–5, translation mine). It is neither the one, nor the other (*ni l'un, ni l'autre*, a phrase repeated throughout Marin's text), but a Hegelian degree zero. Or, to invert Lévi-Strauss's description of the function of myth – a conceptual or imaginary mediation of a real social problem or contradiction (Lévi-Strauss 1989: 229–56; Boer 1996a: 43–4) – utopia is the opening up of such contradictions, a move that allows them free play rather than repressing them. A utopian text 'opens up a space of neutrality in which the contradictions are allowed to play against one another rather than being effaced in a mythic synthesis' (Hill 1982: 172). The utopian project thereby produces a multiplicity of spaces that are incongruous with each other. Only in the *jeux d'espaces*, the spatial play of these contradictory spaces does the possibility of utopia emerge.

(I began to be anxious about the well-being of the others, hoping that an unstable wall would not fall while they were standing near, that one of Zeke's devices would not detonate late, that a pit would not open up and swallow them up, that a projectile would not pierce them. We laboured

*our way over broken concrete, twisted metal reinforcement, shattered glass
and tiles. Pipes hissed and spurted about us. Here and there a fire burned.
With the regular landmarks gone, we could only keep our sense of direction in relation to the river.)*

Apart from figuration and neutralization, there is also the combination of the
Freudian wish fulfilment and death wish. The basic idea here that is pertinent
for the hints of utopia is Freud's suggestion that fulfillment of a wish is often
expressed in its opposite. Thus, the fear of the death of a loved one – in an
accident or through disease, say – is in fact a wish fulfilment, the impossible
wish for the loved one's death that can only be expressed in its inverse because
of the Censor. Alternatively, desire for the continued health and longevity of
that loved one may well be concealing its alternative, a violent and rapid
death. Thus, the fear of a loved one's death, or the desire for their continued
health and well-being, embodies a hope for that death, something that may
well be expressed more directly with less censorship (see Freud 1973: 175–
82; 224–5; 243). But the death itself – now going past Freud – may well be
regarded as the only way that any imagining of another life might find expression. So also with utopia: the fear of the destruction of the present order
being therefore the impossible hope that this order may well destruct, that
such destruction is highly desirable but can only be voiced as its opposite.
Eventually all of this folds back into figuration, for it may then be suggested
that every fear of destruction is in its own way a figure of the utopian wish
despite itself.

So, it is the figuration of utopia in the text, the moment of neutralization,
and the wish fulfilment that I seek in both the work of the Strugatskys and the
text of Lamentations. But there is one final point of a more theoretical nature
that needs to be made before turning to the texts themselves, and that is the
relation between religion and utopia. It seems to me that the language and
imagination of religion are profoundly utopian, although this is too often
reactionary in its content – religion has, after all, been more often a crucial
element in the ideological construction of ruling class discourse. Yet, even this
discourse is not excluded from the figuration of utopia (although this approach needs to be wary of endorsing such reactionary utopias unwittingly).
There are, however, certain distinctly liberative aspects of religious language
and imagination, especially when that has a social dimension. The expectation of some improvement in life, if not a significant leap in whatever follows
this life, has both its reactionary forms – one's advancement in middle class
status, for example – and its liberative forms – such as the demands for equal
distribution in social struggles. But this expectation, and the imagery that is
very much part of it, is core utopia. Perhaps the strongest utopian figure in
religion is the collective, the notion of a group or cooperative that features
repeatedly in many religions, however much it overlaps with the tribal, ethnic,
social and political groupings. For it is in the very assumption of the collective

that religions figure utopia, irrespective of the particular shape such collectives may take.

('It's starting to feel very alien', said Zara, while we stood on the edge of the vast crater of McDonald's former headquarters. She coughed, for the air was full of the smoke and dust of the devastation wreaked on the city. The stores of frozen buns and patties, ketchup, pickles and lettuce lay scattered in the western corner of the crater. A river of shake mix wound down into its centre. Although most had managed to get out, there were still too many bodies and too many cries for help from the injured.)

IN THE 'ZONE'

I sat on the bench, my knees empty, my head empty, my soul empty. Gulping down the strong stuff like it was water. Alive. The Zone had let me out. It let me out …

(Strugatsky and Strugatsky 1977b: 28)

The Strugatskys have the ability to enter a story late and leave it early, to vary style and subject matter, and they have a strong humanity in their work, where science fiction becomes a genre eminently suited for consideration of the contradictions of human existence (see further Fyodorov 1983; Gakov 1982). In contrast to what Suvin calls the 'static utopian brightness' (1988: 162; see also Potts 1991: 19–35) of some of their earlier work, one of the huge attractions of their writing as it has developed is a more negative vision, a pessimistic, dystopian view of human history and society. But it is here that the possibilities of utopia itself begin to emerge. I will attempt to track such possibilities in light of the notions of neutralization, figuration and wish fulfillment that I traced earlier.

A properly dystopian stream begins in the Strugatskys' work when utopia is regarded not so much as a future that requires a few hurdles to be surmounted before it is realized as a near impossible destination that humans persistently sabotage. Thus, in *Escape Attempt*, the main protagonist is caught on a feudal planet, Saula, where the combination of slavery and high technology holds this society in a state of permanent utopian disability. Intervention threatens to worsen the situation, although it is done to trigger the road to a communist future even on this planet. *Far Rainbow* turns the negative into a physical force, the Black Wave, which is unleashed by the scientists experimenting on the frontiers of science on the planet Rainbow. This price of experiment and progress is death for all the inhabitants, barring the children who are squeezed into the only available space craft. In *Hard to Be a God*, the possibility of slow utopian development, as espoused by the Earth's Institute

116

of Experimental History, turns out to be dystopian devolution on the planet in question. The 'gods', ambassadors from the institute to the planet Arkanar, make themselves members of this society in all but their views, assisting where they can within the system, but not using their greater powers to achieve their end, which is the development of the planet to earth's level. In the face of a putsch that targets intellectuals, teachers, musicians, individuals and the stray revolutionaries, Rumata, the hero, finally cracks when his girlfriend is murdered on a night of anti-revolutionary pillage and slaughter. Leaving a swathe of dead behind him, he is returned to earth and remains mentally ill at the novel's close. *The Final Circle of Paradise* follows a similar theme, although this time a socially demoralized and decadent capitalist enclave, the Country of Fools, or the Boob, is placed on earth. In this case, Zhilin, the engineer from the earlier *Space Apprentice* struggles against the electric and chemical modes used to keep the population in subservience, only to find that human weakness leads to decadence, a finding refused by his superiors. A comparable example is the later *Prisoners of Power*, in which Maxim, the hero, finds himself on the isolated, violent world of Saraksh where a military dictatorship maintains power through the use of persuasion technology. In immersing himself in the surrounding obscurantist cruelty, Maxim attempts to set off a coup that looks like making matters worse until the Council for Galactic Security, which has been working there for some time, comes to his aid. Still, in each of these stories, the dystopian element takes place in the context of a vaster utopian assumption. As yet, the negative dimensions are framed by the larger positive.

> *(All of us were silent before the devastation Zeke's bombs had caused. He had slipped into catatonia after his earlier exuberance, and Zara and Hokhma were chewing over the implications. My situational depression felt like it was on its way back. Encased in smoke and dust, eyes and noses running, grimy from the ruins, heads down, shuffling along – we were a dismal group.)*

With *The Second Invasion from Mars* the utopian context of the recalcitrant planet or location has disappeared. Here the self-serving petty bourgeois ignorance of the unnamed town acquiesces before the Martian invasion that seems to be based at nearby but largely unknown Marathon. The point of view of the retired school teacher, Phoebus Apollo (all of the characters have names from Greek mythology), reflects the town's justification for conformism. All that concerns him is his pension and the possibility of some money from the new arrangements. Knowledge of what goes on comes through hearsay and speculation, both within the town and its borders of ignorance: money paid for stomach juice; a new blue grain crop that produces not only delicious blue bread but also blue beer (good for producing stomach juice); black shiny vehicles that glide over the ground; strange characters that appear from the vehicles dressed in suits; and rebels in the country who attack the shiny vehicles and the beings in them.

A similarly bleak picture is presented in *Monday Begins on Saturday* (Russian 1965; English 1977a) and *Tale of the Troika*. The former traces the work of Janus Nevstruev and his Scientific Institute for Happiness in contrast to the work of Amvroz Ambruazovich Vybegallo who wants to create the happy Universal Consumer. With elements of folk-tale, satire and parody, the novel deals with the (ab)use of science. *Tale of the Troika* has Vybegallo as a consultant to the 'troika', which has usurped power from its position as a commission for checking the plumbing. There is little of redeeming value in the prejudices, conflicts, incompetence and scientific despotism of this bureaucracy who would be self-serving if they weren't so stupid. A final forlorn work is *The Kid from Hell* (Russian 1973; English 1982), where the best efforts by humans to transform, through utopian stimuli, a killer drawn out of a war between two disintegrating societies fail. However, the bleakness of these works, which is only reinforced by the satire and humour, may well be understood in terms of Freud's wish fulfilment that I noted earlier. For here, given the distinctly utopian themes of other Strugatsky works, the very negativity of these three novels expresses the desperate wish for the opposites of the pictures presented. Such an interpretation is reinforced by the encounter with the alien in *Tale of the Troika*, in which the bureaucracy shows itself completely unprepared for a utopian future.

> (*'It's hard to know what is worse'*, said Zara, *'all the crap, rip offs and corruption of before, or this hell-hole we have now.'*
>
> *I wasn't sure either; 'Each attempt to make a leap for the better only seems to end up reverting to a situation as bad as, if not worse than, before.'*
>
> *'At least so many people wouldn't have to die'*, wheezed Zara in the smoke. *Hokhma had no wisdom to cast on the matter.*)

In the final group it is precisely the question of the alien that forms the basis of utopian possibilities. However, it is not that the alien provides such an opportunity gratis, but the glimpse of utopia is found in the way people react to the alien presence. Of course, throughout their work the question of the alien is present – it is, after all, a generic requirement – but it tended to be the humans who were the more advanced, benevolent, aliens trying to help others in backward locations. The reverse of this – humans as subject to ambiguous alien contact – already takes place in *The Second Invasion From Mars* and *Tale of the Troika*; in both cases, the humans fare badly in their response (see Potts 1991: 71–89).

The unknown alien presence is crucial to *The Ugly Swans*, in which the existence of a run-down and perpetually drunk town is put out-of-step by the 'slimies', figures with some sort of disease whose contagion – evidenced by marks around the eyes, bandages on head and hands, dark clothing and thin bodies – is avoided at all costs. Mostly told from the perspective of a decorated, inebriated and politically suspect writer called Banev, we learn gradually that the slimies are often ill-treated, that there is a constant fear that the 'contagion' will spread, that the young are slowly being perverted by the slimies, and that the boundaries between a corrupt military and the slimies appears obscure. With only the hint of an alien presence (but is the physical disassembly and reassembly of the slimy before Banev's eyes merely a drunken hallucination?), the town lives in fear that more and more of its citizens are being corrupted by the slimies, especially those in high places. Yet the place in which the slimies live on the outskirts of town is very ambiguously utopian: it is surrounded by fences and barbed wire and under armed guard, it commands resources without seeming to pay for them in any way. Yet in the climax of the story the children of the town voluntarily go there and the perpetual, soaking, rotting, rain is less there. The slimies themselves need books, for without them they will die. They are always calm and long-suffering, never losing their temper and always seeming to be in control. The contrast here lies not only between the town's citizens who fear contagion and the young who choose to follow and evolve into higher beings, but also between the rotting town and the place of the slimies, where even the weather seems to be controlled. This alien zone is qualitatively different from what surrounds it.

(With its craters, piles of rubble, forlorn walls and white, dusty air, Parramatta looked like something on another planet. Distinctly inhuman, apart from our little group, hostile and full of lethal traps.)

The hopes and disappointments of an alien encounter also characterizes *Space Mowgli*, in which a child raised by qualitatively different aliens raises and then dashes hopes for a way to understand the unknown. A similar idea is used in *Beetle in the Anthill*: Leb Abalkin must be hunted down on earth since he is one of a number of space children, deposited on earth as babies with unknown programmes that may threaten earth. While Abalkin, having returned from distant space exploration, seeks to find out more about himself, Maxim Kammerer (from *Prisoners of Power*) has the task of locating him. Maxim's bureaucratic chief kills Abalkin in the end, choosing human survival as the prime ethic. Here at least a utopian possibility (a new step with the help of these figures) has presented itself, although its dystopian underside (human annihilation) remains. It is the sheer unknowability of the aliens – suspected of being the 'Wanderers' of whom only odd pieces of evidence suggest the existence – that generates the dilemma. In the case of *Beetle in the Anthill* it is impossible to know which side of the dilemma is utopian. Such an unknowability also characterizes *Definitely Maybe* (Russian 1984; English 1978), in which the disturbing force that upends the work of the world's leading scientists of utopia is interpreted as the laws of nature reasserting themselves or the presence of an evil super-human civilization. In this case, some people respond with a resistance that functions as a utopian harbinger.

Perhaps my favourite Strugatsky book is *Roadside Picnic*. Apart from the appeal of the title – is it not a grandly utopian suggestion, to stop by the road and enjoy a picnic? – what intrigues me is not only the relation of the book to Tarkovsky's film *Stalker*[1] (1979) but also the very notion and function of the zone. Comparable to the place of the slimies in *The Ugly Swans*, and very faintly to the forest in *Hard to Be a God*, the zones are six areas with a distribution like the spray of bullets into a spinning earth from a vast gun in a medium distant star cluster. The story focuses on one zone in Canada near the town of Harmont and on the reactions of Redrick Schuhart, in first person and then third person, in three main phases of his life as a Stalker. Hardened outlaws with a maverick knowledge who went into the highly lethal zone outside official approval, Stalkers brought out artifacts left behind by the alien visitation and sold them to the black market. Red is variously single, married, drunk, in gaol, rich, poor, exploiter and exploited, but he becomes one of the longest-lived Stalkers, except for Buzzard Burbridge, whom Red saves after Buzzard falls into a pit of 'witches' jelly'. For, in contrast to the pure exploitation by Burbridge of even his own children, Red's response to the zone is to care despite himself for those around him, especially Guta, his spouse, their mutant child, Monkey, his father, 'resurrected' as a result of the zone, and others. (These relations between marginal and disparate characters – mutant, zombie and humans – may be read as a utopian figure.) The zone itself is profoundly alien, vehicles caught in it during the visitation remaining as new, the grass staying green, odd shadows, moving heat patches, the sky, especially at dawn, a different colour. This alienness and its artifacts, the debris of an alien visit, have both an official terminology and a street-level jargon – mosquito mange, empties, bracelets, needles, pins, rings, white whirligigs, bitches' rattles, death lamps, lobster eyes, rattling napkins, so so's, black sprays, Dick the Tramp, the jolly ghost, the wish machine, the meat grinder, and the Golden Ball. Apart from total ignorance as to the meaning of these artifacts – their use being compared to hammering nails with microscopes – the effects of the zone on medicine, agriculture and the military are immense, as are the unexplained effects of those who were present during the visitation, such as catastrophes wherever they emigrate. But what counts in the end is the human response to the zone, whether exploitation by the more communist institute or the capitalist town around it, and the possibilities the zone generates in humans. For the zone is a place to which people are drawn, since they hope for something great from it. The zone produces in people greed and hope, destruction and salvation. It constitutes a *jeu d'espaces*, the opening of a play of contradictions. Its ambiguity is caught in the close, when Red finds the Golden Ball: 'HAPPINESS FOR EVERYBODY, FREE, AND NO ONE WILL GO AWAY UNSATISFIED' (Strugatsky and Strugatsky 1977b: 145) he shouts, unable to say anything else, despite an earlier unexpressed wish for Monkey. Does the Ball compel these words? Will this wish be realized, or is it a cruel joke, a futile wish, especially since he sacrificed Burbridge's son, Arthur, to the meat-grinder in order to get to the Ball? The very openness of the end may be understood as a glimpse of either utopia or dystopia (see Gomel 1995: 103; Salvestroni 1984: 298; compare Jameson 1982: 157). The danger here lies in the obverse of the wish fulfilment.

(On the other hand, one could imagine the city, Parramatta, on earth, visited in some mysterious, highly destructive yet promising way, by a force, malevolent, beneficent, divine, physical, alien, incomprehensible.)

However, what is important about the zone is that it is a locus for both utopian figuration and neutralization, rather than any blueprint for utopia. Thus, the zone in *Roadside Picnic*, or the compound of the slimies in *The Ugly Swans*, acts as a figuration of utopia in a radical, unimaginable alternative to the present, capitalist, social organization, so much so that they are viewed as places of threat, disease and hope. But the primary figuration comes with the responses of people to the zones, for these responses figure more strongly than anything else the utopian promise. The zone is also an empty signifier that throws into question the reality it invades. The zone (and, to a lesser extent, the compound of the slimies in *The Ugly Swans*) is the most highly developed form of neutralization, for within and outside the zone all physical and social patterns are altered in unrecognizable ways. Not only is there a negation of present social and economic relations but also of conventional expectations of what utopia might be; in this very neutralization, in allowing a play of contradictions that are normally repressed, they provide a taste of utopia. At the same time, such neutralization opens up the possibilities for dystopia.

Further, what is interesting about the encounter with the alien, or the encounter with the remnants of an alien visitation, is its connection with religious questions (something I will pursue in the discussion on Lamentations). In this respect, the alien and the divine have some things in common, including absolute difference, lack of knowledge, and their effects are as ambiguous as each other (see Salvestroni 1984: 291–2). Contact with humans is therefore indirect and all information is provisional. Commenting on the alien intelligence of *Beetle in the Anthill*, Gakov writes, 'It can be called neither vicious or kindly; it is simply inexpressibly different, it lives by its own laws and its evaluation of the inhabitants of our globe is very different from ours' (1982: 160). So also with the divine in regard to Jerusalem in Lamentations.

(I wanted to cross the river, get away and nearer to home, at least to see what had happened up that way. All that was left for crossing the river was the bicycle bridge, battered but not broken, so we made our sullen way towards it.)

'Look out!' yelled Zara.

A few steps away a dusty figure leapt out from behind a pile of rubble. Before we could react, a knife was implanted in Zeke's stomach, pushed upwards into his lungs and heart. I gave delayed chase, noting the yellow 'M' on the shoulder of the filthy uniform.

'One of the survivors of the McDonald's security force', I said when I rejoined the group.)

THE DYSTOPIAN DIALECTIC OF LAMENTATIONS

> ... to characterize Lamentations as a hopeful book is therefore to mislead.
>
> (Provan 1991: 23)

What might be the implications of such an approach to dys/utopia for the Hebrew Bible? How might the dynamics of the Strugatsky texts impinge on reading a biblical text? While it is tempting to turn to the prophetic poets of the Hebrew Bible, especially their denunciations of foreign nations as well as Israel and Judah, their bleak depictions of the future as a result of present sins and failings, their proclamation that the only hope comes from a direct irruption of Yahweh into history, they tend to include too much that is positive and hopeful, especially in the final arrangements of the collections. For one of the notable things about the prophetic texts is that no matter how much doom is prophesied in the text, there is a moment of redemption, of salvation, a way out, a *deus ex machina* at the close of the collections.

(Zeke died in a flood of blood. There was nothing we could do but leave him and move on, eager as we were to get out of the destruction zone. But it continued: Church Street had been mined, the banks, petrol stations and private schools destroyed even on the north bank of the river, so we made our way carefully through the back streets. Claudia's Penthouse on Sorrell was still intact, as was the old pub on the northern stretch of Church Street, a favourite haunt of local bikers. Plenty of beer, but no patrons today.)

There is, however, one text in the Hebrew Bible in which such a positive moment is minimal, where the moment of salvation, viewed as the means by which the dreadful present or more immediate future may be overcome, is fleeting. This is of course the text of Lamentations, which may qualify as a properly dystopian text. Here, in bitter terms, the destruction of Jerusalem and the exile to Babylon is lamented through the interplay of a number of voices: poet, Zion as grieving mother, an anonymous suffering 'man', and the citizens of Jerusa-

lem and Judah.[2] Conventionally understood as acrostic laments for the fall of
Jerusalem to the Babylonians in 587 BCE, Lamentations uses imagery of destruction, exploitation, defilement, and hopelessness to depict the destitution
of Jerusalem. I want to suggest that the utopian dimension is not found so
much in the conventional motifs of waiting for God's deliverance, of rescue
from and punishment of one's enemies (see 3:21–41, 55–66; 5:19–22), but in
the very texts of violence and destruction to which the positive sections come as
a reply.[3] To offer such a reading raises inevitable ethical questions, particularly
the highly gendered nature of the violence. Once again, I need to face the vexed
question of the relation between violence and utopia.

The immediate impression when reading Lamentations is of dystopian images
of destruction and desolation. This takes the form of a personified Zion who
has been betrayed and abandoned, of the systematic and total destruction by
Yahweh in which all the features of the contemporary social, political and
cultural structures are dismantled (2:5–10). Shortage of food, disease, death
in the streets and in homes, the scorn of enemies, the emptiness of a desolate
city, the lack of comforters, abandonment by lovers, the abasement of all
people in authority, the punishment of Yahweh – each of these themes appears. Further, Lamentations contains no material in which the restoration of
the city itself is a theme, contrary to the genre of the ancient Near Eastern city-
lament (see Dobbs-Allsopp 1993: 94).[4]

> (Picking our way through the old graveyard on Brickfield Street in which
> some of the early colonial explorers were buried, Zara commented, 'I
> guess, deep down, I always wanted things to stay as they were. I enjoyed
> making money from the judges, police, clergy and government officials
> who were regulars at my house, exploiting them as they exploited every-
> one else. I think I was always a little ambivalent about our plans.')

It is precisely with these depictions of destruction and desolation that I
want to invoke the Freudian notion of the wish fulfilment and the death
wish, that is, the suggestion that the fear of the death of a loved one or the
fear of the destruction of one's known world may actually be a wish
fulfilment, a hope for an alternative situation that can only be expressed
through its opposite.[5] In this light the strongest images of destruction may
have an alternative charge: perhaps the two most powerful sections are 2:19–
22 and 3:1–20. In the first, the breakdown of patterns of family connection
and affection are depicted through images of starving children, cannibal
mothers, dead boys and old men, young men and women in the street, and
the death of the 'those whom I bore and reared' (2:22). And all of this takes
place in the context of a desperate plea to Yahweh; indeed, the accusation is
that such atrocities are caused by Yahweh (see Westermann 1994: 156). Yet
it is here, with images that resonate with those of the contemporary media,
that Freud's suggestion may work. The only way even to begin to imagine

the possibility of an alternative social structure is to do so in terms of graphic and horrific destruction. If we flip the coin, however, the question becomes one of how such a world might look in which bonds of parent and child are no longer demanded, where the structures of family relation and dependence are not the ties that hold people together.

The other passage, 3:1–20, is a detailed depiction of the attack of Yahweh upon someone who appears in the first person. Here the shock is not so much the language itself – with themes of a deaf ear, darkness, physical suffering, enemy (Yahweh), laughing stock and accusation – as the placing of the source of such suffering and destruction at the feet of Yahweh. This is of course not so uncommon in the Hebrew Bible, particularly in the lament and complaint psalms (3:42–66 may in fact be identified as a personal lament (so Westermann 1994: 169[6])), but the utopian possibilities of this in Lamentations are significant. First, Yahweh is identified here as enemy, as the one who sets up a helpless person as a target (compare Job 6:4; 16:11–14; Psalms 38:3/2), as a hostile alien whose intervention or visitation is understood to be destructive (see my comments on the alien above). But the alien is also highly ambiguous and unknowable, and so 3:21–4 presents the alternative – that a visitation from Yahweh may be beneficial. Second, it seems that Yahweh, the enemy, is disavowed: 'Gone is my glory, and all that I had hoped for from Yahweh' (3:18), or, as Provan glosses, 'my lasting hope in Yahweh has perished' (1991: 90). This verse, it seems, is a front contender for the most pessimistic statement; for Provan it is 'perhaps the lowest point of the whole poem' (1991: 90). However, Fuerst finds 3:44 – 'you have wrapped yourself with a cloud so that no prayer can pass through' – 'one of the most drastic and doleful expressions in the Old Testament' (1975: 240).

> (*'I know it's weird', said Hokhma, 'but I really feel this destruction. It's as though the city and I have some sort of relationship, as though I've been devastated as well.' We had passed by the flattened gas stations and KFC on Church Street, a fire feeding on the spilled petrol from the underground tanks. A black cloud of smoke hung over the forlorn intersection of the roads heading north west and north east. In the V of the intersection the eucalypts competed with the smoke. I couldn't smell the gum trees any more.*)

I do not, however, want to argue that every depiction of destruction and desolation operates in the form of such a wish fulfilment, especially those that speak of the destruction of Jerusalem and Zion – now gendered as female – in terms of rape (1:8–10; 2:1). The metaphor of a female Jerusalem subject to the violence of a male Yahweh is perhaps the greatest problem with Lamentations (see Exum 1995), although some care is needed in understanding how gender is constructed in this text.[7] In this case, the disavowal of Yahweh in 3:18 gains greater force.

The second major feature of utopian construction is that of full-scale figuration, the inconspicuous and unexpected hints of a utopia beyond the ruin and devastation (itself a necessary moment in most utopian visions). In other words, the very dystopia that is depicted, the elaborate image of doom and catastrophe, bears in its very construction the glimpses of another world. For the Strugatskys this lay primarily in the human responses to dystopian directions. Lamentations offers a series of such glimpses. There are five major elements or themes that act as figures or traces in the text of Lamentations: the breakdown of the old order; collapse of former religious codes; aloneness and emptiness; asceticism of the acrostic; and hints of a new communalism.

While the end of the old order most often appears in terms of a lament, it may also be read as a hope and a wish (to carry over from my discussion of wish fulfilment above). It is not so much the expression itself of such a breakdown, but the way it is said. Thus, in 2:2 Yahweh 'has brought down to the ground in dishonor the kingdom and its rulers', something with a distinctly anticipatory feel about it. The rulers and princes come in for more comment in 4:7–8, and the wealthy are the topic of 4:5. In their place, 'slaves rule over us' (5:8). In one glorious section (2:5–10) there is a description of the total destruction of all contemporary social, political and cultural structures.[8] Yahweh destroys palaces and strongholds (2:5), tabernacle, festival and sabbath (2:6), having spurned king and priest (2:6). He has 'scorned his alter, disowned his sanctuary' (2:7). Wall, ramparts, gates and bars lie in ruins (2:8–9), while kings, princes, prophets and elders are without guidance, visionless and in mourning (2:9–10). Gone is 'everything that gave the life of the city its glitter' comments Westermann in a somewhat loaded fashion (1994: 127). And the whole picture is cast in an inversion that leads into my discussion of neutralization below: that which once was regarded as valuable, precious and sacred is so no longer:

> How the gold has grown dim, how the pure gold is changed!
> The sacred stones lie scattered at the head of every street.
> The precious children of Zion, worth their weight in fine gold
> – how they are reckoned as earthen pots, the work of potter's hands!
> (4:1–2)

For Hillers, who seems in the end to miss the point here, the 'clay vessel, most common of ancient artifacts ... was proverbial for cheapness' (1992: 146). But is that not precisely what is desired?[9] What was most precious is now treated as common.

(Zeke had made sure that the churches and other places of religious worship had also been destroyed, eternally suspicious of organized religion as he was. Ancient sandstone at one site gave way to postmodern perspex and aluminium at another. Only the cemeteries remained.)

A specific aspect of this more general approach to the breakdown of the old order – the very form of which gives a taste of what may come – is the collapse of the old religious codes and structures. Lamentations is replete with references to both the destruction of the sanctuary and the authority of religious professionals (1:10, 19; 2:6–7, 9, 14; 4:13–16). The priests are, not unexpectedly (since they always seem to suffer criticism for insincerity and corruption) condemned: in 1:19 they perish in the city, in 4:16 it is Yahweh who shows no honour to the priests, and in 4:13 the priests themselves are blamed for shedding the blood of the righteous in Jerusalem, becoming fugitives defiled with blood, scattered and dishonoured (4:14–16). But in the same verses the prophets are blamed for the same thing. Their very task is itself corrupt and empty: they have 'seen for you false and deceptive visions ... have seen oracles for you that are false and misleading' (2:14). Not only this, but Jerusalem itself has attained the status of ritual uncleanness, a category whereby the sacred has entirely disappeared. Indeed, this is cast in terms of menstrual uncleanness in 1:9 and possibly in 1:17, the vividness of the image serving to emphasize a desirable profanity and uncleanness. Is there not a dimension of alternative hope in all of this? Useless priests and prophets and a profane, unclean, Jerusalem provide a utopian moment through the lament.

A third figure that leaks over into neutralization is the depiction of Jerusalem as both alone and empty. The aloneness comes through most strongly in the first chapter when Jerusalem is characterized as a woman who has been abandoned by her lovers and comforters: 'How lonely sits the city' (1:1), 'she has no one to comfort her' (1:2; see 1:17, 19, 21), and 'all her majesty' has departed (1:6). But is aloneness always to be lamented as a loss? It is also solitude, a utopian trace.[10] Alongside this image is the powerful one of the emptying of Jerusalem. Everyone has been killed or driven away. Returning to 1:1: 'How lonely sits the city that once was full of people!' Her 'gates are desolate' (1:4); Mount Zion 'lies desolate; jackals prowl over it' (5:18). Or, if the agency is given to Yahweh, it is like a clearing, cathartic fire: 'he has burned like a flaming fire in Jacob, consuming all around' (2:3). Not only does such a clearing action provide the space for something new, but it is also the space for the 'spatial play', Marin's *jeux d'espaces*, of utopia. I will return to this in a moment.

Fourth, the acrostic, much commented upon, provides a certain linguistic asceticism that may be read as a figure that runs close to the previous one of emptiness. Of course, this suggestion is only provisional, especially in the light of a range of possibilities, including its usage for magic, pedagogy, memorization, completeness (see Gottwald 1962: 32–2; Renkema 1995), stability in the face of chaos and fragmentation (Gous 1996; Landy 1987b: 333) and formal expressions of anguish and pain as a way to hope (Minkoff 1997). But if the suggestion of Gottwald is taken that the acrostic produces an economy of speech that restrains the boundless grief and shock, that it is one of the 'most obtrusively formal books in the Bible' (Landy 1987b: 333), then its asceticism becomes a stylistic figure for utopian possibilities. For in asceticism, in the denial of the present body, is embodied a hope and anticipation.

A final figure is what might be termed a new communalism, something that relates closely with the end of the old order of power and the removal of the religious professionals. Here there are the merest glimpses of what such a situation may be like, an inversion of codes of personal and social value that works towards a radical commonality. Thus, the people 'trade their treasures for food to revive their strength' (1:11), reverting to basic needs as of more value. But it is 3:45 and 4:2 that seem to me to offer the most radical vision:

You have made us filth and rubbish among the peoples.

(3:45)

The precious children of Zion, worth their weight in fine gold –how they are reckoned as earthen pots, the work of a potter's hands!

(4:2)

(Finally, we came close to the dilapidated shelter I called home, an area whose industrial history went back to the back-burning by Aborigines to create open fields for kangaroos and emus, continued through the oldest woollen mill in Australia, through the industrial explosion after Second World War of what were later called rust-belt industries, to the late capitalist industrial parks with their village-like atmosphere, soft-impact buildings, trees, bushes and postmodern floating signifiers – a jumble of signs whose significance was no longer clear. The industrial parks were now heaps of debris and wreckage, but the derelict sites had been left, including my solitary shack at the back of the broken sheds no one wanted, amidst the weeds, piles of tiles and bricks, graffiti, broken windows and pervasive feel of homeless shelter.)

Apart from the acrostic, each of the items of figuration functions by means of a reversal of what has gone before.[11] Although my reading of them in terms of a glimpse of a utopian alternative is distinct, the reversal itself appears to be a common feature of city-laments in the ancient Near East. Thus, according to Dobbs-Allsopp, in 'the so-called contrast motif (*Kontrastmotiv*), the poet compares the glorious past to the desolate present' (1993: 39). Using examples from the Curse of Agade, the Lamentation over the Destruction of Sumer and Ur, the Eridu Lament and the Uruk Lament (compared with Lamentations 1:1, 2:1b, 4:1–10, especially 4:5), Dobbs-Allsopp notes that 'the destruction of the city is described via a succession of literary representations *depicting the reverse of the normal order of things* (Dobbs-Allsopp 1993: 40, emphasis mine). Such images include slaves ruling the people (Lamentations 5:8), criminals on the watch and brigands on the highway (in the Curse of

Agade), familial relations broken (4:10; 5:3), people no longer fulfilling their assigned tasks (5:12–14), and songs and singing becoming weeping and lamentation (see Lamentations 5:15). But it is precisely these sorts of reversal that may also be read as utopian.

It is these inversions, the contradictions that hover everywhere in the text, breaking through at times with a clearer hint, that push towards neutralization. For it is neutralization that is the final indicator of the possibility, rather than necessity, of utopia. Neutralization is not equivalent to the destruction of the old, although it is certainly helped by such a demolition job (my first and second figures a little earlier). Nor is it the production of empty and desolate space (my third figure), nor even a new communalism (fifth figure), but the space that is necessary for the new communalism to have any chance of taking place. Yet that space is generated linguistically, through the language of the poems (the fourth figure of the acrostic). As Landy notes with an unwitting crossover to my argument, '[t]he barrenness and desolation of the poem are, then, also matters of rhetoric; the descriptive voice is direct, unenigmatic, as if the scene spoke for itself, and uses rhetorical techniques – repetition, metaphor, personification, and so forth – in the service of negation' (Landy 1987b: 329).

> (*'I'm fucked', said Zara.*
>
> *'Let's have a rest at my place', I said. 'It's just over there'. With no protest from either Hokhma or Zara, we scaled the aging stone fence to my hidden corner, watching all the while for any security types. We moved silently over the old secrets of the site, although it now lay at rest, awaiting new life. The fallow frames and foundations of the old industrial buildings finally led to my shack. A window hung strangely to the lower left; we clambered through the gaping hole and lowered ourselves with relief to the floor inside. It was time for some refuge and rest.*)

Neutralization therefore involves a linguistic and spatial play, a collocation of contradictory words and spaces, both neutral and plural, in which utopia may or may not take place. And the contradictions in Lamentations turn on the way the ruin and desolation are read – as something that is lost and must be recovered (5:21), or as that which is a good riddance so that something else may grow up in its place (2:5–10). The text is never sure whether it is one or the other, *ni l'un, ni l'autre* as Louis Marin says throughout *Utopiques*. The lament, the dominant poetic form of Lamentations, captures much of this ambivalence about Jerusalem's destruction and its exile. Jerusalem is then a neutralized space, a 'zone', a place of radical destruction and exploitation, but also one of hope and promise, like those of *Roadside Picnic*, and *The Ugly Swans*.

Jerusalem is also a place, like the zone in these works, of alien visitation, in which only the traces of such a visitation are left – destruction, alteration of the social and physical world, a lethal trap and source of amazing possibilities.

What humans do with the results of such visitations will determine the utopian or dystopian possibilities of these zones. So it is not only the ambivalence of the zone and its effects that is at issue, but whether the aliens are to be seen as beneficent (3:21–41, 55–66) or hostile (1:8–10, 17; 2:1–8, 17–22; 3:1–20, 42–9).[12] In the end, it is the absolute difference and the radical provisionality, if not impossibility, of interpreting this alien presence that is so marked in Lamentations. So, after 5:2–18, 'the lengthiest description of misery in the entire Book of Lamentations' (Westermann 1994: 213), comes 5:21–2:

> Restore us to yourself, O Yahweh, that we may be restored; renew our days as of old – unless you have utterly rejected us, and are angry with us beyond measure.

This ending is as ambiguous and open-ended as is the ending of *Roadside Picnic* ('HAPPINESS FOR EVERYBODY, FREE, AND NO ONE WILL GO AWAY UNSATISFIED'). Is the bleak dystopianism of both Lamentations and much of the Strugatskys' work to be read as a utopian harbinger, or not?

> (*I dug a couple of bottles out from under the box in the corner, pried off the tops and passed them around. We drank silently, wearily.*
>   '*Shit, that's good*', *said Zara.*
>   '*Stale bread, anyone?*' *I asked, digging out an old half loaf. Each of us thankfully chewed on a chunk, sipping beer, dozing, as the sky slowly became a lighter blue.*)

7

GRAVES OF CRAVING

Fast food, or, manna and McDonald's

After all, one must eat – when the pantry is empty, one tucks into one's fellow being.

(Lacan 1991: 232)

Short of death, of eternal unconsciousness, any bit, piece, lump, chunk, morsel or bite will do, to suck, chew and hold. The nourishment in question having nothing to do with a homeostasis of health or with the organism's survival … . The mouth's pleasure and the mind's escape lead to fatal excesses, revealing the incompatibility, indeed the opposition, between enjoyment and health.

(Ames 1988: 20, 21)

If only we had flesh to eat!

(Numbers 11:4)

And so I turn, finally, to food: neither death, nor sex, nor violence – only food remains. It is a return to Freud's primary stage of infantile development – the oral.

(Zara smelled it first with the change in the wind. 'Food's being cooked', she said, prodding us awake. Sunlight came in through the broken east window. The wind was gusting from the north-east, and soon we caught it too.

'It can't be', I said. I sniffed patties grilling in their fat, eggs baking, coffee brewing, the bitter mayonnaise, the deep fried fries and the sweet apple pies. Saliva surged in my mouth and my stomach felt cavernous. 'Come on', I beckoned, 'I thought Zeke had hit them all.')

But the oral has its own subtle forms of censorship, especially of a class nature. For nothing is perhaps so culturally un-chic, so proletarian, so anti-bourgeois, so 'westie',[1] as to desire breakfast at McDonald's, especially hotcakes, syrup and juice. I am even prepared, in an early morning rush, to buy hotcakes on a drive-through and eat them on the way, rolling up each hot cake and dipping it in the syrup, held between my legs, which constantly threatens to tip and run all over the seat and my crotch. The (fat) saturated ambiance of McDonald's is my desire. And of course in the profound contradiction of globalization it is my local McDonald's that beckons most strongly, crying out for yet another customer with its characteristic smells of Big Macs, coffee and fries.

If you were to happen past Northmead McDonald's, pausing only for a piss and a soft serve, you might glimpse me in the corner, a tray of half-eaten food before me, note paper scattered over the table, a copy of Lévi-Strauss's *The Raw and the Cooked* in one hand and a volume of the Hebrew Bible in the other. Not only is Lévi-Strauss my constant companion (in the same way that Benjamin's *Arcades* project is in my hip-pocket whenever I descend upon Westfield, Parramatta, the largest shopping mall in the southern hemisphere), but so also is Marx. I can visualize them sitting in the empty chairs opposite me, squaring each other off before absorbing the ambiance that is McDonald's.

What possible theoretical justification can I have for this? It is certainly not healthy food, nor is it particularly au fait with the sort of middle class resistance to fast food and multinationals that bedevils academics, nor is it exceptionally good for the environment, nor are the executives of McDonald's noted for their social conscience, economic justice or their left politics. So, in terms of health, environment, economics and politics, McDonald's loses out. Why am I here?

To explode the idea that fast food is purely capitalist; or rather, to see what fast food signifies in different periods of time. For other socio-economic formations have at various points in their culinary repertoire what may be termed fast food. I am thinking in particular here of the stories of manna and quail in the Hebrew Bible, stories with a distinctly mythical component that Lévi-Strauss enjoys, especially the presence of Yahweh as the provider of fast food (even McDonald's cannot claim this).[2]

HAMBURGEROLOGY[3]

I think there's a *place* for junk sex – it would be: very fast and quick like McDonald's food ...

(Sprinkle 1991: 28)

Two-all-beef-patties-special-sauce-lettuce-cheese-pickles-onion-on-a-sesame-seed-bun.

(McDonald's advertising campaign)

... when we sat by the fleshpots and ate our fill of bread.

(Exodus 16:3)

(Cars had been rendered useless by Zeke's work, so people were out walking mainly, but also riding bicycles and scooters. They seemed to have

overcome their fear of possible explosions – at least the few who were out
– to talk, speculate and see what the new world looked like. Nearly all of
them were heading in the same direction as us. It was November: the
bright purple of the jacarandas was everywhere, as though some vast
hand had spattered the ruined city with purple paint. The heat rose with
the sun and so did the cicadas, uncertain at first and then with a pulsat-
ing crescendo of noise. Having noted the changes, they were keen to get on
with things.)

Perhaps the greatest success of McDonald's[4] has been the expansion of the
hamburger as the basic item of the meal: the combination of dead cow, with
various pieces of vegetation, sauce, sometimes cheese, and a bun have become
the basic components of a ubiquitous meal. Indeed, Mac and Dick McDonald
– owners of the first McDonald's in Pasadena in 1937 and then on the corner
of Fourteenth and E Streets in San Bernadino in 1940 – made the first step in
the early 1940s, focusing on hamburger production after seeing that the burger
accounted for 80 per cent of their sales (Love 1986: 14). Before the arrival of
McDonald's on Australian shores, the hamburger was an item bought at the
Australian equivalent of the diner, the 'fish and chip shop'. Usually run by
immigrants from Kithera (a small island off Greece), it made and sold, apart
from fish and potato chips, hamburgers. Each one was made to order and
you were able to watch it being made. These places still exist,[5] but the explosion of the hamburger has gone beyond them, perhaps the most obvious
signal of this being the presence of the hamburger in nearly every food establishment's menu. The more recent drive to making the hamburger a breakfast
item has had the usual McDonald's success, although now of course it has egg
and bacon in the bun – the bacon and egg McMuffin, a twist on the dreadful
English practice of having bacon and eggs for breakfast. The hamburger has
then become a basic signifier of food, first in European, especially English,
derived locales, but increasingly in other places throughout the world, so
much so that it has remade culture and social relations in its own interests
and, in the process, redefined community life.[6]

One of the conversation partners sitting at my table speaks up, the one with
the confident bearing, stern look and firm mouth with which Lévi-Strauss greeted
the world. In his opinion one of the most significant items in the new dispensation is that the very symbol of food has now become a collection of fast food
items, usually the hamburger and a container of soft drink to its side. In silhouette these two items now signify 'food' virtually anywhere one goes, although
usually as a negative: the silhouette is surrounded by a red circle with a diagonal
line going through it to indicate that no food is to be taken in or consumed here.
Occasionally the positive sign is found, but even in the prohibition the very
signifier of food makes its presence felt. (The structural significance of this is
not only that fast food has become ubiquitous in western society, not only that
McDonald's and its many emulators are a part of capitalist society, but that in

many respects they are crucial to it, especially its late capitalist mutation. Food then acts a central signifier for socio-economics itself.)

But, I respond to Claude, my conversation and meal partner, surely there are other symbols of food that function in a similar way to the burger and coke. Indeed, the verbal slogans of other times and places have their own currency. And perhaps one of the most common in western traditions has been the 'bread from heaven' (Exodus 16:4), of which the manna of Exodus 16 is but the first instance. Its opposite, the equally pervasive 'fleshpots of Egypt' (Exodus 16: 3), may function either as a negative, the slashed red circle over the manna, or the fleshpot stands slightly behind the manna cake, in silhouette of course, and we have something comparable to the coke and burger shadow. 'Bread from heaven' takes on a life of its own, moving via the Wisdom of Solomon into the New Testament and from there through to the patristics. Appearing in Wisdom (see especially 16:15–29) as God's food for mortals, as part of creation, a source of teaching, of prayer and immortality (see Dumoulin 1994), it transforms into the profoundly cannibalistic Eucharist, where bread is (human) flesh, where one tucks, salvifically, into one's fellow being, one's primary being.

('It's probably useless information by now, but the scraps of paper pinned to the left nipples with an "M" scrawled on them probably mean more than one thing ...' I didn't finish, for Northmead Maccas loomed around the corner. It looked as though it had not been touched. Recently bull-dozed and then completely remodelled, Northmead Maccas was one of the earliest in Australia. Its first design presented a vast car park to the commuters on Windsor Road, with a barely discernible building at the back of the block; the only signal that a multinational had landed being the obligatory arches overlooking the road. Only a few weeks ago and many thousands of global franchises later, designers and consumer advisers gave the word and the old Northmead Maccas was a pile of untimely rubble overnight, a harbinger of Zeke's grand day. The new building angled its glassed front to greet southbound travellers; tables and chairs on a reconstructed sidewalk café out front, leading in to an internal servery and eating area that was immediately visible from the road. A multicoloured children's gym slightly to the left, parked cars strategically hidden and a drive through around the back completed the new Maccas in a little over three weeks. Zeke had been planting his devices for some six months, so it probably went out with the rubble. Now it survived, replete with outdoor eatery, open front, shrubs, flowers and a beautiful jacaranda out the front.)

One of the extraordinary features of fast food is its studied blandness – something a Frenchman, especially one who writes about exotic dishes produced while on anthropological fieldwork (Lévi-Strauss 1989: 420–2), would notice acutely. Such blandness is not accidental, nor from a laxness in food production, but rather the result of careful market research and implementation of the results of that research.[7] People will object less to food that has no exotic tastes, that does not challenge one's accustomed palate. Indeed, there are minor variations in McDonald's menu items depending on the locale in which they are found – here, at Northmead Maccas, muffins and salads are not to be found, while they are in the USA, and at Hungry Jack's (a franchise of Burger King) there is an Oz Burger. Most older Australians avoid salads, commonly known as 'rabbit food'. Initially on the menu here, they were removed after market research showed a low demand.

But, as with the symbolization of food, McDonald's does not have a monopoly on blandness either. For the manna from Yahweh, the bread from heaven, is also studiously bland, a 'fine flaky substance, as fine as frost on the ground' (Exodus 16:13). It is 'like coriander seed, white, and the taste of it was like wafers made with honey' (Exodus 16:31), although in Numbers 'its colour was like the colour of gum resin' (Numbers 11:7). After being ground up, beaten and boiled, 'it was like the taste of cakes baked with oil' (Numbers 11:8). Fine for a snack every now and then, but as a staple diet they were to eat it for 'forty years' (Exodus 16:35), as the text, in a moment of surveying hindsight, narrates. As if to reinforce the enslavement of such a diet, the text repeats in a sort of prose parallelism 'the Israelites ate manna forty years, until they came to a habitable land; they ate manna, until they came to the border of the land of Canaan' (Exodus 16:35). This chronic narrative routinization of diet, producing the outcry for flesh in Numbers 11, finally comes to closure in Joshua 5:10–12, when they celebrate the passover in Canaan and eat the produce of the land: 'the manna ceased', reads the text in a parallelism comparable to Exodus 16:35, 'on the day they ate the produce of the land, and the Israelites no longer had manna; they ate the crops of the land of Canaan that year' (Joshua 5:12). And what do they get? The vastly different diet of 'unleavened cakes and parched grain' (Joshua 5:11)!

Yet blandness is not the preserve of mythic stories about nomadic Israelites circling about in the deserts, for in contemporary fast food blandness is of course the culinary partner to routinization. Routine food requires routine workers, and the focus of sociological studies of the fast food industry is precisely on the workers themselves.[8] Thus, in Reiter's study (1991), based on field work in a Canadian Burger King outlet, the main issues are employment and management rather than the food itself or the customers. Leidner's study (1993a), which compares fast food and insurance sales people, is concerned with routinization of both worker and customer/client.

(We weaved a broken path around the tables and chairs out front. To our great surprise, everyone was behaving in an orderly fashion. 'I was expecting a scene of people run amok, pillaging and plundering', Zara said, somewhat disappointed. I thought I heard a French accent from the far corner where a weird guy sat amidst a pile of Maccas debris and books.

We couldn't understand why we did as everyone else did, walking through the glass doors, lining up, reading the menu. Even though I knew that menu, I insisted on reading it once again – McQuail burgers, Manna McMuffins, and Massah water, spurting out of the obligatory rock and into paper containers full of ice.)

Marx's comments on the profound effect of the machine upon the worker's body, time and daily life – reshaped from the feudal rhythms to which it had been accustomed for centuries – take on a new meaning in the context of McDonald's apparent success in the routinization of all activities carried out by McDonald's employees. Thus, already in the 1940s, Dick and Mac McDonald applied the Taylorized 'labour-saving' devices that Henry Ford had applied to automobile manufacturing. By limiting the work of employees to simple, specific tasks, they were able to employ untrained cooks at lower wages, reduce training, and make faster hamburgers (see Love 1986: 18). In today's McDonald's every task for employees is specified in the *Operations and Training Manual* – dubbed 'The Bible' by managers – whose 600 pages include colour photos to show the placement of ketchup, mustard and pickle slices on each type of hamburger (Leidner 1993a: 49). 'The hamburger has become the acclaimed Model T of catering' (Gabriel 1985: 8). This is by no means read always as a negative: for some (Leidner 1993a:134–47, 220–1; see also Worden 1995: 524) routinization has its good points, understood here in terms of confidence boosting, comfort with the job, and psychic protection from difficult aspects of the job.[9]

While workers find themselves in simple stations – patties, buns, fries, cashier and so on – customers undergo a comprehensive effort at routinization. 'Environmental manipulations' are supposed to produce 'desired behaviours' (Foster, Aamodt, Bodenmiller *et al.* 1988: 201–2).[10] Considerable attention is directed to customers in order to make them conform to expected behaviour patterns, at least while on the premises and in the restaurant. McDonald's customers are taught how to behave and respond through the perpetual television advertisements for Maccas, and in the store the various needs of these customers are already pre-arranged and pre-determined. Yet McDonald's is not unique in all of this, since they are merely at the forefront of a profound routinization of every sector of life under late capitalism.

Routinization is closely tied in with uniformity: during the major growth period under Ray Kroc, McDonald's distinguished itself from its competitors by its absolute commitment to uniformity through all its franchises. And that uniformity lay in QSC: quality, service and cleanliness.[11] This extended well beyond the stores to the whole production and supply system for the food. McDonald's inaugurated a massive reshaping of food production and supply – in potatoes, beef, milk and bread. From the 1950s an exorbitant amount of effort was devoted to developing a uniform french fry, thick shake, hamburger patty and bun (see Love 1986: 119–32, 323–56).

Close behind the routinization and uniformity comes speed. According to Mac and Dick McDonald '[o]ur whole concept was based on speed, lower prices, and volume' (Love 1986: 14). They cut their menu to nine items (hamburger, cheeseburger, three soft drink flavours in one twelve ounce size, milk, coffee, potato chips and a slice of pie), prepared food beforehand and handed out food in paper wrappers. Speed has remained a crucial factor in the very notion of *fast* food, although it also highlights a contradiction of capitalism between the individual and routinization. For speed clashes with the other stated aims of fast food that include quality, customer interaction, individual attention and so on (see Leidner 1993a: 134–47; Waldrop 1988). But the contradiction is consciously acknowledged; Leidner reports a slogan from Hamburger University: '[w]e want to treat each customer as an individual, in sixty seconds or less' (1993a: 178).

(We started to notice that things were different. An out-of-uniform middle-aged woman took our orders, there were many more people milling about the preparation area, although the burgers seemed to come out as fast as ever, with all sorts of interesting variations such as triple cheese, no patties, buns anywhere between raw and crisped. And no money was taken for the orders. The food was free.)

As I ponder the tightly controlled way in which the burgers, fries and coke I am ingesting have come off the production line, I point out to Lévi-Strauss that this is not the first time the production and consumption of food has been routinized. For in Exodus 16, Moses reports Yahweh's detailed commands for the collection, preparation, consumption and (non)preservation of the manna. Like the specifications for sesame-seed buns at Maccas, each person is to gather an omer each (which equals, as Exodus 16:36 helpfully states, a tenth of an ephah), taking account not for different metabolic rates but for the various numbers of people in each tent (16:16). They were to consume it all on the same day (16:19), although such a law is based on its assumed transgression (16:20). In a division between the raw/rotten and cooked to which I will return below, the whole arrangement reverses on the sabbath: that which would have been rotten on the next day if kept is not rotten on the sabbath, while there is none to gather on the sabbath (16:22–6). More blatantly now is an increasingly arbitrary law based on its transgression (16:27–9). Finally, there is a complete overturning of the initial rule about immediate consumption, for one omer is placed 'before Yahweh, to be kept throughout your generations' (16:33). Claude is of course itching to put a structuralist throw on this, but I hold him back, indicating of course that the preserved omer has been read Christologically, for Christ is the bread from heaven, preserved, pickled perhaps, and then eventually torn open and devoured at the Eucharist. But, as manna, he was tasted, chewed and ingested by the Israelites before ever the Church got its teeth into him. It is necessarily a big body, for the Israelites fed off him for forty years, and the church has been doing so for some 2,000 years. Like father, like son, it seems (on God's gigantic body see Stephen Moore 1996: 86–91).

While routinization is good for business,[12] both it and blandness act as figures for what I termed neutralization in chapter 6. There is something radically levelling about such routinization, something with a utopian flavour that is more than the grease and the coke and that makes McDonald's a pleasant experience despite itself. By utopian I refer not to the vision of futurists, in which the globe is covered in fast food outlets as a solution to world hunger (Molitor 1984). Rather, routinization and blandness act both as figures – not so much in terms of the explicit content but in what alternatives are suggested by that content and its form – of collective alternatives and as a profound neutralization of liberalism itself. In the very realization of the ultimate logic of late capitalism, fast food shows up the deep contradiction in which the socio-economic dimensions of capitalism contradict one of the central tenets of its ideological elaboration – the individual.

> *(By the trash bin were a couple of crumpled uniforms. 'Hey', I said to Zara and Hokhma, 'look at that.' I bent over the uniform to fold out the left breast of one of the shirts. It confirmed my suspicions, for upon it was embroidered a dirty 'M'.*
>
> *Zara paused, 'So, here we are in the middle of the last Maccas and it turns out they took out the other four last night and Zeke this morning.' 'Wouldn't it give you the shits?'[13] I said.)*

GRAVES OF CRAVING

> The turd slides into his mouth, down to his gullet. He gags, but bravely clamps his teeth shut. Bread that only would have floated in porcelain waters somewhere unseen, untasted – risen now and baked in the bitter intestinal Oven to bread we know, bread that's light as domestic comfort, secret as death in bed.
>
> (Pynchon 1973: 235–6)

> You shall eat not only one day, or two days, or five days, or ten days, or twenty days, but for a whole month – until it comes out of your nostrils and becomes loathsome to you …
>
> (Numbers 11:19–20)

The other half of the fast food equation is the food itself, the focus of intense energy, much time and endless money. Contrary to the impression of a stable staple, a basic menu, McDonald's food has undergone perpetual change. For instance, the infamous Big Mac was invented in 1968, copied by McDonald's franchisee Jim Delligatti from Bob Wian's 'Big Boy' of the 1950s Big Boy chain. After a string of failures in finding a desert that would sell, another franchisee, Litton Cochrane, hit upon the apple pie in 1969. And the Egg McMuffin came from the mind and hands of Herb Petersen in 1971 (on these, see Love 1986: 295–300). The simple french fry took a number of years to develop, for what was sought was a product with consistent colour, texture, moisture and one that came out the same from the cooking process every time. The final product became highly specialized: Idaho Russets grown under specific conditions were found to have the right consistency and moisture content, sugar and salt coating ensured a brown colour, and the frying vats were found to cook the fries to the same specifications if the temperature of the oil after the immersion of the fries rose three degrees, no matter what (within reason) the initial temperature was. Similarly, the move from the old milkshake – labour intensive and time consuming – to the shake, with its combination of vegetable gum and dairy fats, enabled prior preparation and storage in bulk, awaiting its dispensation in stores. These sorts of expectations have forced McDonald's to establish complete structures, or expect local providers to do so, for the basic items of the McDonald's production line – patties, buns, potatoes, pickles, sauce. For example, in the former Yugoslavia, it took three seasons to develop conditions for the production of Idaho Russets before they were found to be acceptable (*The Economist* 1988b), whereas the store in Moscow relies on a huge processing plant that provides patties, fries, rolls and milk. The plant still needs to import bull semen and Russet potatoes (*The Economist* 1989b).

Further, one of the major battlegrounds for the fast food industry has been nutrition. The designation 'junk food' and attacks about the high content of fat, salt and sugar have generated continual efforts to 'prove' that fast food is good for one. According to studies commissioned by McDonald's, a burger, fries and a shake (the 'three-corner' meal) comprises a large part of the daily requirements (Love 1986: 369). Apart from the leaflet, entitled *McDonald's Nutrition Facts* and available in any contemporary McDonald's, the web site (www.mcdonalds.com) contains detailed nutrition menus for all its products, as well as the Nutritionist's page (replete with photo of aforesaid person) and advice about 'eating right'.

> (*I felt an urge to crap, so I slipped into the toilet, which had clearly not been cleaned since yesterday. The turd slid quietly into the water, and I reached for the paper, only to find the dispenser empty. A pile of papers were stacked on the cistern for precisely such an emergency. The first one, with nutrition information, was a bit harsh, but the soft one on Maccas' concern for the environment was much more pleasant.*)

Food itself is also at the centre of Exodus 16, Numbers 11, and Lévi-Strauss's *The Raw and the Cooked*. In the biblical texts there are in fact two comparable stories/myths that deal with the rapid production of food. In Exodus 16 the interest is, alongside a number of other things, in an early morning deposit that meets one's needs in a functional sort of way and allows one to get on with the business of the day (like the Bacon and Egg McMuffin, or hotcakes and syrup). Numbers 11, by contrast, is a more substantial affair (although the story is also a vegetarian's delight), being concerned with the dinner order, the quail, that kills. By Joshua 5:10–12, the time of poor diets while on the run, of divine (state) handouts, was over. Indeed, each account is strategically placed: Exodus 16 at the beginning of the wilderness wandering, after the crossing of the Re(e)d Sea and the Song of Miriam and Moses in Exodus 15; Numbers 11 at the moment before the abortive effort to enter Canaan and the condemnation to more wandering; Joshua 5:10–12 at the final entry into Canaan.

In Exodus 16[14] the first mention of food concerns the 'fleshpots' of Egypt in 16:3: 'If only we had died', say the people, 'by the hand of Yahweh in the land of Egypt, when we sat by the fleshpots and ate our fill of bread; for you have brought us out into this wilderness to kill this whole assembly with hunger.' The issue, then, is hunger in the desert. There follows some dialogue between Yahweh and Moses, or rather, Yahweh speaks to Moses and he and Aaron speak to the people. As always with these transferred speeches and instructions, there is some alteration. Yahweh begins (and I am focusing only on the food) by promising to rain 'bread from heaven' (16:4), with some instructions on how it is to be gathered in order to test the people. Moses, however, mentions 'flesh to eat in the evening and your fill of bread in the morning' (16:8). Then, after the glory of Yahweh appears in a cloud, he speaks again to Moses, now mentioning the flesh at 'twilight' and the fill of bread in the morning (16:12). It is as though Moses has triggered the inclusion of flesh, which turns out to be quails, who are not mentioned again until Numbers 11.

> (*I made my way back to the counter to pick up my order. During my absence, an argument had broken out and someone had climbed a step ladder and was plastering some paper over the McDonald's sign. On it she wrote 'Graves of Craving'. Now I felt at home. As she did this she talked with Hokhma and Zara. 'This is Miriam', Zara said. Before I could reply, Ben Moses came over from the grill station to argue with Miriam about the sign. The rag-tag revolutionary group was trying to sort its directions out, it seemed.*)

As for the themes of Numbers 11,[15] here we meet again the grumbling people, although this time the 'alien rabble' (11:4) is at least partly to blame, for they had 'cravings' (11:4) not satisfied by the manna. Here the (literally) burning anger of Yahweh features strongly, held to the fringes of the camp in 11:1–3, but breaking out again at the close of the story in 11:33–5. The quail (burgers?) were not quite what everyone imagined – a massive plague breaks out. Hence the name *Kibroth-hattaavah*, Graves of Craving. One can picture the scene: the people have journeyed for a long time, eating what they can scrounge from empty burger wrappers and discarded fries, when one calls aloud: 'Look, *hinneh*, the golden K and H!' All of them rush forward, inciting Yahweh to anger. He retaliates by giving them some plagued meat to feed the hungry hordes. What comes through in Numbers 11 is the punishment of Yahweh:[16] in Exodus 16 the food is the occasion for a test; in Numbers 11 the test turns to punishment for greed. In one food is for discipline, in the other for punishment and death. If McDonald's were to choose a myth for itself, then it would hardly be Numbers 11.

For Lévi-Strauss, half-way through an apple pie, the role of food in these stories is a little different, particularly its various stages from fresh as the dew in the morning, to its function as immediate (and nomadic) gratification, to worms, rottenness and death-dealing meat. But it is not his moment just yet.

In both stories there is an enabling tension, a conflict between the people and the leadership, a dissatisfaction that is finally directed at Yahweh. In Exodus 16 they 'murmured (*lwn*) against Moses and Aaron' (16:2; see also 15:24), which is then thrown back at the people by Moses and Aaron (16:7) and then by Moses on his own (16:8). And in Numbers 11:1, 'when they complained (*'nn*) in the hearing of Yahweh about their misfortunes (*r'*)', then Yahweh responded immediately with fire. Both acts, or murmuring and complaining, function as narrative triggers for the stories that follow, one a test, the other punishment. But the tension remains, for the test in Exodus 16 becomes more complex, while the punishment in Numbers 11 continually breaks out, barely contained. The friction between Yahweh and the people now feeds into the distinctions between raw, cooked and rotten, for it seems that what is blessed by Yahweh may be eaten, but what is not becomes rotten or leads to death.

(Not wanting to get involved in any conflict, I moved away from the counter and surveyed the walls. The usually spotless tiles on the walls were a little dusty and grimy, since there was still a lot of air-borne grit from Zeke's efforts. The photographs were still there: pictures of dirt roads, trams, cottages, old hotels, wool trains, orange orchards, children with grimy faces, worn mothers and bearded men, all in sepia and black and white. Northmead more than a century ago, in whose history the former Maccas, in proper multinational identification with the local environment, had attempted to reconstruct itself. The photos said more about the aesthetics of photography than anything else.)

But there has been murmuring within and without McDonald's as well. Internally, a large revolt was led by the McDonald's Operators Association (MOA) in the mid 1970s. The key here was market saturation and competition between McDonald's restaurants (*The Economist* 1990). Even though McDonald's appointed an ombudsman and a National Operators Advisory Board was established, there was a raft of court cases (see Love 1986: 382–412). Sporadic conflict and court cases still happen around this issue, particularly with expansion into new outlets, such as hospitals, universities, aeroplane flights, in-store snack bars and prisons (*The Economist* 1993; Reiter 1991: 59). However, tired of criticism from disgruntled franchisees, environmentalists and nutritionists, McDonald's launched what has become known as the McLibel case in 1996 (it was still in progress during the writing of this book).

While Exodus 16 is not overly concerned with these questions, the issue of franchise relations is found in Numbers 11. Moses uses Yahweh's fiery response to the people's complaint to launch his own tirade against his franchise boss: 'Why have you treated your servant so badly? Why have I not found favour in your sight, that you lay the burden of all this people on me?' (Numbers 11:11). He rants on for a few more verses, giving vent to a transgendered wish: 'Did I conceive all this people? Did I give birth to them, that you should say to me, "Carry them in your bosom, as a nurse carries a sucking child", to the land that you promised on oath to their ancestors?' (Numbers 11:12). Yahweh realizes that this solitary franchisee is highly strung and that he needs some more franchisees, so he suggests the appointment of seventy branch managers upon whom he puts some of his spirit (Numbers 11:16–17, 24–5). However, two – Eldad and Medad – are not present for the training course at the tent, but they set up branches anyway, infringing on Joshua's franchise (Numbers 11:26–28). Moses tells Joshua to stop *his* whining (Numbers 11:29), and the problems are solved.

The other form of conflict for McDonald's – opposition to its global expansion – has been more widespread and more difficult to contain. Indeed, a favourite topic of popular economics magazines, such as *The Economist* or the *Far Eastern Economic Review*, or the economics pages of newspapers, is the effect of the expansion of McDonald's into ever new areas (along with stories about prostitution). Thus, before the events of 1989 in eastern Europe, and before the global economic crisis of 1998, the arrival of McDonald's in communist countries was celebrated, as with the first one in Belgrade in 1988 and the Moscow McDonald's on 31 January 1989 on Gorky Street, Pushkin Square (*The Economist* 1989b). Crowing that 'Communist Europe, however, has millions of frustrated fast-food freaks' (*The Economist* 1988b: 54), the desire for fast food was understood in the ideologically bereft West as part of the cause of the events of 1989. The Cold War aside, other conflicts include those with local culinary traditions, which either begin to erode, such as the Spanish siesta (*The Economist* 1984b), or respond by developing fast food versions of their own food, as in China (Yang Ji 1996; Huang Wei 1993; *Beijing Review* 1985) and Japan (*The Economist* 1989a; Noguchi 1994). Of course, in overdeveloped capitalist countries, McDonald's is a raging success, as in England (*The Economist* 1984a) and Hong Kong (*The Economist* 1988a), although opposition in all forms continues to dog the corporation. For instance, in

Australia and Ireland there was strong union pressure, as well as rebuttals of sponsoring offers (as with the Ronald McDonald House at Royal Melbourne Children's Hospital) and early losses. It took eight years to begin making a profit in Australia (see Love 1986: 445–7).[17]

(I sat down with my odd-smelling bundle. They weren't going to make any more money in this store. The fixed aluminium chair and hard plastic table were as uncomfortable as ever. The weird blond guy in the corner, talking to himself in French, had rolled a cigarette and lit up. I breathed in the smoke with relish. But my own meal had a similar aroma.)

However, the conflicts I have been tracing also have a deeper resonance with the ideology of liberalism and capitalism itself. For liberalism, the ambivalence of admiration at economic success alongside opposition to McDonald's is based on the tension between routinization and individual choice, multinational expansion and the viability of small business and local cultures, as well as exploitation and benevolence (they are doing the world a favour while making piles of money). For McDonald's embodies the profound contradiction at the heart of such an ideology: the paradox is that as customers are treated more and more in terms of a fundamental routinization, they demand more personal services from employees; the inviolability of the individual conflicts with the collective drive of capitalism itself. By contrast, a dialectical Marxist perspective sees the extraordinary collective potential of what Ritzer (1996; 1998) calls the 'McDonaldization' of society: here, as nowhere else – as yet – in late capitalism is there such a large scale effort at a collective imagination. To be sure, it leaves much to be desired in terms of the narrowness of that imagination, but the very act of thinking about, planning for and attempting to influence the collective behaviour of so many people must have a profound fascination for any concept of collective life. Of course, the possibility that McDonald's might be the precursor of socialism is anathema to liberals and socialists alike, but it is more the figure of collectivism that McDonald's signals rather than any specific content of such a collective experience that interests me here.

THE RAW AND THE COOKED

Fried chicken is a comfort food. When life is rough, a bargain bucket of fried chicken and biscuits can soothe stressed-out souls.
(Bill Roenigk, vice president of the National Broiler Council, USA, quoted by Crawford 1992)

… and it bred worms and became foul.
(Exodus 16:20)

Fast food is, as I have argued, primarily concerned with food and its ingestion. And this is where I pick up Lévi-Strauss's *The Raw and the Cooked* from
among the increasing debris of my meal. There is still some coke left (I could
really do with a cigarette, so I roll one despite the prohibition), but I feel a
craving for apple pie and shake coming on. For Lévi-Strauss the language of
food is a mythical language, one that finds itself expressed as central elements
of the myths that a society produces. Thus, in *The Raw and the Cooked*, he
traces 187 myths (numbered from M1) from South American indigenous
tribes, relating them all in an extraordinary structuralist performance to the
myth with which he begins, 'The macaws and their nest' (1994: 35–7). It is a
Bororo myth about a young man who rapes his mother, is sent on dangerous
expeditions by his father, is left behind by his father while hunting macaws,
has his buttocks and anus eaten out by vultures, which results in an inability
to keep in his food, shapes another behind out of clay, returns to his village
where he lodges with his grandmother (the only one to have fire after a violent wind), kills his father during a hunting expedition by taking on the form
of a deer, and then returns to the village to take revenge on his father's wives.

This is the key myth, to which all the others are related:

> I propose to show that M1 (the key myth) belongs to a set of myths
> that explain the origin of the cooking of food (although this theme
> is, to all intents and purposes, absent from it); that cooking is con-
> ceived of in native thought as a form of mediation; and finally, that
> this particular aspect remains concealed in the Bororo myth, because
> the latter is in fact an inversion, or a reversal, of myths originating in
> neighbouring communities which view culinary operations as me-
> diatory activities between heaven and earth, life and death, nature
> and society.
>
> (Lévi-Strauss 1994: 64–5)

('I suspect there's more to the stapled "M"s than Maccas hit squads', I said
to Zara as she sat down opposite me.

> *'They can sort out their own problems', she said, referring to the argu-*
> *ment she had left about the new sign. 'Why, what are you thinking?' she*
> *asked.*

> *'There are endless possibilities: Maccas, the myth of the revolution,*
> *myths themselves, the desire for mammaries ...'*

> *'It looks like they shouldn't try to pin down their signifiers too quickly',*
> *she replied.)*

What is so attractive about this book, apart from the pure systemic brilliance
it displays, is that not only is a whole series of apparently unrelated items
connected with food and eating – jaguars, crocodiles, lizards, birds, and so on
– but the language of food, its preparation and ingestion, is what may be

termed a master narrative (despite the unpopularity of such a term at the present moment). Food speaks of society as a whole and is central to the myths by which a society perceives itself. In fact, the process of food preparation, from raw food to cooked, is a fundamental transitional moment for social inauguration and formation. However, while the process from raw to cooked is a mark of culture, of social formation, there is another transition that belongs to nature – that from fresh to rotten.

If food, and especially its preparation and eating, is structurally tied up with social inauguration and self-perception (more notably in some societies than others, such as the Chinese and French – Lévi-Strauss's own ethnic identity must play a role here as well), what then of fast food? What does the Lévi-Strauss sitting across from me think? I assume of course that he is highly intrigued, although perhaps not overjoyed, to occupy a seat for a few minutes at my McDonald's restaurant. What sort of socially significant messages would he read at Maccas, especially given his inspiration from Marx in the development of his own work and theories?

McDonald's may be regarded as an inaugural moment for what is now termed late capitalist society, giving its own particular name to a whole process of food production in, first, the USA and then throughout the world. Ritzer (1996; 1998) has of course provided a term – McDonaldization – that signals such an inauguration. But this inauguration inevitably takes concrete forms: McDonald's, and the host of those who follow in the same path, is the first step in the job market for many young people – in fact, it is probably one of the few growing areas for young people to begin work in late capitalism. One estimate suggests that one out of fifteen first-time job seekers in the USA starts at McDonald's (Leidner 1993a:46; Wildavsky 1989: 32).[18] The fast food industry is something like a vast transitional space, operating at the minimum wage level (see Card and Krueger 1994; Ihlanfeldt and Young 1994; Katz and Krueger 1992), into which an increasing number of school leavers, older and semi-retired people, mothers, the long term unemployed, impoverished and 'illegal' immigrants for whom no insurance and tax needs to be paid (Dawson 1992), now move before passing on to other forms of (un)employment.[19]

It is not merely the crucial, if somewhat dubious, role that the fast food industry plays in job production that connects with Lévi-Strauss's argument; in addition, the extraordinarily massive, long and detailed procedure from seeding to mastication and digestion is perhaps the longest and most prodigious for the process of 'cooking' food in any society. In other words, not only is Maccas a marker of the commencement of late capitalism (its initial establishment and surge took place in the 1950s), but the phenomenal process of food production, or 'cooking', signifies the highly mediated form of social interaction and industrial production that constitutes late capitalism. Fast food production has usurped the place of traditional production-line industries in the present mutation of capitalism (Reiter 1991: 75–6), taking on the mutant characteristics of both a core and peripheral industry (Parcel and Sickmeier 1988).

(I opened the grease-stained wrapper. Inside was a burnt bun piled up with lettuce, tomato, onion, pickle and, strangely, beetroot. Everything bar the lettuce was also burnt. 'Charcoal is good for your teeth', I said to Zara, hopefully. The fries were also dark brown to black at the tips and had a distinctly crispy texture.)

Even though all about me I hear, in many languages, my local McDonald's reverberating with 'what is it?' (Exodus 16:15) as customers look inside their burgers, this is not, as Lévi-Strauss is quick to tell me, the only connection with the story of the manna (Exodus 16:15, 31). Let us return, he continues, to some of the threads of our earlier discussion. The manna appears with the dew in the morning, or rather, when the dew dries (Exodus 16:13–14; Numbers 11:9). It is small, flake-like, 'like coriander seed' (Exodus 16:31; Numbers 11:7). It may be eaten on the same day, as is, or ground, boiled and baked into cakes (Numbers 11:8). However, it only lasts one day, for in the morning there is a new batch, while any that is kept becomes rotten, full of worms and foul (Exodus 16:20)[20] – apparently any preparation does not prolong the life of the manna. There are two exceptions to this: the manna gathered for the sabbath on the sixth day lasts for two days instead of one (Exodus 16:23–6), and the omer of manna that is collected and placed 'before the testimony' ('*eduth*, Exodus 16:34). What is interesting about the various stages of the food is the relation between what is fresh, or 'raw', and that which rots or has worms in it, and then that which escapes becoming rotten. Although there is not an explicit reference to preparation and cooking in Exodus 16, except by way of comment on sabbath practices (Exodus 16:23), Numbers 11 assumes that this is a daily practice (Numbers 11:8). This is, however, significant, for the main concern of Exodus 16 is the role of food in human obedience to the divine, whereas fire, food and anger are the concerns of Numbers 11. In fact in Exodus 16 cooking does not affect the longevity of the food: it still rots and becomes wormy. The raw food is fine if eaten hand-to-mouth, on a daily basis. The lesson here seems to be a reliance upon Yahweh, for when people try to store up things for the future they come adrift. Yet, it is only when Yahweh commands differently that the food does not rot. In both cases – sabbath and memorial – the food comes into sacred territory or time. That is to say, only in Yahweh's presence does the food keep (like some sort of divine refrigerator or preservative). The difference, then, between what is raw and rotten is the connection with the divine: although Yahweh gives the bread, it is only Yahweh's connection with it that prevents its putrefaction, either on the sabbath or before the testimony. For Lévi-Strauss, this is a fresh/decayed axis, to be distinguished from the raw/cooked axis.[21]

In Numbers 11 it is the turn of the quail, who appear and then disappear in Exodus 16:13. Indeed, in Numbers 11 the people have become sick of the daily fare of manna, groaning about its blandness, developing an indiscriminate desire for flesh (Numbers 11:4). Yahweh burns some of the aforesaid people with fire, a crucial item of this story. Curiously, the fish, cucumbers, melons, leeks, onions and garlic that they used to eat in Egypt (Numbers 11:5) do not quite constitute 'flesh'. These are not really the 'fleshpots' of Exodus 16:3. Could it be that the flesh they desire is that of Moses himself, or their fellow beings, or Yahweh? The questions of Numbers 11:21–3 throw up precisely this problem: Moses suggests that, with 600,000 on foot, there is no resource for flesh, not enough herds, flocks or fish, except that of the people themselves. Like the human sacrifice of Genesis 22, Yahweh intervenes with the quail, which soon arrive in abundance, a day's journey in any direction and two cubits deep. Given the small size of quail, this is a significant amount. Yet, what is notable about this account of the quail is that there is no reference to the preparation or cooking of the birds. It is as though the people eat them from the ground, tearing out feathers, ripping out the crop, squeezing out the blood and picking the scarce meat from each bird. But, while 'the flesh was still between their teeth' (Numbers 11:33), Yahweh afflicts them and they die. The raw meat is now full of disease.[22] For Lévi-Strauss disease and rottenness signify the same thing – raw food that has undergone a natural process to putrefaction.[23]

> (*Apart from the lettuce, the only other thing not burnt was the patty, the compressed dead cow. In fact, it did not even look as though it had been near the grill. I picked it up by a corner and held it up for Zara to see. 'It's squirming', she said, with relish. I dropped it on the table and looked closer.*
>
> *'I think you are right', I said, 'it seems to be moving of its own accord.' There were little white moving parts all over it. I decided to leave it to its own devices and eat the rest.*)

Thus far, I have touched on only one part of the equation mapped out by Lévi-Strauss:

> It is thus confirmed that the Ge myths about the origin of fire, like the Tupi-Guarani on the same theme, function in terms of a double contrast: on the one hand, between what is raw and what is cooked, and on the other, between the fresh and the decayed. The raw/cooked axis is characteristic of culture; the fresh/decayed one of nature, since cooking brings about the cultural transformation of the raw, just as putrefaction is its natural transformation.
>
> (Lévi-Strauss 1994: 142)

This means that so far Exodus 16 and Numbers 11 follow the fresh/decayed axis of nature, and the raw/cooked axis is absent. However, before pursuing this axis, I want to focus for a few moments on the depiction of Yahweh.[24] Yahweh's presence threatens perpetually to break out and consume, a barely controllable power that manifests itself in the outbreak of fire on the edges of the camp (Numbers 11:1), in the prophecy of Eldad and Medad (Numbers 11:26–9), and with the death in the meat (Numbers 11:33). Yahweh seems to have jurisdiction over the fire: it burns, or cooks, some of the people when they complain earlier in the story. Yet the people eat their meat raw and die of disease as a punishment for their whining. Since the disease and the fire both act as punishment, it would seem that they are one. Yet, for Lévi-Strauss, disease is on par with putrefaction, a natural process, whereas fire is associated with cooking, a cultural process. Yet, death by fire and disease follows another opposition in Numbers 11. In the myths discussed by Lévi-Strauss, this pair is determined by the presence and absence of the sun, for whom Yahweh is an appropriate replacement. Too great a presence, an over-presence, of the sun produces a burned world, whereas absence of the sun or total disjunction leads to rottenness and disease (1994: 293–4). The problem here is to achieve a balance between burning and disease, both of which are destructive. And the way in which that mediation is achieved is through the cooking of food, which is absent in Numbers 11, except with reference to the manna (Numbers 11:8). This involves a domesticated presence and use of the fire that Yahweh brings.

Such a domestication is found precisely with the manna. In Numbers 11:8 it is boiled in pots and cakes are made of it; in Exodus 16:23 it is also baked and boiled. Is this the key to the preservation on the sabbath and before the testimony? Although it is not explicitly stated to be so, if I follow Lévi-Strauss then we might expect such cooking to be the domestication of the divine fire, especially when it is connected with the divine command to keep some over for the sabbath. Thus, preservation, fire and cooking belong to Yahweh, whereas raw food, rottenness and disease belong to the people. For Lévi-Strauss such an opposition is fundamental to social formation itself. Only those who remain in the social structures for which Yahweh is the enclosing force and symbol will remain whole – preserved, cooked and with fire – whereas those who threaten those structures come outside such support and fall away – rotten and diseased. Finally, there is also an originary dimension to this, for the process from eating raw food, being rotten and diseased to one of having fire, cooked food and wholeness is one that speaks of the very process of social formation itself. It symbolizes the inaugural moment of human society.

Given that both Exodus 16 and Numbers 11 are concerned with natural processes, that is, from fresh to rotten, raw to disease, and that Yahweh holds fire, as it were, and is thus the key to social inauguration, then these two chapters may be read as a site of tension between natural and cultural processes; something that is entirely appropriate in that both Exodus 16 and Numbers 11 mark the start and restart of the wandering in the wilderness. This means that the wilderness period, as far as this narrative is concerned, is socially ambiguous, a conflict between the nature and culture.

('At least mine are cooked', said Zara as she looked inside hers, 'so they won't be squirming.' She had three patties interlaced with cheese; sauce oozed out of the sides and dropped from the edge of the bun onto the table as she lifted it to her mouth. They were properly cooked and I envied her as she sunk her teeth into the burger.

'Do you think this is the beginning of something new?' I asked her.

'Maybe, except they're going to run out of supplies in a few days.')

While Exodus 16 and Numbers 11 broach the question of the beginning of cultural inauguration within the context of natural processes, McDonald's may be read at the other extreme of overcooked and overdeveloped. I have mentioned both the question of work and that of processing itself, but is there another inaugural feature of fast food? It seems to me that it might be found in the distinctly populist note about places like McDonald's (and shopping malls for that matter) that appeals to me. Not that populism necessarily entails anti-intellectualism (although there is something distinctly healthy about that too), but it seems to me that any viable left politics needs to consider seriously the mass patronage of places like McDonald's. For in many areas there is a distinct class divide that manifests itself in the choice of places to eat: the clothes, appearance, and age of those in McDonald's and, for example, a more expensive restaurant, mark a difference between youth and elderly over against the more well-heeled young and middle aged, between relative poverty and wealth, between places where the patrons live, and so on. But McDonald's is not merely a place for wandering youth or lonely elderly, for people with less money who live in poorer areas. It is also a haven for harried parents, coaches celebrating a win or commiserating over a loss with their teams, for travellers wanting a quick stop and some food, and even for those who can't see any reason to pay more than they need to for a coffee. McDonald's is, then, a popular intersection, a place where people, especially from certain groups, are to be found: it is a distinct example of mass or popular culture, the irony being that it is one of the most aggressive and expansive multinational companies out of all of them.[25] Endless studies seek to locate the appeal of fast food – convenience (Balzer 1993), taste (Waldrop 1993), location, speed, consistency, cleanliness (Kasdan 1996) – yet it seems to me that the utopian dimensions of fast food are there despite and not because of these elements. It is like a lover, as soon as one begins to list the reasons for being attracted to a person – voice, politics, eyes, hair ... – then you lose sight of what is appealing about that person.

Finally, Marxists have always been interested in the way internal contradictions of a system lead to its downfall and supersession. Ritzer's (1996) recasting of Weber's rationalization process in terms of 'McDonaldization' identifies four features – efficiency, calculability, predictability and control (1996: 9–10, 35–120) – the precursors of which he finds in bureaucratization, the Nazi Holocaust, scientific management, the assembly line, shopping malls and new suburban housing. Although he identifies the irrationalities and problems of this process and although he argues for an alternative vision, his analysis would be strengthened by being incorporated into a Marxist framework in which the ubiquity of McDonaldization is read as a marker for the ubiquity of capitalism itself – the domination of the market, commodification and reification. However, there is an embryonic argument that is contained within its Weberian limits: Ritzer traces a contradiction within McDonaldization that may be read as a marker of the contradictions of capitalism. The drives to efficiency, calculability, predictability and control end up producing their opposites. Although vitiated by a humanist argument, what is interesting here is that the contradiction of food is not only a trace of contradictions within capitalism but an effort to overcome those contradictions – the drive to freedom produces enslavement, democracy produces anything but, efficiency leads to inefficiency. ... It is precisely these sorts of contradictions that can lead to a breakdown of a socio-economic system and either its restructuring or its collapse.[26]

(So there we sat, on some metal chairs at a plastic table in a slightly jaded fast food restaurant at the edge of the world; piles of rubble surrounded us, the smoke of explosions and fires hung in the air, and yet there were people here, eating what could still be made for them. Zara was engrossed in her burger, Hokhma had joined us with hers, Miriam had succeeded in getting her sign up. I put aside the patty and bit into my burger. It was crunchy, but satisfying.)

POSTSCRIPT

The exploding elephant

(That night I dreamt. I was travelling through the desert. Having done so for a while I arrived at an abandoned cabin. The place was under siege, as it were, by an elephant who galloped around the cabin repeatedly. With the threat of the elephant, we closed a large door made of planks kept together by some cross-beams in order to keep out the rampaging elephant. However, while we were securing the door, the elephant leapt over it – through a space between the top of the door and the roof – with a grimacing face and into the cabin. Next, I was in a holiday house with the rest of a family I didn't know, but I recall that the house was not our own and that there was some anxiety about keeping it in reasonably good condition. The house was two storeys high, or at least my dream focused on a large room that was on the second storey, although there were some strange things associated with the room's construction. The walls and floor were made of some shingle substance that was not stationary: it had a tendency to move about. It was possible to look out of a window in this room into the neighbour's dusty yard. At some point in the proceedings an elephant got in downstairs. We had just left the house when the elephant exploded and there was quite a mushroom cloud behind us. We rushed back, since I was anxious about damage to the house. The shingles in the upstairs room were disrupted with a huge hole in the floor. All of the family was clawing through the shingles and there seemed to be a lot of them, much like a pile of leaves. The third phase was at a beach close to the house, although its precise distance was uncertain. I recall a few old trees that had fallen down en route between house and beach. On the beach, there was group of people, and as we were there, an elephant came galloping down onto the beach, only to explode in a plume of sand quite close to us. We were left with a huge, bloated carcass, and bits and pieces of exploded elephant scattered about the beach.)

My phantasy, my impossible desire, is that at least some of the bad debts of biblical criticism may have been paid with this book. These bad debts are the ones I mentioned in my discussion of the much under-rated Michel de Certeau in my introduction. But such an argument relies, as I noted there, on the massive premise that the contemporary disciplines of the sciences and humanities gained their initial impetus from theology and, I added, biblical studies. What has happened is that the methods of these various disciplines developed their forms as a logical progression from theology and biblical studies, but their content, in proper Enlightenment fashion, was made avowedly non-religious. Now these methods demand, like schizophrenic voices in the head, to be unleashed upon the Bible. They are the bad debts of biblical criticism, the overdue and bounced cheques left for so long unpaid.

In making use of cultural criticism – although that in itself involves sociology, psychology, historiography, ethnography, structural anthropology, film criticism, literary criticism, queer theory, porn theory – I have pursued some of these bad debts. Indeed, it seems that any 'method' is not so much a pristine zone of engagement, but rather a point of intersection for a swarm of other methods, which are themselves similar intersections. ... Which brings me to the point that only certain elements unleashed after the Enlightenment have in fact returned to influence biblical criticism; there has been, in other words, a process of censorship of the applicability of the many methods with which biblical criticism has some connection and is not so foreign. In seeking to pay some bad debts, then, I have sought to bypass such a Censor.

A further point beckons: where various methods and disciplines have returned to biblical studies it has been quite genteel. Even a considerable amount of cultural studies – the main methodological focus of this volume – might be described as 'nice' criticism. That is to say, the gritty, visceral desires and fears of everyday life and popular culture – inevitably spinning around the staples of violence, sex and food – are less often the zones where cultural (and for that matter biblical) critics work out their own obsessions. For it is precisely in these areas that the swarming, turbid and impossibly narcissistic source of social and individual consciousness may be found. There are of course, two ways in which this may be read. On the one hand, all that seems to belong to the higher levels of historical and social strivings, all of the most genuine social motives and aims, are none other than manifestations of the basest and most selfish motives, of an unconscious that seeks only its own gratification at the expense of others, of an ineradicable radical evil. On the other hand, all of the most intensely personal desires and wishes, from the incredibly mean to the most altruistic, are but expressions of internalized dimensions of various ideological formations that play a crucial role in any social, political and economic situation. It seems to me that these two positions are both contradictory and true.

And so it is that I regard what I have done here as a step towards a grotesque biblical criticism, by which I mean a biblical criticism that provides the intertwined and writhing swarm of methods with no restraint in application to the Bible, and one that makes the most of the coarse, instinctual and indecent dimensions of popular culture and everyday life. For this type of biblical criticism is finally the most satisfying.

(Within a day and a half the food stores at my Maccas had run out. The idiosyncratic burgers and fries and drinks no longer appeared, the crowds

were left hungering for more, the makeshift cooks dispersed, the store became ramshackle and filthy, with people availing themselves of the moveable chairs and tables for their own uses. Eventually the cicadas finished their frantic spring searches for a mate, the jacarandas lost their bell-shaped purple petals and the long hot summer began in earnest, with its flies and high humidity. On the second day of the Destruction I returned to my shack to find it destroyed by a stick of dynamite. The anal window was gone, but I was worried about Hokhma and Zara. With nowhere else to go, they had bedded down under my temporary shelter for the last couple of nights; they had been asleep when I had set off to look for food in the morning, and now the place was rubble. I left a shred of my shirt tied around a splintered doorpost and slunk out of the place, suddenly suspicious.

At my last Maccas breakfast that morning, I had met Michal. I thought she had gone with the first bomb in the police station, but she had been out on the bicycle patrol. 'Have you heard about the army and police units?' she asked, after we sat down together with some odd looking hot cakes.

'No, why?' I replied.

'They are moving on Sydney from Melbourne and Canberra.'

'Isn't anyone standing in their way?'

'There's a guerrilla force, mainly city slickers with a few rural types, but they are heavily outnumbered and outgunned. At least they know the territory and have been training for a while.'

'So what are you going to do, Michal?'

'I think I'll join the rebels.'

'Not the police?' I asked, puzzled.

'Hardly', she said. I wished her all the best and a charmed life as we parted. I wondered whether I too should join the rebels, but first I had to find Hokhma and Zara.

Later in the day I carefully worked my way around the back of what was home for a little while at least. In the backyard of a demolished house I lay down and waited for dusk. Finally, when the sun was about to set, two figures came slowly towards the ruins. I waited, but no one confronted them or shot at them. They sat for a while, unmoving and not noticing my shred of clothing, so I crept out, limbs stiff and weary, and then, to minimize the shock value, stood up and walked over. They leapt back, startled, until they realized who it was. 'You scared us shitless', said Zara, edgy and tired.

'You didn't see who did this?' I asked. Neither had I, and I was keen to get moving. 'It's late and I think I know a place', I said.

Across the now deserted freeway we crossed quickly and silently, the whole environment now sinister and potentially lethal. We followed Darling Mills Creek downstream until it linked with Toongabbie Creek for the headwaters of Parramatta River. A much neglected place even before the Destruction, it was now thoroughly desolate, although full of rubbish and debris. A few eucalypts mixed it in with the weeds and other low brush. A flat piece of land, somewhat flood prone, appeared in the other side of the lagoon at the river's headwaters. There was nothing for it but to strip and swim, all the bridges having been blown. On the other side we emerged, dripping and cold, on a nondescript piece of land that had once been an aboriginal camp. All we could see of the place were the low bushes: there was nothing very special about it.)

NOTES

INTRODUCTION: IN DEBT TO THE CENSOR

1 See Bach (1996), Marsh and Ortiz (1997), Martin and Ostwalt (1995), May and Bird (1982), Scott (1994). These volumes also have a more popular dimension in the regular reviews found in journals and magazines like *Sojourners, Christian Century* and *The Fourth R.*

2 The bulk of these studies has been on film; see Cheryl Exum (1996) and Babington and Evans (1993) on biblical epics, Kreitzer (1993; 1994) on representation in general, and Bach (1996).

3 Many of the essays in the series of volumes edited by Aichele and Pippin (1992; 1997; 1998) follow this approach, making use of fantasy theory to interpret the Bible. See also *Biblical Interpretation* (2(1), 1994), edited by Alice Bach.

4 Some of the essays in Aichele and Pippin (1992; 1997; 1998) do this, as well as an issue they edited of *Journal for the Fantastic in the Arts* (8(2), 1997). See also Moore (1998).

5 I have consciously chosen de Certeau and Lefebvre since their crucial contribution to cultural criticism is often overshadowed by the – often less inspiring and softly Marxist – work of Stuart Hall and Lawrence Grossberg and the Birmingham School. Morris of course has close connections with Grossberg, but her preference is for de Certeau.

6 This is also the time of the transformation of the Church by new, secular, political forms and the corresponding rise of 'mystics' in response (see Ahearne 1995: 30–1).

7 Similarly, mystic motifs appear now in historiography, philosophy, psychiatry, and so on (see de Certeau 1992: 16).

8 See also the reflection on this paper of Morris by Chambers (1994–5).

9 The English translation of this appeared in *Heterologies* (1986: 119–136), although when collated in French, it appeared as chapter 3 in *La Culture au Pluriel* (1994, originally 1974). It was not included in the English translation of *Culture in the Plural* (1997b), although, as in some senses the precursor to *The Practice of Everyday Life*, this is its proper place.

10 Anthropology follows a similar pattern: 'The Bororos of Brazil sink slowly into their collective death, and Lévi-Strauss takes his seat in the French Academy. Even if this injustice disturbs him, the facts remain unchanged. This story is ours as much as his. In this one respect (which is an index of others that are more important), the intellectuals are still borne on the backs of the common people' (de Certeau 1984: 25).

11 It then easily becomes 'mass culture', the popularization of the conceptions of an elite. Mass culture was, for some two centuries, that which was spread by education for the benefit of the political and economic elite (de Certeau 1997b: 119).

1 QUEER HEROES

1 I have argued elsewhere (Boer 1996b) that anti-essentialism should not be understood merely in terms of the constructionist/essentialist opposition, but that a third term in the discussion is, as Fredric Jameson suggests (1991: 217–59), a retooled nominalism. I also argued that the final referent and enabling condition for the whole debate may well be capitalism.

2 Part of this exercise is work on the origins and socio-economic constructions of homosexual and heterosexual identities; see especially Adam (1996), Bravmann (1996), Greenberg and Bystryn (1996), Halperin (1990a), McIntosh (1996) and Weeks (1996). As Peter Ray (1996) points out, until 1869 'homosexuals' did not exist, just people who performed 'unnatural' acts. The trials of Oscar Wilde in 1895 also played a crucial role in the construction of the (male) homosexual as well as camp (so Meyer 1994; Savoy 1995).

3 So Gamson (1996: 404): 'The ultimate challenge of queerness, however, is not just the questioning of the content of collective identities, but the *questioning of the unity, stability, visibility, and political utility of sexual identities* – even as they are used and assumed.' However, some have argued for the greater political power of constructionism: 'While [universalist positions] seem to have more immediate political power to mobilize people round an identity apparently rooted in an essential human type, social constructionism returns control over same-sex sexuality to those who live it' (Dyer 1991: 186).

4 Doty takes up the oppositional dimensions of queer rather than constructionist questions, assuming that queer designates what is 'contra-, non-, or anti-straight' (1993: xv; see also 2–3).

5 Straayer's fascinating book (1996) is thus not an example for me here, being given over to overtly queer cultural products. Examples of some of the more appealing queer readings of popular culture include those of the Simpsons (Hall 1997) and of *2001: A Space Odyssey* (Hanson 1993); Hal, of course, is queer.

6 For Meyer (1994: 7) Sontag's essay had the effect of confusing camp with irony, satire, burlesque and travesty. For a considered defence of Sontag in the context of critiques by Miller (1989) and Moon (1989), see Michasiw (1994). See also Babuscio (1977) and Kleinhans (1994).

7 Although I share political assumptions with Donald Morton, I find that his critique of such a recasting of camp and then the strategy of queering texts as an obscuring – through being 'at play' – of crucial issues of social and political circumstances is misdirected (see especially Morton 1996). The move that needs to be made is one that asks for the cultural and socio-economic situation in which precisely these strategies are enabled.

8 In sliding from queer to gay male in my discussion, I do not want to make an implicit claim that the two are synonymous. Rather, such a slide recognizes the significant differences in terms of 'sexual history, experience, fantasies, desire, or modes of theorizing' (de Lauretis 1991: 10) between lesbians and gays, let alone other forms of sexuality apart from the heterosexual.

9 I borrow the phrase from Burston (1995: 31).

10 Tasker (1993a: 73) notes the intrinsic connection between the male body-builders and action films in the last two decades.

11 Indeed, the body of the action figure evokes working class male bodies, which are a major feature of gay desire and iconography, although with a twist: apart from the 'clone' – cropped hair, singlet or plaid work shirt, jeans, Doc Martens and the obligatory handkerchief – the most popular manifestations are the various Village People characters – construction worker, police officer, cowboy, soldier – whose identities were 'hyperboles of fantasies of phallic masculinity' (Bredbeck, 1996: 89).

12 A similar logic applies, it seems to me, to the sports hero. It is not the oft-remarked bum-slapping, embracing, and kissing (see Harper 1994: 125–8) that is at issue, but that the

hetero/homosexual definitional divide emerges at the same time that modern sport was being established (see Messner 1996). In many respects the gay sports hero epitomizes the divide of modern sport, perhaps the signal example of this being the Australian rugby league star and international, Ian Roberts, who played first with South Sydney, moved, appropriately, to Manly and now captains the North Queensland Cowboys (!) (see Freeman 1997). Roberts simultaneously overturns the ideological relation athleticism = masculinity = heterosexuality and shows the base logic of modern sport's masquerade of masculinity, namely that it relies on the homo/heterosexual divide for its operation.

13 A similar motif appears in a very different film, *The Devil's Advocate* (1998), which also signals the impossibility of heterosexual union (the Hollywood narrative). Here Reeves's lawyer character, Kevin Lomax, is on the verge of mating with his half-sister, Christabella (Sophia Nielsen): the two demon spawn will produce the anti-Christ. But Reeves *chooses* not to.

14 Of course, Rock Hudson – 'the last guy you'd have figured' (Dyer 1993) – with his pedestrian, rather than ostentatious, masculinity, embodies an earlier version of a similar logic. See also Richard Meyer (1991).

15 Earlier in the film he escapes castration by hamming up the role of a religious fanatic.

16 Another group of buddy films is the 'sword and sandal' epic, such as *Ben Hur*, *El Cid*, *Spartacus*, *Barabbas*, and *Fall of the Roman Empire*. See further Leon Hunt (1993).

17 Fuchs discusses *Off Limits* (Christopher Crowe, 1988), *Lethal Weapon* and *Lethal Weapon 2* (Richard Donner, 1987 and 1989), *The Rookie* (Clint Eastwood, 1991), *New Jack City* (Mario van Peebles, 1991), *Black Rain* (Ridley Scott, 1989) and *Heart Condition* (James D. Parriott). She leads in with *Butch Cassidy and the Sundance Kid* (George Roy Hill, 1969). See also Holmlund (1993) and Tasker (1993b) on *Tango and Cash* (Andrei Konchalevsky, 1989) and *Lock Up* (John Flynn, 1989). See Tasker's fuller treatment of action films in her disappoiting and superficial *Spectacular Bodies* (1993a). An indispensable resource on action movies is Julius (1996).

18 Van Damme himself has been a gay icon for some time. 'Those people obviously have lots of taste', was his response to being asked how he feels in such a role. Immensely proud of his butt, he has at the centre of every film the butt shot, showing off, in his own words, his 'very up, strong butt' (see Burston 1995: 47)

19 The allusion here is to David Halperin's famous statement on Michel Foucault: 'As far as I'm concerned, the guy was a fucking saint' (Halperin 1995: 6).

20 See the extensive references in Moore and Anderson (1998: 249–51).

21 '[S]ex between members of the superordinate group was virtually inconceivable, whereas sex between a member of the superordinate group and a member of any one of the subordinate groups mirrored in the minute details of its hierarchical arrangement the relation of structured inequality that governed their wider social interaction. Sex, in this system, was not a private quest for mutual pleasure that absorbed, if only temporarily, the social identities of its participants; it was rather a declaration of one's social identity, an expression of one's public status: it served to position social actors in the places assigned to them (by virtue of their political standing) in the hierarchical structure of the Athenian polity. Defined by reference to an assymetrical gesture – the penetration of the body of one person by the body (and, specifically, by the phallus) of another – sex was not conceived as a collective enterprise in which two or more persons jointly engaged, but as an action performed by one person upon another; sex therefore effectively divided, classified, and distributed its participants into distinct and radically opposed categories ("penetrator" vs. "penetrated"). Sex was not only polarising, however; it was also hierarchical. For the insertive partner was construed as a sexual agent, whose phallic penetration of another person's body expressed sexual "activity", whereas the receptive partner was construed as a sexual patient, whose submission to phallic penetration displayed sexual "passivity". Sexual "activity", moreover, was thematized as domination: the relation between the "active" and the "passive" sexual partner was thought to be the same kind of relation as that obtaining between social superior and social inferior.

Finally, the total aggregates of these congruent functions (penetration/activity/dominance, on the one hand, and being-penetrated/passivity/submission, on the other) were constructed, respectively, as "masculinity" and "femininity"' (Halperin 1990b: 266).

22 Stephen Moore and Janice Anderson (1998), while agreeing with the basic assumptions of social-sexual domination and subordination, suggest that this is a continuum rather than a sharp bifurcation and that one's position on the continuum is always precarious, as 4 Maccabees shows with its victory through self control of a 'feeble, flabby old man, a gaggle of boys and an elderly widow' (273) over Antiochus Epiphanes.

23 The Philistines are of course the paradigmatic enemy of all action heroes, a source of endless bodies and stupid, macho-enhancing threats.

24 I am presuming the singular 'Philistine' refers to Goliath, although this is not explicitly spelled out.

25 One of the things Halperin fails to notice is that the relation between David and Jonathan is but a heightened form of David's relations with others as well.

26 Incessant harp-playing may indeed have this effect on anyone, especially by one who practises 'day by day' (1 Samuel 18:10).

27 Similarly, Pleins (1992; 1995) and Lawton (1993) suggest that the Saul–Jonathan–David trio enables a transferal from Jonathan, through his affection, to David as Saul's 'son' (pursuing 1 Samuel 17:55–8 – 'whose son are you?'), and then as heir.

28 Less interesting examples include Klein (1983: 182), who speaks of a 'personal and political' love. For Miscall (1986: 130) Jonathan's 'sincere love for his friend' is coupled with 'his fear of David's violence' as reasons for the covenant, but he makes nothing more of this.

29 Stefan Heym (1972: 52) reads this as a euphemism for castration: in his story David brings back a pile of Philistine penises.

30 This is what the Hebrew literally reads. By contrast, NRSV translates 'David wept the more'. Does it mean that he wept more, or that he restrained himself, plucked up courage, or perhaps that his position was enhanced through Jonathan's devotion?

31 This has been used as a text in gay religious ceremonies of dedication, marriage and funerals. Similarly, Ruth 1:16–17 is used for lesbian marriage ceremonies, blessings and funerals (see Howes 1993: 703).

32 Polzin notes eleven 'if ... then' statements in 20:5, 7–10, 12–14, 21–2.

33 Also, in 18:10 an evil spirit from Yahweh does something to Saul. The verb here, ṣlḥ, covers two meaning clusters surrounding 'penetrate' and 'prosper'. There is some debate over whether there is one verb (running through split > force entry > penetrate > succeed) or two (see Koehler and Baumgartner 1994–: 1026), the dual sense of penetrate and succeed now places Yahweh and Saul in an intriguing relation: the evil spirit forces entry or penetrates Saul.

34 Polzin (1993: 193–4) notes, for different reasons, the doubleness of language in chapter 20. But do not David's devious plan and Jonathan's double-voiced stratagem with the arrows also signal, formally, the doubleness of a queer reading?

35 For both characters, Fuss's comment is highly applicable: '[t]he homo in relation to the hetero, much like the feminine in relation to the masculine, operates as an indispensable interior exclusion – an outside which is inside interiority making the articulation of the latter possible, a transgression of the border which is necessary to constitute the border as such' (Fuss 1991: 3).

2 COWS WITH GUNS: SADISTIC HEGEMONY, HITCHCOCK AND BIBLICAL DISMEMBERMENT

1 The title of the theme song for my course, 'The Politics of Meat: Sacrifice in the Hebrew Bible and Contemporary Thought'.

2 Sloan identifies methods used for the study of Hitchcock in terms of auteur theory, structuralism, social and political concerns, psychoanalysis, feminism, and film history.

3 In fact the *Out in Culture* anthology devotes a whole dossier of almost one hundred pages to Hitchcock (Creekmur and Doty 1995: 183–281)

4 Hitchcock worked hard at enhancing his own critical status after 1960, as Kapsis has argued (1986; 1989; 1992), although he was assisted by the rise of auteur theory.

5 Against the idea, 'a prison officer revolts against his job of hanging a man' the problem is that 'capital punishment is part of our [British] law, and we mustn't propagate against it' (Hitchcock 1995: 160–1).

6 This was to show 'fistfights between strikers and undergraduates, pickets, and all the authentic drama of the situation' (Hitchcock 1995: 198) but it was vetoed by the British Film Board.

7 It appears in the 1934 *The Man Who Knew Too Much*, although the censor still objected. Hithcock's initial plan was to show the militia and the house in Sidney Street surrounded by machine guns: all he was allowed to do was 'depict the policemen being handed rifles and shown how to use them' (Hitchcock 1995: 198).

8 All the same, for Corber Hitchcock is complicit with the anti-Stalinist programme of post-war liberals, seeking to explain psychoanalytically what were firstly social and historical conditions (Corber 1993).

9 A similar argument applies to the Law: the Law exists not because of a desire to maintain order, but exists through the very breaking of the Law, it is constituted by the transgression of the Law (see Žižek 1991: 209).

10 This is not the first time sadism has been used as an interpretive tool for Hitchcock. Modleski based much of the argument of *The Women Who Knew Too Much* (1988) on the sadism–masochism dialectic for understanding the male viewer's response, without considering the unstable construction of 'male'.

11 The phrase is Kay Sloan's (1985: 91).

12 Odabashian argues that Jeff witnesses the 'primal scene', the copulation of his father and mother that conceived him (1993: 6). Indeed, all of the scenes enacted across the courtyard deal with the presence or absence of sex.

13 My emphasis differs from the conventional reading of *Rear Window* as a mise en abyme for the cinema itself, eg. Harris (1987) and Stam and Pearson (1983).

14 I am indebted to Julian Smith (1992) for this argument.

15 On another level, the various people in the apartment building reflect different dimensions of the relationship between Lisa (Grace Kelly) and Jeff. Thus, Thorwald is a mirror of Jeff's darker side (so Jeanne Allen 1988: 34–6).

16 'I've always been interested in establishing a contrast, in going against the traditional and in breaking away from clichés. With *Harry* I took melodrama out of the pitch-black night and brought it out into the sunshine. It's as if I had set up a murder alongside a rustling brook and spilled a drop of blood in the clear water. These contrasts establish a counterpoint; they elevate the commonplace in life to a higher level' (Hitchcock in Truffaut 1986: 341).

17 'I undertook *Rope* as a stunt; that's the only way I can describe it. I really don't know how I came to indulge in it' (Truffaut 1986: 259).

18 Similarly, Durgnat comments (1974: 208) that in contrast to proper track or pan, the camera 'slides from one fairly conventional set-up to another, rather than moving in relation to the primary visual elements … the incessant visual glissando creates, in this context, an appropriately creepy, slithery and serpentine mood, as unpleasant as a softly excessive attentiveness'.

19 My close family often greets me in this fashion, especially in the morning – 'Get up, cocksucker!'

20 Similarly, 'When I was working in the city of London, they had a social club and as part of the activities of the club we were given the opportunity to learn to dance – waltzing or what have you. I suppose I was about eighteen or nineteen at the time, and a middle-aged

gentleman taught me to waltz. Three or four years later his daughter [Edith Thompson] was not only arrested as a murderess but was hanged as well' (Hitchcock, interviewed by Schickel 1995: 21–2). And then, 'It's [the town in *Shadow of a Doubt*] like the town near where we live in northern California, Santa Cruz. You would have felt that this was a [quiet] little seaside resort town and yet they had the most bizarre murder. I don't think the man has been sentenced yet, he may have been – killed five people and tied them up and threw their bodies into a pool' (23). Zirnite (1986) reads this in terms of spatial layering: one is banal, complacent, shallow; the other, upper, level is oppressive, malignant, destructive. Stairs and towers therefore play a crucial role in the films, although this is not always the case. See also Weis (1982: 101) on the way innocent songs and tunes like the Merry Widow Waltz in *Shadow of a Doubt* are through their innocence constitutive of the villain.

21 An elaborateness enhanced, along with illustrations of body parts and altars, by the laborious and thorough commentary of Milgrom (1991).

22 Levine (1989: 7) argues that the verb translated as 'flayed' (*nth*) is normally used with regard to live animals.

23 The obligatory cross reference is with the dish of quail in *Frenzy* and the story of the quail in Numbers 11 (see Chapter 7).

24 The following rhythm is thereby established:

1 presentation (3, 10, 14);
2 putting a hand on the animal's head (4a);
3 slaughter (5a, 11ab);
4 blood works (5b, 11b);
5 dismemberment (6, 12a);
6 washing of intestines and legs (9a, 13a);
7 burning (9b, 13b, 17ab).

25 Hartley, it seems, is himself turning on the exegetical and theological spit, desperately denying Yahweh's desire for his flesh: 'Usually a whole offering was presented not to cool God's wrath but to seek his goodwill before his wrath might be kindled. Furthermore, this metaphor serves well to say that God himself must accept each offering in order for it to be efficacious without in any way indicating that God is dependent on these offerings for sustenance' (Hartley 1992: 22–3). Yet Hartley cannot escape such an outcome, stressing Yahweh's actual presence (1992: lxiii–lxiv). Similarly, Levine is taken with the realism of the instructions (1989: xxi).

26 With cannibalistic fervour, Hartley writes: 'The ancients prized the liver and the kidneys both as centers of emotional life and as delicacies' (1992: 40).

27 Even the fat of animals who have died or been killed by wild animals must not be eaten (7:24), although it may be put to other uses, 'such as the greasing of equipment or instruments' (Noth 1965: 64).

28 Goodwin (1981: 224) argues against most that Stevie's death is perfectly logical, given viewer identification with him.

29 Modleski (1988: 55) is incorrect when she argues that identification with characters is first exploited with *Rebecca*.

30 '[T]he point is to draw the audience right inside the situation instead of leaving them to watch from outside, from a distance. And you do this only by breaking the action up into details and cutting from one to the other, so that each detail is forced in turn on the attention of the audience and reveals its psychological meaning' (Hitchcock 1995: 256–7).

31 Further, *Sabotage* also has the recurring theme of the structural relation between police and criminal (see Cohen 1994: 200). Winnie Verloc, the 'innocent murderer' (Leitch 1986: 66), is pressed against her will not to confess her murder by the police officer who

has himself been investigating Verloc. Thereby he also gets the girl, although in a highly ambiguous fashion. *Blackmail* follows a very similar format.

32 '*Psycho*'s shower-murder scene has passed into the consciousness of the world. An uninitiated viewer – one who does not already know Norman's story or Marion's fate – can scarcely be found' (Rothman 1982: 266). However, Linda Williams (1994) saw it, and attempts to reconstruct those days. She suggests that it was the inaugural film for new cinema and viewing habits, what she calls the roller coaster – tension and release, assault and escape.

33 Bellour speaks of the 'Hitchcockian constant according to which, given a certain order of desire, it is above all women that get killed'. This is because 'woman, the subject of neurosis, becomes the object of the psychosis of which man is the subject' (1986: 317). See also the bleak article by Carson (1986). Paula Cohen (1995: 25), by contrast, argues for an ambiguity surrounding the depiction and treatment of women in Hitchcock's films: this mix of sympathy and sadism evoked in male viewers is a result of bringing in a Victorian concept of subjectivity into a space where that is suppressed. Modleski (1995; also 1988: 5) makes a similar argument for the ambiguity of female representation: it is a misogyny that opens up the possibility of critique, however unintentionally.

34 Although Durgnat asks whether the murder itself or cleaning up afterwards is the more gruesome (1974: 326).

35 Critics have speculated over Norman's sexuality. Hepworth (1995: 188) finds Norman conveniently set up as a crowd-pleasing scapegoat. For Wood the homosexual identity is much harder than it seems (Wood 1995: 197, 205). Wood traces a tendency both to aggression against gay men and to identification with them. Hitchcock also identified with his female leads/parts. Rothman (1982: 82) argues that no major figure in Hitchcock's corpus takes himself to be a homosexual. Some men are bound together in the mutual denial of the love of women, but they are not cognizant of their homosexual affections. In other words, there is no redemptive homosexual love in Hitchcock's films.

36 Even though the whole scene is approximately 1.5 minutes long, it took over a week to shoot.

37 Thus critics have sought to make connections between the two halves; see, for example, Bellour (1986), Klinger (1982), and Petlewski (1988). Critics have also read the hole in the wall/eye/shower/mouth/drain as a voyeuristic 'murderous gaze' (Rothman 1982: 292–31) and as anal (Edelman 1995; Sterritt 1992: 50).

38 Wood (1995: 205) argues that Hitchcock identifies with both the terror of the shower and the thrusting knife, but that terror overrides sadistic violence.

39 'When Perkins is looking at the car sinking in the pond, even though he's burying a body, when the car stops sinking for a moment, the public is thinking, "I hope it goes all the way down!" It's a natural instinct' (Hitchcock in Truffaut 1986: 420–1).

40 'All very businesslike' drones Boling (1975: 276).

41 Bal (1988: 92) names her 'Beth' while Exum (1993:176) prefers Bath-sheber, 'daughter of breaking'. 'The Hebrew *shabar* means "to break" or "to break in pieces"; the noun *sheber* can mean "breaking", as in the breaking of pottery into pieces (Isaiah 30.14), or "fracture", as in the fracture of a limb (Leviticus 21.19; Leviticus 24.20); it can also refer to anguish or brokenness of spirit (Isaiah 65.14). ... The word *sheber* can refer to interpretation, as in the phrase, "breaking of a dream" (Judges 7.15)' (Exum 1993: 176–7).

42 Bal (1988: 119) reads the killing in four stages: handing her over to the sons of Belial, rape and torture, dragging her home on the donkey and the slaughtering.

43 So, for example, Moore (1908: 419): the man's speech makes the impression of indescribable brutality, but the author had no such intention.

44 A signal effort in this regard is Stone (1995), who connects the honour/shame social dichotomy with a reconstruction of sexuality in the ancient world to argue that penetration of the Levite or the concubine constitutes social belittlement for the Levite; hence the revenge.

45 Many take the narrative hint – 'when there was no king in Israel' (19:1) – reading the story as symbolic of Israelite divisions (Boling 1975: 277; Lasine 1984; Niditch 1982: 371) and as a contrast with the proper way to summon the tribes, as shown later by Saul (1 Samuel 11:5–7; see Gray 1967: 379).

46 So Bal (1988: 119–27). For Exum (1993: 181) it is an effort to desexualize the woman: she must be opened and dispersed.

47 For Jones-Warsaw (1993) the Levite is also a victim.

48 He tells the Israelites: 'The lords of Gibeah rose up against me ... they intended to kill me. Then I took my concubine and cut her into pieces, and sent her throughout the whole extent of Israel's territory; for they have committed a vile outrage in Israel' (Judges 20:5–6).

49 She also reads it as a signal of social tension, a marker of social change from what she calls patrilocal marriage (husband lives in wife's father's home) to virilocal marriage (wife lives in husband's home). This tension works itself out on the bodies of women, often in violent terms.

50 The film is also notable for the layering of stories – a crime writer (Grace's lover), a plot by Tony, that goes wrong, another story by Tony to frame the Kelly character, an almost right guess (except for the key placement) by the crime writer, another story by Tony after he has told the 'preposterous' true story to the police inspector, and then finally the discovery of what 'really' happened by the detective.

51 'Hitchcock himself believed that this stomach-churning bit of footage was one of the most frightening murder scenes that he ever devised' (Phillips 1984: 128). Durgnat (1974: 234) suggests that the scissors recall the knife in *Blackmail* with which the Anny Ondra character (Alice White) kills her attacker. Phillips (1984: 128) notes the ambiguity of the scissors as an instrument of murder and of the expert film cutting that achieved the scene, as with *Sabotage* and *Psycho*.

52 At first he claims to have carried out the command of Yahweh (15:13), and then, in the face of Samuel's sarcastic question (15:14), Saul shifts the onus onto the people, who have spared the best to sacrifice to Yahweh (15:15). A third time, in response to Samuel's increasing frustration and anger, Saul still claims to have followed Yahweh's command, insists the people kept the best sheep and cattle to sacrifice to Yahweh, and admits that he still has Agag the king of Amalek (15:20–21). Samuel now tells Saul, after some poetic comments about obedience being better than sacrifice, that he has been rejected from being king (15:22–3). But, apparently having learned a few political tricks of the trade, Saul shuffles some more, admitting that he did not in fact obey Yahweh's command, but only because of his fear of the people, over whom he is supposed to be king (15:24–5). A sixth time Saul attempts to retrieve something, grasping and tearing Samuel's garment as he turns to leave. A reinforcement of Saul's denial of the kingship by Yahweh brings one last effort by Saul: 'I have sinned; yet honour me now before the elders of my people and before Israel, and return with me, so that I may worship the Lord your God' (15:30). In his attempt to be honoured, to save face, before the elders and Israel, Saul finally succeeds, having worn an angry and frustrated Samuel down. This, it seems, is the only way Samuel will be rid of Saul.

53 So Miscall (1986: 112). Hertzberg (1964: 129) prefers to see it as the fulfillment of the ban against Amalek.

54 Durgnat (1974: 397) argues that masochism runs through the film: Rusk's preferences in women; Inspector Oxford's acquiescence before his wife's gastronomic disasters; the sado-masochistic secretary of Mrs Blaney.

55 Hepworth (1995: 189; so also Modleski 1988: 44) argues that there is a persistent equation of corrupt and violent sex and carnivorous eating: the shot of Rusk forcing apart Mrs Blaney's legs is juxtaposed with Mrs Oxford (the wife of the inspector) opening her dish of quail with its legs spread; the protruding foot of the corpse in the potato sack is set against the Inspector's efforts to skewer some pig's trotter; the snapping of the corpse's

fingers by Rusk is paralleled by the cracking of the breadstick by Mrs Oxford. It is here, in the potato truck where Rusk must find some incriminating evidence on a body locked in rigor mortis (hence the snapping fingers) that involuntary sympathy is generated, for viewers begin to hope that he won't be discovered, that he will find the incriminating evidence (so Garrett 1991: 31).

56 Peele (1986: 213) alone suggests that Gromek is likeable.

57 For a critique of the perpetuation of auteur theory with regard to Hitchcock, and the consideration of him as a discursive subject in history, see Corber (1993: 111–53). See also Jameson (1990: 198–201), who connects auteur theory with modernism.

58 Others, like Peele (1986), disagree, suggesting that Hitchcock kept his personal and artistic sides separate.

3 NIGHT SPRINKLE(S): PORNOGRAPHY AND THE SONG OF SONGS

1 Another way of translating Song 5:2 (*rss lylh*). NRSV reads 'drops of the night'.

2 As pornography gets harder, men begin to appear more frequently (so Kuhn 1985: 45), both with women and with other men.

3 My argument is close to, but not the same as, Ellis's (1988), for whom the auratic quality of pornography is generated by its censored status. The genius of Kendrick's proposal is that censorship comes into play in response to the democratization of culture.

4 Aretino also produced *Ragionamenti* (1534–6), a pornographic dialogue between an older, experienced, woman and a younger one without experience. Such dialogues became a generic marker for three centuries (see Hunt 1993a: 24–5). On Aretino, see Findlen (1993: 51–2).

5 By comparison the inaugural moment in England is connected with the 'bishop's ban' of 1599 (see Boose 1994).

6 'The whole male intellectual tradition that I was involved with in fact refused to face the relationship between pornography and women's real lives. Women's lives were worth nothing, and the pornography itself was very misrepresented whenever it was written or talked about. The reality is that men commit acts of forced sex against women systematically' (Dworkin in Elizabeth Wilson 1987: 162).

7 In this light, pornography is that which has as its specific aim the generation of desire; it is 'literature that must be read with one hand', to gloss the French descriptor of porn. Pornography and masturbation go hand in hand, so to speak (see Queen 1996). It is a small step to argue that pornography incites sex acts and crimes.

8 '[G]iven the way the research is conducted, it cannot be relied upon to make a judgment on anything' (King 1993: 57).

9 Now largely discarded, the distinction between erotica and pornography also plays with the Censor: pornography, insofar as it is depicts sexual domination, must according to this argument be censored while erotica must not. It also operates with a high/low culture opposition, porn being suspect because of its direct appeal to the body (so Clover 1993: 3).

10 I resist here the overwhelming tendency to define pornography as that which arouses the reader/viewer, for this trades on the cause–effect split: rather, pornography is the representation of sexually explicit material.

11 Indeed, Hunt suggests (1993a: 43) that the use of pornography for arousal is a development after its initial use as a political weapon.

12 The 'Grub Street Jacks', the writers, publishers and printers of Holywell Street in London – Thomas Spence, George Cannon, John and William Dugdale foremost among them – developed the area of 'obscene libel' as a progression of the long tradition of popular

literature of preceding centuries, including the novels of Rabelais, bawdy songsheets and chap-books (precisely what Nisard confiscated in France).

13 There was a Solomon Wiseman in the Parramatta area who, in the early 1800s, ran a ferry over the Hawkesbury River at Wiseman's Ferry, on the main route north for travellers in the early colony. Since he had a monopoly he could, and did, charge what he liked.

14 An allusion to Shannon Bell's interview of Sprinkle, 'Ejaculator Meets Slut Goddess! Or, Deep Inside Annie Sprinkle's Heart, Mind and Pussy', in *Spectator: California's Weekly Sex News and Review* 27/9 (1991): 5, 16 (see Bell 1994b: 215).

15 As Marxists have argued, pornography is also commodified sex (see Berger, Searles and Cottle 1991: 57–9; Williams 1989: 93–119). Arcand goes a step further and points out that it was inevitable that sex would be commodified under capitalism (1993: 146–66). Williams also argues that the central feature of modern hard core is *scientia sexualis*, the compulsion to speak incessantly about sex (1989: 2).

16 On the history of pornography, particularly its rise in sixteenth century Italy and seventeenth and eighteenth century France and England, see the collection edited by Hunt (1993c). See also Arcand (1993: 125–46), Kendrick (1996), Somers and Pogel (1981), Webb (1982); for the rise of the pornography industry in the 1960s and 1970s, see Goldman (1983), and on the development of the porn feature film see Williams (1989). On the way the representation of sex has been an early exercise for each new medium – poetry, novel, postcard, photographs, film, internet – see Trumbach (1993) and Kuhn (1985: 25).

17 Except for Stadelman (1992), a literal – that is, erotic, non-theological and often female perspective if not authorship – reading of some sort or other is pursued by all the commentators I have consulted (Bekkencamp and van Dijk 1993: 79–81; Brenner 1989; 1993b; 1993c; Cotterell 1996; Falk 1993a; Fox 1985; Goitein 1993; Goulder 1986; Keel 1994; Munro 1995; Murphy 1981; 1990; Pope 1977). It is an underlying feature of the *Feminist Companion to the Song of Songs* (Brenner 1993a) and of Pope's massive commentary (1977), although he also notes the history of allegorical readings in smaller type. Even fundamentalists like to read the Song as a sex guide, verses like 2:6 justifying clitoral stimulation (see Weaver 1989: 73). Only Trible (1978: 144–65) and Landy (1983; 1987) pursue the implications of poetic language although, romantics that they are, they are more concerned with 'love'. One of the problems with all these readings is a rampant heterosexual focus, although Trible's has a decidedly queer tone.

18 See the vast survey of the history of interpretation of the Song in Pope's commentary (1977: 89–229).

19 Indeed, Keel's commentary (1994), with its conjunction of text and the various graphics of which he is enamoured, approximates the layout of text and picture in pornographic publications.

20 Any desire to investigate the construction of sexuality in the Song would need to consider the primary role of the whole range of fluids, both bodily and otherwise.

21 Fox's warning (1985: 298–9) against limiting the search for references to genitalia is well taken, although I suspect he was trying to restrict such activities, rather than open them out to the range of 'sexual organs' I have in mind.

22 Similar terms were already in use in eighteenth century French pornography: 'vit' (dick), 'foutre' (to fuck), 'cocu' (cuckold), 'branler' (to wank) and many variations of the word 'cul' (ass) (Goulemot 1994: 67).

23 '[W]idespread replacement of masculine for feminine pronouns, verbs and suffixes; the pleonastic use of the personal pronoun with the finite verb; and the employment of the anticipatory suffix followed by the relative particle and possessive *l*. The Song is also the only biblical book that uses the relative particle *se-* consistently throughout the book' (Grossberg 1989: 57).

24 While biblical critics note the crucial role of such imagery (e.g. Meyers 1993), there is a curious repression of the fetish.

25 Lavoie (1995) suggests that the animal and plant references, particularly since so many are edible fruits and grains and game, find their proper reference in erotic eating. Perhaps it is better to see them as food fetishes.

26 On the money shot – so named because male actors get paid more for ejaculation – and its history see Bell (1994b); Champagne (1991: 201); Kaite (1995: 55–6); Pendleton (1992: 156–8); Williams (1989: 70–6, 93–119).

27 On female ejaculation, see Bell: 'How did it cum to be that male ejaculation has never been questioned, debated, analyzed; just accepted as a given feature of the male body and male sexuality?' (Bell 1994b: 529; see further, Bell 1995: 49, 261–6). On Annie Sprinkle's ejaculatory efforts see Thomas (1996: ch 2), Straayer (1993: 168–74) and Williams (1993b: 185–6).

28 '[A]lthough the physical act of sex obviously must take place in order to be filmed, the visual spectacle of external penile ejaculation is a tacit acknowledgment that such real-live sex acts can be communicated to viewers only through certain visual and aural conventions of representation' (Williams 1989: 121).

29 The trick is that film and photography are coded in order to seem uncoded. 'The truth/ authenticity potential of photography is tied up with the idea that seeing is believing. Photography draws on the ideology of the visible as evidence' (Kuhn 1985: 127).

30 Alan Soble (1986: 55–102) has a Marxist turn – unfortunately too simplistic – on this argument: pornography consumption (the assumption is heterosexual males) signals defeat by males in their economic, social and sexual lives. It is not a signal of power, but rather its lack. However, he argues for a distinct place for pornography in communist society, since it will be produced communistically and have sexual value for communist people (1986: 103–49).

31 See also Ecstavasia (1993) on the construction of the call girl as 'cyborg subject-position "fantasy girl"' (178).

32 This is the case particularly with the stag film, with its narrative discontinuity, although Williams argues that the innovation of the porn feature film was to string sexual encounters together in a crude narrative, *Deep Throat* being the first example of this (Williams 1989: 63, 99–100). What she fails to note is that the narrative remains crude – all it ever can be.

33 Ross (1993: 238) suggests that the structure of most contemporary pornography is set to male patterns of masturbation: peep shows, 8mm loops, stroke books, and feature films with intervals between sex acts.

34 Grossberg (1994), in a moment of domestic nostalgia, even suggests that the Song concerns home and family.

35 Bosshard-Nepustil (1996) likes it both ways – two identifiable couples, one a king and queen, the other a woman and a shepherd.

36 Indeed, transvestite pornography expresses the 'truth' of heterosexual pornography, for the penetrated she–male is also the phallic mother. See further Kaite (1995: 61–6).

37 Kaite (1995: 49–50) traces the differential effect of the anus, especially the 'rear view' of a vaginally penetrated female, for the anus is lit up and spread, a site of both expulsion and penetration.

38 '[I]n an erotic text the important thing is to move from one episode to another' (Goulemot 1994: 74). See Williams on the various 'sexual numbers' of straight porn films (1989: 126–8).

39 On the *wasf* (Arabic for 'description'), see Soulen's paintaking history of the genre and the emergence of the term (1993); also Falk (1993b).

40 Fox analyses as an example the reference to kisses in 1:2 and its connection with 8:1; 8:2; 1:4; 4:10; 4:3; 2:3; 5:16; 7:10; 1:3; 7:14 (Fox 1985: 71–4).

41 It then becomes interesting to ponder what an allegorical or spritiual interpretation might do with such a move, particularly when critics such as McGinn (1992) argue for a conjunction of divine and human erotics. On the other hand, the contribution of the Song in light of my reading to a modern sexual ethic (so Lüthi 1993) would be an intriguing endeavour.

42 'When it is the liquid consistency of the oils rather than their scent that is emphasized, the language is powerfully evocative of desire' (Munro 1995: 49).

43 A consistent and somewhat worn image of the vagina and its labia is a flower.

44 For the association in pornography between fruit and testicles, see Kaite (1995: 57).

45 Although not quite with this in mind, Watson (1995: 262) refers in passing to an 'exchange of bodily fluids'. He also mentions Mesopotamian texts that speak of 'vulva from which urine comes', a 'spittle-laden mouth', and 'armpits stinking of mushrooms'.

46 In fact, as with this chapter, 'god' does not appear in the Song of Songs, although, as Blumenthal suggests (1995), this is forgotten because of the sexual valences in the Song.

47 'The bodies of the lovers are disassembled and reconstructed in the Song, each constituent metaphorically combining with heterogenous elements to give the impression of a collage' (Landy 1983: 73).

48 Murphy is restrained: 'The translation understands him to be feeding on the lilies, which presumably are a symbol for the woman herself' (Murphy 1990: 141 on 2:16).

49 The gender neutral first person of this section (3:1–5) allows either a man or a woman, or whatever.

50 Hermon's dick evokes memories of Yahweh, stunt cock extraordinaire, and purveyor of the column of smoke in the wilderness. See Boyarin (1990), who argues that the Song was read by the rabbis as an allegory of the Exodus.

51 For Goulder (1986: 37–9) 4:8–5:1 is a royal fucking scene, part of the celebration of a royal wedding, until entry and orgasm in 5:1. While I appreciate his insight, my reading and demarcation are a little different.

52 I am indebted to Fiona Black for this insight; her PhD thesis focuses on the grotesque body in the Song of Songs. However, see the staunchly realist reading of Waterman (1948), who proposed a grotesque body without realizing its sexual potential.

53 Many commentators read this as a reference to breasts: so Goulder (1986: 37).

54 This word (*šlḥyk*, from *šlḥ*) has puzzled many. Considering its base in a root which means 'to let loose', or 'to send', and considering that its denominatives variously mean 'missile' and 'water channel', it makes sense to translate it as 'ejaculation', with specific reference to female ejaculation. See the discussion in Pope (1977: 490–1) who notes the propulsive sense of the root but prefers 'groove' in reference to the vagina. In a curious double-take, Keel (1994: 175–6) likes 'canals', understood euphemistically. Landy (1983: 192) reads as both shoots/canals.

55 Confusion reigns over the word for 'hole' (*ḥr*). Murphy (1990) reads it as a door-latch, while Gordis (1974: 91) suggests it means that he withdraws his hand from the gate-hole, for 'vagina' is nonsense here. Keel's flat reading (1994: 189–90) sees here merely the locked out lover. Pope (1977: 517–18), however, reads 'hand' as a euphemism for penis, and, in characteristically restrained tones, suggests that 'the statement "my love thrust his 'hand' into the hole" would be suggestive of coital intromission' (1977: 519).

56 Murphy is brilliantly obtuse: 'The myrrh on the lock comes either from the man or the woman [!]; it seems more reasonable that the man is responsible. When she says that her fingers dripped myrrh, she means that she placed her hands on the anointed lock. The precise symbolism of the myrrh is not easy to determine. At the very least this is a sign from the lover. He put it there, perhaps as a token of his love and a tangible sign of his presence (cf. 1:13), even though he disappears' (1990:171). See Pope (1977: 521–5) on the elaborate speculation over this dripping myrrh and Keel (1994: 193–4) for brilliant literal obtuseness.

57 Once again, these verses (5:10–16) do not indicate the gender of the speaker.

58 The man is also described in terms of a lily (2:1, 16). Does this then signify his anus?

59 Here again the gender is indeterminate, and the sociality of these verses is distinctly female. Even 6:11–12 do not preclude lesbian sex, the *ndb* (a prince? Aminadab?) of 6:12 being sufficiently ambiguous to allow such a reading.

60 This is the basic sense of the Hebrew *ndb* in 6:12.

61 Debate has also raged over *šrr*, 'valley' or 'navel'. For Landy it means 'vulva' (1983: 89) as part 'of a metaphorical fusion of sex and suckling, teat and vagina' (90). Murphy notes that it is meant as a 'euphemism for the pudenda. The presence of "mixed wine" in this anatomical vessel has been understood as a reference to fecundation, or even to "love water"' (1990:185). For Pope it is without a doubt 'vulva' filled with 'punch' (1977: 617–20). 'If the vessel in question is the vulva, the spicy mixture probably does not refer to semen but to what the Indian erotologists call "love-water" (*kama-sulileh*) which in the ideal lotus woman is perfumed like the new-burst lily' (Pope 1977: 620). Pope, it seems, wants his taste of these secretions. Keel (1994: 234) reads 'navel' as a euphemism for vulva, replete with illustrations.

62 I am indebted to Athalya Brenner (1993c) for pointing out the caricature of the normal *wasf* in these verses.

63 On the long association between breasts and fruit, see Kaite (1995: 57).

64 Goulder (1986: 60–2) reads 7:11/10–8:4 as a sexual romp in the country.

4 STOLEN WATER IS SWEETER, STOLEN BREAD TASTES BETTER: ON REPRESENTING SEX WORKERS

1 Yet, the third, revised edition, under the auspices of Trébuchet and Poirat-Duval, appeared at the time of Nisard's work, 1857.

2 Alexandre Parent-Duchâtelet. *Hygiène publique, ou mémoires sur les questions les plus importantes de l'hygiène appliquées aux professions et aux travaux d'utilité publique.* 2 vols. Paris: Baillière, 1836.

3 So also, almost 150 years later and half-way around the world in Australia, Daniels notes that '[o]ften the policeman mediates between prostitute and historian' (Daniels 1984: 5)

4 Not only did his work spark a series of comparable studies in France, but in the 1840s English writers followed (Walkowitz 1980: 36–9). As Nash notes, 'it was in the 1850s and 1860s that interest in prostitution became so widespread as to cause a veritable explosion of information on this subject'. It had become 'an urgent social problem, which threatened the Victorian family, their health, and the good order of their public life' (Nash 1994: xxiv). Parent-Duchâtelet's ambivalence becomes itself a topic of study in social patterns of the simultaneous acceptance and vilification of prostitution (see Connelly 1980; Gilfoyle 1992). See also Barbara Hobson on the 'discovery of prostitution' (1987: 11–76). Novelists made use of his material in their work: see Brooks (1980: 132) on such use by Balzac, Dumas and Sue.

5 Sex work, like money and the commodity, is one of those things that capitalism has appropriated and made its own (in terms of the sale of labour power/body). This means that sex work is neither eternal due to desire (libertarian position) nor purely the creation of the conjunction of capitalism and patriarchy (vulgar Marxist; see Shrage 1994). A whole stream of historical and sociological works continue to identify the widely divergent forms in which the sale of sex has operated. See, for example, Perkins and Bennett (1985: 3–14) on Australia until the early eighties; Lie (1995) on the changes in twentieth century Korea; Manderson (1992) and Muecke (1992) on Thailand; Werner (1984) on the Brazilian Mekranoti tribe; and Shrage (1989) who compares temple prostitution in Babylon, fifteenth century work in France and contemporary USA. Also, see the volume edited by Davis (1993) for an indication of the variety and commonality of contemporary issues in different countries. A distinctive feature of capitalist prostitution is the increasing range of services: for heterosexual female work there are streets and brothels, massage parlours, bondage and discipline specialties, escort agencies, hotel and ship prostitution, call girls, and

courtesans. For male homsexual work there are street and bar hustlers, parlour prostitutes, private escorts, call boys, specialists and trade workers (hetero men in homosexual prostitution). The smaller areas include lesbian, transsexual and heterosexual male prostitution, S/M fetish services and fantasy work, telephone sex, stripping, porn performance, sexual facilitation or therapy, and cross-dressing (see Bell 1995: 8).

6 Indeed, Perkins (1994: 144) notes that between 1539 and 1977 some 5500 works on prostitution were published, and that since 1977 (she writes in 1994) as many have been published again. Categories include autobiographies; biographies; quantitative studies, of which Parent-Duchâtelet's was the first; and qualitative work.

7 Some references might include: Keuls (1985: 204–228) on the sharp bifurcation between the whore and housewife, between Hera and Aphrodite, in ancient Athens; Nussbaum (1995) on the relation between these binaries in Victorian society and the construction of the imperial world, in which the 'nether' regions are torrid and female over against a temperate and sober male England.

8 For example, in the older sociological study directed by Winter may be found this gem: 'Far too often the prostitute is found to be unintelligent, inarticulate, illiterate, lazy, selfish, bad-tempered, poorly educated, emotionally unstable, socially irresponsible, financially dishonest, politically naive, devoid of any sense of humour and immoderate in her consumption of alcohol, tobacco and other drugs. ... [P]rostitution is the manifestation that criminality most often takes in women' (1976: 131).

9 Rather than legalized, which has led, in countries like Germany and states like Nevada in the USA, to more regulation in favour of clients. On the debate, see Rio (1991).

10 Heterosexual sex workers in developed countries have, according to available studies, a very low incidence of HIV (see McKeganey and Barnard 1996: 58–69). However, male street prostitution has been identified as a high risk group (see Boles and Elifson's 1994 study of 224 males in Atlanta, Georgia), although Pleak and Bahlburg (1990) argue on the basis of Manhattan evidence for significant safe sex practices. Other examples of the focus on sex work and HIV/AIDS include the Davis anthology (1993), Kane on the military in Belize (1993), Markos, Wade and Walzman on adolescent male prostitutes (1994), and Zalduondo (1991) on methods of research in the relation between prostitution and HIV/AIDS.

11 See Barry (1979; 1991; 1995), the founder of WHISPER; on the battle see Bell (1994b: 99–136). In Australia, the wider sex industry, including film and video, magazines, the internet and phone sex, along with sex workers themselves, has organized itself into a much broader coalition known as the Eros Foundation. Apart from the advocacy work that the Eros Foundation undertakes, it has a much wider agenda, including social activities, literary and film awards, and the support and protection of those involved in the sex industry.

12 See McClintock (1992: 87–95). In a different arena, Lizzy Borden in *Working Girls* portrays prostitution as work: 'I wanted to place prostitution solidly in the context of work as opposed to sex ... . Prostitution is a business transaction, pure and simple, between prostitute and john' (quoted in Jackson 1987: 5). Some have argued that the wide variety of types of sex work renders a catch-all such as 'sex work' problematic (see Sullivan 1994: 259) but it is no more problematic than other forms of work.

13 Satz (1995) argues that if sex were not connected to gender inequality there would be no problem.

14 Indeed, sex work has been part of the ideological construction by the middle class of the uninhibited and 'dangerous' sexuality of the working class as a whole.

15 'The money is important ... somehow when the money is there we can have a fabulous time with these people, really give and be loving and totally be of service. And if the money isn't there, forget it, don't want you in the same room with me... . What is it that the money provides? Maybe it's just a clear exchange, especially if you are with someone that you don't like that much, somehow if they give to you, you can give to them. You've been compensated in a clear, clean way' (Annie Sprinkle, quoted by Chapkis 1997: 92).

16 Overall agrees: 'What is essential to prostitution is not sexual activity itself but the buying of sexual activity' (1992: 717; so also McCaghy and Hou (1991) on Taiwan; Rio (1991: 210) on the USA; Earls and David (1989) on male sex work). However, against Overall I agree with Shrage (1994) that sex work is not inherently sexist, racist, classist and ageist in all cultures (see also Overall 1994).

17 Given that socialism is the only viable alternative to capitalism at this time, the question of Marxism and sex work has had a steady stream of studies (Gil, Wang, Anderson and Lin 1994; Guy 1988; Henriot 1995; 1996; Hershatter 1989; 1996; Shrage 1996; Waters 1989).

18 This is to be distinguished from the literary representation of the courtesan as one who provides culture and excitement for males outside the home: she is therapist, psychiatrist and marriage sustainer, a venue for sexual experiment that the wife is not expected to provide or participate in.

19 To quote Annie, 'Maybe there's a little porn star in you. Maybe not. But I can tell you from a whole lot of experience that there's a lot of you in every porn star' (Sprinkle 1998: 121).

20 For Bell, in the work of Sprinkle and others (Gwendolyn, Veronica Vera, Janet Feindel, Scarlot Harlot, and Candida Royalle) the broader binary division of women into feminist/ mother/good girl and male-identified/slut/bad girl has been destabilized. 'It is in this destabilized space, the space in which the male-defined division of woman into madonna/ whore is already deconstructed, that any new philosophical theory of prostitution needs to find its point of departure' (1994b: 188). Williams (1993b: 181–8) traces this already in the 1981 porn film *Deep Inside Annie Sprinkle* (no longer available).

21 Once again the literature on sex work in the Ancient Near East and the Bible is extensive. See, for instance, Lerner (1986) and Schulte (1992).

22 Murphy (1995: 225) notes the 'erotic fashion' of wisdom's representation. To speak of both figures as 'values' of wisdom and foolishness (Domeris 1995) signals a nervous avoidance of such an erotics.

23 Indeed, McKane himself seems to give voice to a desire for male penetration. 'They (*lehabin, bina* in 1:2)', he pants, 'describe intellectual virtues of discrimination and penetration …' (McKane 1970: 264).

24 Often the two are taken as symbolic registers in order to talk about women in Ancient Israel and the Hebrew Bible (so Brenner 1995:51–6).

25 See the discussion in Yee (1995: 111–12) over multiple or single identities. Yee favours a single figure, the *zara*, or strange woman; so also Bellis (1994: 194). Murphy, however, regards her as a composite (1995: 225), as does Camp: 'the layering of different kinds of sexual misbehavior, as well as ritual offense, generates a portrait of idealized evil in its multiple dimensions' (1997: 93).

26 On 5:15–17, McKane writes, 'springs and channels or water equate with male sperm; not to be wasted' (1970: 319).

27 Fox (1994) usefully reminds us that other evil influences also appear, such as the evil man of Proverbs 2:12–15, who is paired with the strange woman in 2:16–19.

28 In an almost orgasmic moment, McKane writes that '[w]hat is envisaged [in 5:1–14] is an extremity of destitution and exhaustion which evokes an elemental, animal cry of anguish' (1970: 317).

29 Indeed, McKane (1970: 314) feels that the aura of the prostitute dominates the descriptive material in Proverbs 1–9.

30 McKane is not so keen on such a connection: 'The woman in 7.10f. invites the youth to take his fill of love until morning. She is interested in him for his virility, through which she can fulfil her service to Astarte. The young women of ch. 9 have an educational mission; they invite young men not to bed, but to school' (1970: 360). Bellis (1994: 195) sees only a stark contrast between the two figures; not so Camp (1997: 94), at least in terms of sex: 'whatever negative opposition is constructed in these texts between the good

woman and the bad, it is *not* an opposition based on sexual experience versus its negation'
(1997: 99).

31 McKane obtusely regards this as the depiction of 'Wisdom as Preacher,' especially in
1:20–33 (1970: 272), while for Daniel Williams, she is the 'town crier' (1994: 277). In a
similar vein, Lang (1986: 22–4) argues that here Wisdom is public life. At least Newsom
(1989: 156) notes the 'traces of the erotic' in the depiction of Wisdom; so also Camp
(1997: 99).

32 Yee (1995: 112–124) focuses on the speech itself as crucial, as that which seduces. Here
she follows Aletti (1977).

33 The images of 6:25 and 7:6–27 structure the very image of the prostitute in later writings
on sex workers. Mahood quotes the nineteenth century evangelical Tait, who notes the
temptation of prostitution:

> From boyhood to manhood his life is one continued fight against it … he
> cannot pass along the street in the evening without meeting with, and being
> accosted by women of the town at almost every step. Their fascinating smile –
> their artful and familiar conversation, are sure to attract his attention. The
> freedom with which they approach him, the affection and friendly manner in
> which they ask after his health and invite him to their lodgings, together with
> their handsome figure and beautiful appearance, are too much for any one
> whose conduct is not governed by powerful religious principles.
> (Mahood 1990: 72, quoted from W. Tait, *Magdalenism: An Inquiry into*
> *the Extent, Causes and Consequences of Prostitution in Edinburgh,*
> Edinburgh: P. Richards. 1840)

34 Shirley Wurst finds significant commonality between the two houses in her PhD (in
progress at the University of South Australia and graciously given to me in draft form):
they are woman's houses (*byth*), men are included, they are on the heights, woman is table
host, men are guests, and they are inclusive. She also traces the common characteristics of
the two women: they are assertive, self-defined, authoritative, life-givers, nurturers, teachers,
willingly share knowledge, are irrepressible, go out to meet people, honest and up-front,
seductive and attractive. My reading stays a little closer to textual intersections.

35 The depiction of Wisdom and the prostitute/foolish woman has echoes in the practices of
Athenian sex workers. They looked for clients in the agora and at the gates, played a
crucial role at symposia, where they partook of eating, games, philosophical talk and
public sex (see Keuls 1985: 160–8).

36 Lang (1986: 97–8) reads the strange woman as a prostitute but Wisdom as a goddess. He
does not seem to notice the transference between the two. Not so Yee: 'Both women are
described in dangerously similar terms; both speak perilously similar messages to beckon
the young man to their repective houses. However, … the speeches of '*iššâ zarâ* lead to
death, as Wisdom's call leads to life' (1995: 111). Camp also (1995: 134–8) notes the
duality of the two figures which are yet one.

37 Note the warning by Keuls (1985: 188–200) on the sentimentalization of the hetaira in
Greece through the legend of the wealthy and witty courtesan. Sprinkle also is ambivalent
about her evocation of the ancient spirits of the sacred prostitute: 'I make this shit up, but
then I find later that it is real' (quoted in Bell 1995: 35).

38 The mythological focus is marked among Scandinavian critics, beginning with Boström
in 1935. Apart from connecting the strange woman with Astarte, Burns (1995) suggests
that the man in Proverbs 7 is connected with Adonis, Melqart or Eshmun. Hadley (1995)
suggests that the construction of a female wisdom figure in the Bible functions as a late
literary compensation for the excision of goddesses from Israelite belief and practice.

39 Redressed a little in the recent study by McKeganey and Barnard (1996: 50–3)

40 Newsom quotes Toril Moi: 'It is this position that has enabled male culture sometimes to

vilify women as representing darkness and chaos, to view them as Lilith or the Whore of Babylon, and sometimes to elevate them as the representatives of a higher and purer nature, to venerate them as Virgins and Mothers of God' (Toril Moi, *Textual/Sexual Politics: Feminist Literary Theory*, London: Methuen, 1985: 167; Newsom 1989: 157). Van Dijk-Hemmes (Brenner and van Dijk-Hemmes 1993: 54) insists on the dominant 'androcentric discourse' of Proverbs 1–9. For an effort to locate the ideological issues of these chapters in post-exilic Judah, see Washington (1994).

5 EZEKIEL'S AXL, OR, ANARCHISM AND ECSTASY

1 Fourier (1772–1837) is strictly identified as a utopian socialist, although his ideas are distinctly anarchist and he strongly influenced Proudhon and Kropotkin.

2 Pierre-Joseph Proudhon (1809–65) worked as journeyman printer and then writer and revolutionary. He published more than forty works, left eleven volumes of notebooks, fourteen volumes of correspondence and many unpublished manuscripts.

3 Prince Peter Alexeivitch Kropotkin (1842–1921) broke away from his upper class situation in Russia to become a leading anarchist. After imprisonment in Russia and France and much travel, he settled in London in 1836, where he became the major theorist of anarchism for the next thirty years.

4 Auguste Vaillant, on 9 December 1893, hurled a bomb into the Chamber of Deputies in Paris. No one was killed, but he was executed.

5 François-Claudius Ravachol (1859–92) was executed after a series of murders and bombs in Paris, including bombs targeted at judges who had sentenced workers after the 1891 May Day demonstrations.

6 Emile Henry (1872–94) was executed for a bomb in the Café Terminus near Gare Saint-Lazarre that killed one person and injured nineteen.

7 I follow David Shumway in speaking of a 'cultural practice'. It is not exclusively records, lyrics, written music, videos, performers, listeners, clothes, appearance, attitudes – it is all of these things and more that come together to represent a way of life lived by those young people who choose to do so.

8 Weinstein argues that the eruption of heavy metal took place between 1969 and 1972, its crystallization between 1973 and 1975, a golden age from 1976 to 1979 and then diversification from 1983 (1991: 21). Such periodization is always open to suspicion.

9 Dan Rubey (1991: 879) notes that heavy metal as such is the most popular music for MTV viewers.

10 In this respect it carries on the class connection of rock and roll itself (see Frith 1981). Weinstein (1991: 66) notes a later influx of black and hispanic musicians.

11 The mix of heteroerotic and homoerotic imagery here is interesting in itself. According to Viegener, Axl Rose's dress and manner are identifiable derivatives of gay leather style (Viegener 1992: 125). See Garratt (1990: 402–3) on the ambiguous sexual construction of pop stars. Drukman (1995: 91) suggests that heavy metal video, like televised sports, both offers up the 'male spectacle for eroticization' and then disavows the gaze.

12 See especially the songs on *Appetite for Destruction* (1987).

13 On this see my *Novel Histories*, 1997, especially chapter 4. See also Rosemary Jackson's *Fanstasy: The Literature of Subversion* (1988).

14 Zimmerli, in a restrained manner, allows only 'a strangeness of psychic experience' (1979: 17) by someone who 'was overwhelmed by images and visions up to the point of actual physical emotional participation' (20), otherwise refusing to speak of ecstasy or possession, a refusal also found in Greenberg's commentary. Brownlee, in a moment of breathless insight, mentions the effects of 'trauma' (1986: 58), and an 'internal-emotional' state that coincides with Yahweh's 'internal-volitional' hand and the 'physical' sensation of the 'spirit-wind' (41).

15 The date of this piece should indicate that I am resurrecting a hoary thesis, one that I would like to redirect to literary construction of the prophet in the Hebrew Bible.

16 Is the command to use human dung to cook the food (4:12) intended to deal with this problem?

17 Others have suggested a physical disease such as catalepsy or mental illness (see the discussions in Eichrodt 1970: 83–4 and Zimmerli 1979: 17–18).

18 Although it is the association with symbolic magic that has bothered more than one commentator (see, for example, Eichrodt 1970: 81).

19 Reading the more difficult *Hif'il* participle of שמם instead of the often emended שׂם שׂי, the easier *pol'el* participle.

20 LXX has no comparable word for מר, prompting many commentators to omit it from translation. The sense remains the same: 'in the [angry] heat of my spirit'. So Zimmerli 1979: 94. Brownlee (1986: 36, 38) reads רם instead of מר, basing the emendation on the Hexaplaric μετέωρος 'in midair'. So: 'I soared aloft in the ecstasy of my spirit', yet Brownlee takes a low view of ecstasy.

21 Axl Rose also mentions that the Bible was 'shoved down my throat, and it really distorted my point of view' (Rose 1992b). Cooke (1936: 37) relates 3:1–3 to 2 Esdras 14:38–41, where Ezra drinks a cup 'full of something like water', but with 'a color like fire' (v. 39) with the effect of increased understanding, wisdom and memory.

22 The interviews with Axl Rose indicate something of his troubled psyche (Rose 1992a).

23 On the other hand's Curtis's (1984) McLuhanite analysis of rock music, with its strong technological determinism, leaves no room for any consideration of oppositional possibilities.

24 Straw argues against a heavy metal subculture, largely due to the suburban habitation of its audience, a situation that removes intermediary strata between groups and audiences that are needed to foster a subculture (club circuit, social marginality). Straw writes about the 1970s, and he admits the growth of such intermediary strata in the 1980s, including small-scale magazines, speciality stores and the paraphernalia of fandom.

25 See further Peterson and Berger (1990) and Stratton (1983) for a detailed study of the commercial business of rock music. The volume *Rock and Popular Music* as a whole attests to the intricate ways in which rock music is part of the complex web of capitalist society and politics.

26 A later development of this (Grossberg 1993) is to speak of the contradictory patterns of the 'mattering maps' that rock enables through its rhythms: a territorializing pattern is set over against deterritorializing 'lines of flight' which place rock outside the mainstream of everyday life. Born (1993: 281–8) attempts to use 'alterity' as a possible category for resistance.

6 PAWING THROUGH GARBAGE: ON THE DIALECTICS OF DYSTOPIA IN LAMENTATIONS AND THE STRUGATSKY BROTHERS

1 Highly controversial inside and outside the USSR and distinctly different from the book, *Stalker* picks up the last trip of Red Schuhart into the 'zone', turning the trip into an existential quest replete with Christian symbolism. Although Johnson and Petrie (1994: 141–2) argue that it carries over a good deal from the book, especially since the Strugatskys had a hand in the script, the general feeling, which I share, is that the film fails to convey the danger and alienness of the zone.

2 Gottwald (1993: 172) suggests that the voices operate as follows: lament 1 has the poet and lady Zion; lament 2 has the same voices, but Zion's is much more mute; lament 3 comes from the anonymous 'man'; lament 4 involves the poet and Zion, although Zion

speaks as a communal lament; and lament 5 is that of the community. See further Grossberg (1989: 88–9) who notes that the five personae do not correspond with the five laments.

3 Most commentators read the positive moment, or salvation/restoration, as something beyond or later than the text (so Linafelt 1995; Krasovec 1992). Helberg (1990), in a moment of conventional piety, argues that the poems indicate the negative effects of not having a living relationship with God, in terms of land, covenant and history; what is required then is a restoration of that relationship. Gottwald (1962: 47–62, 108–10) reads doom and hope in terms of 'tragic reversal' where the hope involves universal judgement, satisfaction of guilt, and end of the exile. By contrast, Dobbs-Allsopp states that 'it seems more likely that the poems of Lamentations were composed to give voice to the community's profound grief and to protest the injustice of the city's destruction and the people's suffering. Indeed if there is any hope in Lamentations, it lies in the book's eloquent protest' (1993: 94).

4 Many city-laments close with an appeal for restoration, and there are sections that assume, narrate and pray for the return of the deity. However in the Curse of Agade these themes are absent, like Lamentations. Agade, it is hoped, will not be restored: 'Agade is destroyed! Praise Inanna!' (Dobbs-Allsopp 1993: 94). For comparative material on the city-laments of Sumer and the *ersemmas* and *balags* of Babylon, see also Gwaltney (1991: 251–8).

5 My reading of psychology through Freud is a little less domesticated than that of Joyce (1993), who reads the clash of negative and positive images in terms of the psychological stages of bereavement (shock, control, regression, adaptation) and of dying (denial and isolation, anger, bargaining, depression, acceptance).

6 The sections, according to Westermann are: introduction (1); accusation against God (2–17a); personal complaint (17b–19); avowal of confidence (20–5).

7 Dobbs-Allsopp (1993: 75–90) argues that the weeping goddess of ancient Near Eastern city-laments is transferred to Jerusalem in Lamentations.

8 Dobbs-Allsopp compares the breakdown of social, religious, and political customs with ancient Near Eastern texts (1993: 73–5).

9 Commentators also lament the loss of what are read as the 'inhabitants' (Provan 1991: 111) or the 'young men', the community's hope for the future (Westermann 1994: 201), without noting the differences of class and wealth that the gold and sacred stones suggest. With an eye to class dynamics, Gottwald's reading is closer to mine: 'Chapter 4 as a whole lays bare the physical, sociopolitical, and moral fragility of the upper classes. Political and religious leaders failed equally. Perfidious prophets and priests are rejected as though they are lepers. The lamenting populace acknowledges their misplaced trust in political allies and in their own king' (1993: 170).

10 Is this a way to recast the negative images of a female Jerusalem subject to an aggressive male Yahweh?

11 Droin (1995) reads Lamentations in terms of catastrophe and anastrophe, the inversion of word order and of world order, so as to open up possibilities of a new wor(l)d.

12 Like most commentators, Gous (1996) is too confident that he knows what Yahweh is on about. Thus, in a study of Lamentations 2, which he reads with psychological categories, he traces the beginnings of a new 'cognitive chart' in which the national monuments are bypassed with a focus on God.

7 GRAVES OF CRAVING: FAST FOOD, OR, MANNA AND McDONALD'S

1 'Westie' is a very local term, designating an inhabitant of western Sydney. Used variously with pride and derision, it is primarily a class signifier, since western Sydney is the city's working class heartland, shunned by the middle class sectors of north and east and

championed by westies themselves. Parramatta is distinctly westie, as is Northmead. Class consciousness shows its presence in clothing, language, patterns of daily life, and, of course, eating habits.

2 This is not to say that it hasn't been tried. Ray Kroc (founding CEO of McDonald's): 'I've often said that I believe in God, family, and McDonald's – and in the office that order is reversed' (quoted in Leidner 1993a: 52–3).

3 Hamburger University, McDonald's training institute, teaches about 3,500 students every year, most taking the Advanced Operations Course. Upon completion they receive diplomas proclaiming them Doctors of Hamburgerology, often with a minor in Fries (Leidner 1993a: 57). Burger King's equivalent is Burger King University, formerly Whopper College (Reiter 1991: 70–1).

4 Every second study of fast food in general and McDonald's in particular feels obliged at the beginning to trot out the latest available figures of sales, profits, number of stores, percentage increase, food eating patterns, share of the market. In resisting such a trend, all that interests me is that there seems to be twice as many adult book stores as McDonald's.

5 My personal favourite is 'Fly Point Take Away', hard by the trawling run near Little Beach, about 200 km north of Sydney. Surviving against the odds, it continues to serve food even more unhealthy than Maccas. Much of this book was pondered there.

6 On manipulation of diet and taste see Kinsella (1982: 61, 64).

7 On the stereotyped and predigested nature of popular culture and fast food see the bland article by Kinsella (1982: 62, 64–6).

8 The work is, however, belated and still quite thin. Social scientific studies tend to prefer studies of manufacturing and production rather the service industry (so Leidner 1993b; Parcel and Sickmeier 1988: 44).

9 Ritzer (1996: 225, n. 255) disagrees, suggesting that people may merely accept McDonaldization as part of their work.

10 This study is concerned with the function of signs in fast food stores and the effect on ordering time and errors. It makes the astonishing finding that one sign produces an average of 23.82 seconds to order with .26 errors, while two signs lead to an average 6.48 seconds to order and .08 errors.

11 Burger King swears allegiance to VAST for its property decisions – visibility, accessibility, signage and traffic. Taco Bell professes FACT: fast food, accurate orders, cleanliness, and right temperature (Kasdan 1996).

12 For this reason, most of the studies on fast food have been quantitative, attempting to assess its success, economic impact, employee motivation and how it might be improved: thus Card and Krueger (1994) and Katz and Krueger (1992) are concerned with the minimum wage; Krueger (1991) with franchising; Ihlanfeldt and Young (1994) with incomes, wage variation, urban/suburban and racial differences; Van Giezen (1994) with employment patterns; Waldersee (1991) with management/employee relations; Waldersee and Luthans (1991) with the perenniel problem of employee motivation; Ekelund and Watson (1991) with the relation between income and time (convenience) in household meal production; Brown (1990) with the competition between restaurants and fast food; Fass (1995) with the comparison in the demand for fast food between poor (Haiti) and rich (USA) countries (they are the same!); Juni, Brannon and Roth (1988) with sexual preference/discrimination in service provision and customer preference for service; Schori (1996) with the use of the total image in order to maximize sales; and Wagner and Winett (1988) with the use of signs and flyers to get customers to reduce fat and increase a low-fat, high fibre diet (a self-defeating enterprise).

13 A colloquial Australian expression, denoting annoyance and anger.

14 Exodus 16 is curiously surrounded by water stories: the Re(e)d Sea before, and then the story of bitter water at Massah and Meribah (Exodus 17:1–7). A little like the coke one must have with a burger, perhaps? Historical critical efforts focus, as expected, on the origins and pieces of the story. For Van Seters (1994: 187–8), Exodus 16: 1a, 2–3, 4–7,

13b-15, 21, 27–31, 35a comprises the original J story which functions as an etiology for the sabbath, as well as a test of obedience. P modifies this, since it already has such an etiology in Genesis 1, and extends the miraculous.

15 Van Seters argues for two stories in Numbers 11, one of divine provision and the other of leadership (1994: 227–34). I deal with the leadership question later.

16 Culley (1990) sees two punishment stories: Numbers 11:1–3 concerns punishment by fire; Numbers 11:4–25 punishment by quails. The second has two variations, one through the 'apparent rescue' by the quails that becomes the punishment, and the other through the mitigation of the punishment by Moses.

17 Unions seem to share their opposition with old money, although the nature of the opposition differs: for unions, it is the denial of adequate worker representation, while for old money nostalgia for an artificial past has kept burger outlets out of Suffolk County, NY and Windsor County, VT (see Edmondson 1994).

18 In the USA, McDonald's employs more people that the steel industry (Gabriel 1985: 8). Writing in 1989, Wildavsky notes that many of the 18 million new jobs generated since the 1982 recession are in the fast food industry (1989: 31).

19 The benefits and drawbacks of jobs at McDonald's are debated by advocates such as the unknown writer in *The Futurist* (1985) and Wildavsky (1989) and opponents like Gabriel (1985), Van Giezen (1994) and Reiter (1991: 70–1, 164). The debate turns on issues such as job skills, turnover, satisfaction, union presence and whether the jobs are used as sources of extra cash or as main incomes. Of course, the crucial question is whether McDonald's will lead to salvation or doom.

20 McDonald's has not been without its own putrefaction scares. In the fall of 1976 the famous rumour began that McDonald's was adding worms to its hamburger meat. It was a media disaster for McDonald's, despite Ray Kroc's disavowel -'We couldn't afford to grind worms into our meat. Hamburgers cost a dollar and a half a pound, and night crawlers cost six dollars' (Love 1986: 358). In 1982 the federal Center for Disease Control linked rare bacteria and intestinal illness to McDonald's in the Miami area. As usual McDonald's defended this accusation vigorously.

21 This also means that the resurrection of Christ may be read as divine preservation of his body so that it may be eaten. To avoid putrefaction, God removes Jesus' body, but does this mean that the body is also cooked?

22 One would expect the same with the body of Christ, having been kept for some 2,000 years, but it seems that it may well have been cooked and preserved.

23 Note that disease reappears in the following story, the revolt of Miriam and Aaron (Numbers 12). Miriam's skin turns as white as snow – until she repents and is healed.

24 It seems that Yahweh, or at least a later version, may have a presence in contemporary fast food. For some time, the CEO of Domino's Pizza was a right-wing Catholic, supporting the right-to-life movement and establishing a conservative lay organization called Legatus ('Ambassador'). Of course, 'Domino' itself is Latin 'for the Lord' – Pizza for the Lord (see Baker 1994: 22).

25 It is also ironic that in some places McDonald's sets in train a whole different set of reactions, since it is regarded as a place of privilege, of the glowing promise of capitalism, for which one must pay more than other food stops. In these cases – the early Moscow McDonald's fell into this category – McDonald's mutates significantly from its basic form.

26 I am thinking of neither the 'post-hunger society' – the need to keep the mouth full while doing something else (Mort 1989: 18–19) – nor solving the world's food problems by fast food (Molitor 1984).

BIBLIOGRAPHY

Adam, Barry D. 1996. 'Structural Foundations of the Gay World', In *Queer Theory/Sociology*, ed. Steven Seidman. Twentieth-century Social Theory. Cambridge, MA: Blackwell, pp. 111–26.

Adorno, Theodor. 1990. 'On Popular Music', in *On Record: Rock, Pop, and the Written Word*, eds Simon Frith and Andrew Goodwin. London: Routledge, pp. 301–14.

Ahearne, Jeremy. 1995. *Michel de Certeau: Interpretation and Its Other*. Cambridge, England: Polity.

Aichele, George, and Tina Pippin, eds. 1992. *Semeia* 60. *Fantasy and the Bible*. Atlanta, GA: Scholar's Press.

———. 1997. *The Monstrous and the Unspeakable*. Playing the Text, 1. Sheffield: Sheffield Academic Press.

———. 1998. *Violence, Utopia and the Kingdom of God: Fantasy and Ideology in the Bible*. London: Routledge.

Aletti, J. N. 1977. 'Séduction et Parole en Proverbs I–IX', *Vetus Testamentum* 27:129–44.

Allen, Jeanne. 1988. 'Looking Through *Rear Window*: Hitchcock's Traps and Lures of Heterosexual Romance', In *Female Spectators: Looking at Film and Television*, ed. E. Deidre Pribram. Questions for Feminism. London: Verso, pp. 31–44.

Allen, Jeanne, and R. Barton Palmer. 1986. 'Jeanne T. Allen Responds to R. Barton Palmer's "The Metafictional Hitchcock: The Experience of Viewing and the Viewing of Experience in *Rear Window* and *Psycho*"', *Cinema Journal* 25 (Summer):54–8.

Allen, Mike, Dave D'Alessio, and Keri Brezgel. 1995. 'A Meta-analysis Summarizing the Effects of Pornography, II: Aggression After Exposure', *Human Communication Research* 22 (December):258–83.

Ames, Sanford. 1988. 'Fast Food/Quick Lunch: Crews, Burroughs and Pynchon', In *Literary Gastronomy*, ed. David Bevan. Rodopi Perspectives on Modern Literature 1. Amsterdam: Rodopi, pp. 19–27.

Arcand, Bernard. 1993. *The Jaguar and the Anteater: Pornography Degree Zero*. Trans. Wayne Grady. London and New York: Verso.

Attali, Jacques. 1977. *Bruits: essai sur l'économie politique de la musique*. Paris: Presses Universitaires de France.

———. 1985. *Noise: the Political Economy of Music*. Trans. Brian Massumi, foreword by Fredric Jameson, afterword by Susan McClary. Theory and History of Literature, vol. 16. Minneapolis: University of Minnesota Press.

Axlbio.html. 1997. Biography of Axl Rose. http://www.students.uiuc.edu/~t-gray/axlbio.html

Babington, B., and P. W. Evans. 1993. *Biblical Epics: Sacred Narrative in the Hollywood Cinema*. Manchester: Manchester University Press.

Babuscio, Jack. 1977. 'Camp and the Gay Sensibility', In *Gays and Film*, ed. Richard Dyer. London: British Film Institute, pp. 40–57.

Bach, Alice, ed. 1996. *Semeia 74. Biblical Glamour and Hollywood Glitz*. Atlanta, GA: Scholar's Press.

Baker, Ross. 1994. 'Fast Food Conspiracies: Demogaffes', *American Demographics* 16 (May):22–3.

Bakhtin, Mikhail Mikhailovich. 1984. *Rabelais and His World*. trans. Hélène Iswolsky. Foreword by Krystyna Pomorska. Prologue by Michael Holquist. Midlands Book. Bloomington, IA: Indiana University Press.

Bal, Mieke. 1988. *Death and Dissymetry: The Politics of Coherence in the Book of Judges*. Chicago, IL: Chicago University Press.

——. 1993. 'A Body of Writing: Judges 19', In *A Feminist Companion to Judges*, ed. Athalya Brenner. The Feminist Companion to the Bible 4. Sheffield: Sheffield Academic Press, pp. 208–30.

Balzer, Harry. 1993. 'The Ultimate Cooking Appliance', *American Demographics* 15 (July): 40–4.

Bannon, Barbara M. 1985. 'Double, Double, Toil and Trouble', *Literature Film Quarterly* 13(1):56–65.

Barry, Kathleen. 1979. *Female Sexual Slavery*. Englewood Cliffs, NJ: Prentice Hall.

——. 1991. 'Women for Hire', Review. *American Journal of Sociology* 96 (May):1606–7.

——. 1995. *The Prostitution of Sexuality*. New York: New York University Press.

Barton, Sabrina. 1991. '"Crisscross": Paranoia and Projection in *Strangers on a Train*', *Camera Obscura* 25–6 (January–May):75–100.

Bauso, Thomas M. 1991. '*Rope*: Hitchcock's Unkindest Cut', In *Hitchcock's Rereleased Films: From Rope to Vertigo*, eds Walter Raubicheck and Walter Srebnick, foreword by Andrew Sarris. Contemporary Film and Television Series. Detroit, MI: Wayne State University Press, pp. 226–39.

Beijing Review. 1985. 'Fast-food Joint Ventures Set Up', *Beijing Review* 28 (April 1):29.

Bekkencamp, Jonneke, and Fokkelien van Dijk-Hemmes. 1993. 'The Canon of the Old Testament and Women's Cultural Traditions', In *A Feminist Companion to the Song of Songs*, ed. Athalya Brenner. The Feminist Companion to the Bible 1. Sheffield: Sheffield Academic Press, pp. 67–85.

Bell, Shannon. 1994a. 'Feminist Ejaculations', In *Living with Contradictions: Controversies in Feminist Social Ethics*, ed. Alison M. Jaggar. Boulder, CO and Oxford: Westview, pp. 529–36.

——. 1994b. *Reading, Writing and Rewriting the Prostitute Body*. Bloomington, IL and Indianapolis: Indiana University Press.

——. 1995. *Whore Carnival*. Brooklyn, NY: Autonomedia.

Bellis, Alice Ogden. 1994. *Helpmates, Harlots, and Heroes: Women's Stories in the Hebrew Bible*. Louisville, KY: Westminster/John Knox.

Bellour, Raymond. 1986. 'Psychosis, Neurosis, Perversion', trans. Nancy Huston, In *A Hitchcock Reader*, eds Marshall Deutelbaum and Leland Poague. Ames: Iowa State University Press, pp. 311–31.

Bennett, Tony, Simon Frith, Lawrence Grossberg, John Shepherd and Graeme Turner (eds). 1993. *Rock and Popular Music: Politics, Policies, Institutions*. London and New York: Routledge.

Bensinger, Terralee. 1992. 'Lesbian Pornography: The Re/making of (a) Community', *Discourse: Journal for Theoretical Studies in Media and Culture* 15 (Fall): 69–93.

Berger, Ronald J., Patricia Searles, and Charles E. Cottle. 1991. *Feminism and Pornography*. Westport, CT: Praeger.

Bernheimer, Charles. 1989. *Figures of Ill Repute: Representing Prostitution in Nineteenth-century France*. Cambridge, MA: Harvard University Press.

Berry, Chris, and Annamarie Jagose. 1996. 'Australia Queer: Editors' Introduction', *Meanjin* 55(1):5–11.

Blenkinsopp, Joseph. 1990. *Ezekiel*. Interpretation: a Bible Commentary for Teaching and Preaching. Louisville, KY: John Knox.

Blonsky, Marshall. 1992. *American Mythologies*. Oxford: Oxford University Press.

Blumenthal, David R. 1995. 'Where God is Not: The Book of Esther and Song of Songs', *Judaism* 44:80–93.

Boer, Roland. 1996a. *Jameson and Jeroboam*. Semeia Studies. Atlanta, GA: Scholar's Press.

——. 1996b. 'Green Ants and Gibeonites: B. Wongar, Joshua 9, and Some Problems of Postcolonialism', *Semeia* 75:129–52.

——. 1997. *Novel Histories: The Fiction of Biblical Criticism*. Playing the Text, 2. Sheffield: Sheffield Academic Press.

——. forthcoming. 'The Resurrection Engine of Michel de Certeau', *Paragraph*.

Boles, Jacqueline, and Kirk W. Elifson. 1994. 'Sexual Identity and HIV: The Male Prostitute', *The Journal of Sex Research* 31(1):39–46.

Boling, Robert G. 1975. *Judges: Introduction, Translation and Commentary*. The Anchor Bible. Garden City, NY: Doubleday.

Boose, Lynda E. 1994. 'The 1599 Bishops' Ban, Elizabethan Pornography, and the Sexualization of the Jacobean Stage', In *Enclosure Acts: Sexuality, Property, and Culture in Early Modern England*, eds Richard Burt and John Michael Archer. Ithaca, NY: Cornell University Press, pp. 185–200.

Born, Georgina,1993. 'Afterword: Music Policy, Aesthetic and Social Difference', In *Rock and Popular Music: Politics, Policies, Institutions*. eds Tony Bennett, Simon Frith, Lawrence Grossberg, John Shepherd and Graeme Taylor. Culture: Policies and Politics. London and New York: Routledge, pp. 266–92.

Bosshard-Nepustil, Erich. 1996. 'Zu Struktur und Sachprofil Des Hohenlieds', *Biblische Notizen* 81:45–71.

Boswell, John. 1980. *Christianity, Social Tolerance and Homosexuality: Gay People in Western Europe from the Beginning of the Christian Era to the Fourteenth Century*. Chicago, IL: University of Chicago Press.

——. 1995. *Same-Sex Unions in Premodern Europe*. New York: Vintage.

Boughton, Lynne, C. 1992. 'Biblical Texts and Homosexuality: A Response to John Boswell', *Irish Theological Quarterly* 58:141–53.

Boyarin, Daniel. 1990. 'The Song of Songs: Lock or Key? Intertextuality, Allegory and Midrash', In *The Book and the Text: The Bible and Literary Theory*, ed. Regina Schwartz. Oxford: Blackwell, pp. 214–30.

Boyer, Debra. 1989. 'Male Prostitution and Homosexual Identity', *Journal of Homosexuality* 17(1–2):151–84.

Brammer, Marsanne. 1992. 'Thinking Practice: Michel de Certeau and the Theorization of Mysticism', *Diacritics* 22 (Summer):26–37.

Bravmann, Scott. 1996. 'Postmodernism and Queer Identities', In *Queer Theory/sociology*, ed. Steven Seidman. Twentieth-century Social Theory. Cambridge, MA: Blackwell, pp. 333–61.

Bredbeck, Gregory W. 1996. 'Troping the Light Fantastic: Representing Disco Then and Now', *GLQ: A Journal of Lesbian and Gay Studies* 3(1):71–107.

177

Brenner, Athalya. 1989. *The Song of Songs*. Old Testament Guides. Sheffield: JSOT Press.

——, ed. 1993a. *A Feminist Companion to the Song of Songs*. The Feminist Companion to the Bible 1. Sheffield: Sheffield Academic Press.

——. 1993b. 'To See is to Assume: Whose Love is Celebrated in the Song of Songs', *Biblical Interpretation* 1:266–84.

——. 1993c. '"Come Back, Come Back the Shulammite" (Song of Songs 7.1–10): A Parody of the Waṣf Genre', In *A Feminist Companion to the Song of Songs*, ed. Athalya Brenner. The Feminist Companion to the Bible 1. Sheffield: JSOT Press, pp. 234–57.

——. 1995. 'On Prophetic Propaganda and the Politics of "love": the Case of Jeremiah', In *A Feminist Companion to the Later Prophets*, ed. Athalya Brenner. The Feminist Companion to the Bible 8. Sheffield: Sheffield Academic Press, pp. 256–74.

——. 1996. 'Pornoprophetics Revisited: Some Additional Reflections', *Journal for the Study of the Old Testament* 70:63–86.

Brenner, Athalya, and Fokkelein van Dijk-Hemmes. 1993. *On Gendering Texts: Female and Male Voices in the Hebrew Bible*. Biblical Interpretation Series 1. Leiden: E. J. Brill.

Brigman, William E. 1983. 'Pornography as Political Expression', *Journal of Popular Culture* 17 (Fall):129–34.

British Social Biology Council. 1955. *Women of the Streets: A Sociological Study of the Common Prostitute*, ed. C. H. Rolph. London: Secker & Warburg.

Brooks, Peter. 1980. 'The Mark of the Beast: Prostitution, Melodrama, and Narrative', *New York Literary Forum* 7:125–40.

Brown, Douglas M. 1990. 'The Restaurant and Fast Food Race: Who's Winning?' *Southern Economic Journal* 56 (April):984–95.

Brownlee, William H. 1986. *Ezekiel 1–19*. Word Biblical Commentary. Waco, TX: Word Books.

Brueggemann, Walter. 1993. 'Narrative Coherence and Theological Intentionality in 1 Samuel 18', *Catholic Biblical Quarterly* 55:225–43.

Buchanan, Ian. 1997. 'de Certeau and Cultural Studies', *New Formations* 31:175–88.

Burns, John Barclay. 1995. 'Proverbs 7,6–27: Vignettes from the Cycle of Astarte and Adonis', *Scandinavian Journal of the Old Testament* 9:20–36.

Burston, Paul. 1995. *What Are You Looking At? Queer Sex, Style, and Cinema*. London and New York: Cassell.

Butler, Judith. 1990. *Gender Trouble: Feminism and the Subversion of Identity*. New York: Routledge.

——. 1991. 'Imitation and Gender Insubordination', In *Inside/Out: Lesbian Theories, Gay Theories*, ed. Diana Fuss. New York: Routledge, 13–31.

——. 1993. *Bodies That Matter: On the Discursive Limits of 'Sex'*. New York and London: Routledge.

——. 1994. 'Against Proper Objects', *Differences: A Journal of Feminist Cultural Studies* 6 (Summer–Fall):1–26.

Buxton, David. 1990. 'Rock Music, the Star System, and the Rise of Consumerism'. In *On Record: Rock, Pop, and the Written Word*, eds Simon Frith and Andrew Goodwin. London: Routledge, pp. 427–40.

Cameron, Deborah. 1992. 'Pornography: What is the Problem?' *Critical Quarterly* 34 (Spring):3–11.

Camp, Claudia. 1995. 'Wise and Strange: An Interpretation of the Female Imagery in Proverbs in Light of Trickster Mythology', In *A Feminist Companion to Wisdom Literature*, ed. Athalya Brenner. The Feminist Companion to the Bible 9. Sheffield: Sheffield Academic Press, pp. 131–56.

——. 1997. 'Woman Wisdom and the Strange Woman: Where is Power to Be Found?' In *Reading Bibles, Writing Bodies: Identity and the Book*, eds Timothy K. Beal and David M. Gunn. Biblical Limits. London and New York: Routledge, pp. 85–112.

Card, David, and Alan B. Krueger. 1994. 'Minimum Wages and Employment: A Case Study of the Fast-food Industry in New Jersey and Pennsylvania', *American Economic Review* 84 (September):772–93.

Carroll, Robert P. 1995. 'Desire Under the Terebinths: On Pornographic Representation in the Prophets – a Response', In *A Feminist Companion to the Latter Prophets*, ed. Athalya Brenner. The Feminist Companion to the Bible 8. Sheffield: Sheffield Academic Press, pp. 275–307.

——. 1996. 'Whorusalamin: A Tale of Three Cities as Three Sisters', In *On Reading Prophetic Texts: Gender Specific and Related Studies in Memory of Fokkelein van Dijk-Hemmes*, eds Bob Becking and Meindert Dijkstra. Biblical Interpretation Series 18. Leiden: E. J. Brill, pp. 67–82.

Carson, Diane. 1986. 'The Nightmare World of Hitchcock's Women', *Michigan Academician* 18 (Summer):349–56.

Chambers, Ross. 1994–5. 'Reading and Being Read: Irony and Critical Practice in Cultural Studies', *The Minnesota Review* 43–4 (Fall–Spring):113–30.

Champagne, John. 1991. 'Interrupted Pleasure: A Foucauldian Reading of Hard Core/a Hard Core (Mis)reading of Foucault', *Boundary 2* 18 (Spring):181–206.

Chapkis, Wendy. 1997. *Live Sex Acts: Women Performing Erotic Labor*. New York: Routledge.

Childress, Steven Alan. 1991. 'Reel "Rape Speech": Violent Pornography and the Politics of Harm', *Law and Society Review* 25(1):177–214.

Chow, Rey. 1993. 'Listening Otherwise, Music Miniaturized: A Different Type of Question About Revolution'. In *The Cultural Studies Reader*, ed. Simon During. London and New York: Routledge, pp. 382–99.

Clover, Carol. 1993. 'Introduction', In *Dirty Looks: Women, Pornography, Power*, eds Pamela Church Gibson and Roma Gibson. London: BFI, pp. 1–4.

Cohen, Keith. 1989. 'Psycho: The Suppression of Female Desire (and Its Return)', In *Reading Narrative: Form, Ethics, Ideology*, ed. James Phelan. Columbus: Ohio State University, pp. 147–61.

Cohen, Paula Marantz. 1994. 'The Ideological Transformation of Conrad's *The Secret Agent* Into Hitchcock's *Sabotage*', *Literature Film Quarterly* 22(3):199–209.

——. 1995. *Alfred Hitchcock: The Legacy of Victorianism*. Lexington, KY: University Press of Kentucky.

Connelly, Mark Thomas. 1980. *The Response to Prostitution in the Progressive Era*. Chapel Hill, NC: University of North Carolina Press.

Cooke, G. A. 1936. *A Critical and Exegetical Commentary on the Book of Ezekiel*. The International Critical Commentary. Edinburgh: T. & T. Clark.

Cooke, Lez. 1990. 'Hitchcock and the Mechanics of Cinematic Suspense', In *Twentieth-Century Suspense: The Thriller Comes of Age*, ed. Clive Bloom. Insights. New York: St. Martin's, pp. 189–202.

Corber, Robert J. 1991. 'Reconstructing Homosexuality: Hitchcock and the Homoerotics of Spectatorial Pleasure', *Discourse: Journal for Theoretical Studies in Media and Culture* 13 (Spring–Summer):58–82.

——. 1993. *In the Name of National Security: Hitchcock, Homophobia, and the Political Construction of Gender in Postwar America*. New Americanists. Durham, NC: Duke University Press.

Corbin, Alain. 1990. *Women for Hire: Prostitution and Sexuality in France After 1850*. Trans. Alan Sheridan. Cambridge, MA: Harvard University Press.

Cotterell, Peter. 1996. 'The Great Song: Some Linguistic Considerations', *Bible Translator* 47:101–8.

Cowan, Gloria, and Kerri F. Dunn. 1994. 'What Themes in Pornography Lead to Perceptions of the Degradation of Women?' *The Journal of Sex Research* 31(1):11–21.

Crawford, Franklin. 1992. 'Fried Chicken Still Rules the Roost', *American Demographics* 14 (July):17.

Creekmur, Corey K., and Alexander Doty, eds. 1995. *Out in Culture: Gay, Lesbian,and Queer Essays on Popular Culture*. Series Q. Durham, NC: Duke University Press.

Culley, Robert C. 1990. 'Five Tales of Punishment in the Book of Numbers', In *Text and Tradition: The Hebrew Bible and Folklore*, ed. Susan Niditch. Semeia Studies. Atlanta, GA: Scholar's Press, pp. 25–34.

Curtis, James M. 1984. 'Toward a Sociotechnological Interpretation of Popular Music in the Electronic Age'. *Technology and Culture* 25 (January): 91–102.

Daniels, Kay. 1984. 'Introduction', In *So Much Hard Work: Women and Prostitution in Australian History*, ed. Kay Daniels. Sydney: Fontana/Collins, pp. 1–14.

Davies, Chris Lawe. 1993. 'Aboriginal Rock Music: Space and Place'. In *Rock and Popular Music: Politics, Policies, Institutions*. eds Tony Bennett, Simon Frith, Lawrence Grossberg, John Shepherd and Graeme Turner. Culture: Policies and Politics. London and New York: Routledge, pp. 249–65.

Davis, Nanette J. 1993. 'Preface', In *Prostitution: An International Handbook on Trends, Problems, and Policies*, ed. Nanette J. Davis. Westport, CT: Greenwood, vii–xiii.

Dawson, Tim. 1992. 'Quick Bucks from Fast Food', *New Statesman and Society* 5 (January 31):20–1.

Dean, Tim. 1993. 'Transsexual Identification, Gender Performance Theory, and the Politics of the Real', *Literature and Psychology* 39(4):1–25.

de Certeau, Michel. 1984. *The Practice of Everyday Life*. Trans. Steven Rendall. Berkeley, Los Angeles and London: University of California Press.

——. 1987. *La Faiblesse de Croire*, ed. Luce Giard. Collection Esprit/Seuil. Paris: Éditions Du Seuil.

——. 1988. *The Writing of History*. Trans. Tom Conley. New York: Columbia University Press.

——. 1992. *The Mystic Fable, Volume One: The Sixteenth and Seventeenth Centuries*. Trans. Michael B. Smith. Religion and Postmodernism. Chicago, IL: University of Chicago Press.

——. 1994. *La Culture Au Pluriel*, ed. Luce Giard. 2nd edition Paris: Éditions Du Seuil.

——. 1997a. *The Capture of Speech and Other Political Writings*. Trans. and afterword by Tom Conley. ed. and introduction by Luce Giard. Minneapolis: University of Minnesota Press.

——. 1997b. *Culture in the Plural*. Trans. and afterword by Tom Conley. ed. and introduction by Luce Giard. Minneapolis: University of Minnesota Press.

de Certeau, Michel, and Jean-Marie Domenach. 1974. *Le Christianisme éclaté*. Paris: Éditions Du Seuil.

de Certeau, Michel, Jacques Revel, and Dominique Julia. 1986. 'The Beauty of the Dead: Nisard', In *Heterologies: Discourse on the Other*, trans. Brian Massumi, foreword by Wlad Godzich. Theory and History of Literature, vol. 17. Minneapolis: University of Minnesota Press, pp. 119–36.

Deckers, M. 1993. 'The Structure of the Song of Songs and the Centrality of *nepes*', In *A Feminist Companion to the Song of Songs*, ed. Athalya Brenner. The Feminist Companion to the Bible 1. Sheffield: Sheffield Academic Press, pp. 172–96.

DeCurtis, Anthony. 1991. 'Introduction: The Sanctioned Power of Rock & Roll'. In *Rock & Roll and Culture*, ed. Anthony DeCurtis. Durham, NC: Duke University Press.

DeJean, Joan. 1993. 'The Politics of Pornography: L'École Des Filles', In *The Invention of Pornography: Obscenity and the Origins of Modernity, 1500–1800*, ed. Lynn Hunt. New York: Zone Books, pp. 109–24.

De Lauretis, Teresa. 1991. 'Queer Theory: Lesbian and Gay Sexualities: An Introduction', *Differences: A Journal of Feminist Cultural Studies* 3(2):iii–xviii.

Deleuze, Gilles, and Félix Guattari. 1987. *A Thousand Plateaus: Capitalism and Schizophrenia*. Trans. and foreword by Brain Massumi. Minneapolis: University of Minnesota Press.

De Zalduondo, Barbara O. 1991. 'Prostitution Viewed Cross-culturally: Toward Recontextualizing Sex Work in AIDS Intervention Research', *The Journal of Sex Research* 28 (May):223–48.

Dobbs-Allsopp, F. W. 1993. *Weep, O Daughter of Zion: A Study of the City-lament Genre in the Hebrew Bible*. Biblica et Orentalia, 44. Roma: Editrice Pontificio Istituto Biblico.

Domeris, W. R. 1995. 'Shame and Honour in Proverbs: Wise Women and Foolish Men', *Old Testament Essays*:86–102.

Doty, Alexander. 1993. *Making Things Perfectly Queer: Interpreting Mass Culture*. Minneapolis: University of Minnesota.

———. 1995. 'There's Something Queer Here', In *Out in Culture: Gay, Lesbian,and Queer Essays on Popular Culture*, eds Corey K. Creekmur and Alexander Doty. Series Q. Durham, NC: Duke University Press, pp. 71–90.

Dowsett, Gary. 1996. 'What is Sexuality? a Bent Answer to a Straight Question', *Meanjin* 55(1):16–29.

Droin, Jean-Marc. 1995. *Le Livre de Lamentations*. 'Comment?' Une traduction et un commentaire. Geneva: Labor et Fides.

Drukman, Steven. 1995. 'The Gay Gaze, or Why I Want my MTV', In *A Queer Romance: Lesbians, Gay Men, and Popular Culture*. eds Paul Burston and Colin Richardson. London and New York: Routledge, pp. 81–95.

Dudash, Tawnya. 1997. 'Peepshow Feminism', In *Whores and Other Feminists*, ed. Jill Nagle. London and New York: Routledge, pp. 98–118.

Dumoulin, Pierre. 1994. *Entre la Manne et L'Euchariste: Etude de Sg 16,15–17,1a*. AnBib 132. Rome: PBI.

Durbin, Jen. 1996. 'Confessions of a Feminist Porn Teacher', In *Tales from the Clit: A Female Experience of Pornography*, ed. Cherie Matrix, for Feminists Against Censorship. Edinburgh: AK Press, pp. 52–9.

Durgnat, Raymond. 1974. *The Strange Case of Alfred Hitchcock: Or, The Plain Man's Hitchcock*. London: Faber & Faber.

Dworkin, Andrea. 1981. *Pornography: Men Possessing Women*. New York: Perigree.

Dyer, Richard. 1990. 'In Defense of Disco'. In *On Record: Rock, Pop, and the Written Word*. eds Simon Frith and Andrew Goodwin. London: Routledge, pp. 410–18.

———. 1991. 'Believing in Fairies: The Author and the Homosexual', In *Inside/Out: Lesbian Theories, Gay Theories*, ed. Diana Fuss. New York: Routledge, pp. 185–201.

———. 1993. 'Rock – the Last Guy You'd Have Figured?' In *You Tarzan: Masculinity, Movies and Men*, eds Pat Kirkham and Janet Thumim. New York: St. Martin's, p. 27–34.

Earls, Christopher M., and Helene David. 1989. 'A Psychosocial Study of Male Prostitution', *Archives of Sexual Behavior* 18 (October):401–19.

Ebert, Teresa L. 1996. 'The Matter of Materialism', In *The Material Queer: A Lesbigay Cultural Studies Reader*, ed. Donald Morton. Boulder, CO: Westview, 352–61.

Economist (The). 1984a. 'Fast Food: Vatburger to Go', *The Economist* 292 (July 7):62.

———. 1984b. 'Take Away Olé', *The Economist* 292 (September 22):72.

——. 1988a. 'Sweet and Sour Pizza to Go', *The Economist* 306 (March 5):72.

——. 1988b. 'McComrades', *The Economist* 307 (April 16):54.

——. 1989a. 'Pushkin, Coke and Fries', *The Economist* 313 (November 18):44.

——. 1989b. 'Teriyaki McBurger', *The Economist* 311 (April 29):64.

——. 1990. 'Fast-food Wars: Drive In, Run 'em Over', *The Economist* 314 (February 17): 88–90.

——. 1993. 'Big Mac's Counter Attack',*The Economist* 329 (November 13):69–70.

Ecstavasia, Audrey. 1993. 'Fucking (with Theory) for Money: Toward an Introduction of Escort Prostitution', In *Essays in Postmodern Culture*, eds Eyal Amiran and John Unworth. New York: Oxford University Press, pp. 173–98.

Edelman, Lee. 1995. 'Piss Elegant: Freud, Hitchcock, and the Micturating Penis', *GLQ: A Journal of Lesbian and Gay Studies* 2(1–2): 149–77.

Edmondson, Brad. 1994. 'Burger Breaks', *American Demographics* 16 (July):60.

Eichrodt, Walther. 1970. *Ezekiel: A Commentary*. Old Testament Library. London: SCM.

Einsedel, Edna F. 1989. 'Social Science and Public Policy: Looking at the 1986 Commission on Pornography', In *For Adult Users Only: The Dilemma of Violent Pornography*, eds Susan Gubar and Joan Hoff. Everywoman: Studies in History, Literature, and Culture. Bloomington: Indiana University Press, pp. 87–107.

Ekelund, Robert B., Jr., and John Keith Watson. 1991. 'Restaurant Cuisine, Fast Food and Ethnic Edibles: An Empirical Note on Household Meal Production', *Kyklos* 44(4):613–27.

Ellis, Richard. 1988. 'Disseminating Desire: Grove Press and "The End(s) of Obscenity"', In *Perspectives on Pornography: Sexuality in Film and Literature*, eds Gary Day and Clive Bloom. Houndmills, England: Macmillan, pp. 26–43.

Ericsson, Lars O. 1980. 'Charges Against Prostitution: An Attempt at a Philosophical Assessment', *Ethics* 90 (April):335–66.

Evans, Caroline, and Lorraine Gamman. 1995. 'The Gaze Revisited, or Reviewing Queer Viewing', In *A Queer Romance: Lesbians, Gay Men, and Popular Culture*, eds Paul Burston and Colin Richardson. London and New York: Routledge, pp. 13–56.

Exum, J. Cheryl. 1973. 'A Literary and Structural Analysis of the Song of Songs', *Zeitschrift für die Alttestamentliche Wissenschaft* 85:47–79.

——. 1993. *Fragmented Women: Feminist (Sub)versions of Biblical Narratives*. Journal for the Study of the Old Testament Supplement Series 163. Sheffield: Sheffield Academic Press.

——. 1995. 'The Ethics of Biblical Violence Against Women', In *The Bible in Ethics: The Second Sheffield Colloquium*, eds John W. Rogerson, Margaret Davies, and M. Daniel Carrol. Journal for the Study of the Old Testament Supplement Series 207. Sheffield: Sheffield Academic Press, pp. 248–71.

——. 1996. *Plotted, Shot, and Painted: Cultural Representations of Biblical Women*. Gender, Culture, Theory 3. Sheffield: Sheffield Academic Press.

Fabian, Cosi. 1997. 'The Holy Whore: A Woman's Gateway to Power', In *Whores and Other Feminists*, ed. Jill Nagle. London and New York: Routledge, pp. 44–54.

Falk, Marcia. 1993a. *The Song of Songs: A New Translation*. San Francisco, CA: HarperSanFrancisco.

——. 1993b. 'The *wasf*', In *A Feminist Companion to the Song of Songs*, ed. Athalya Brenner. The Feminist Companion to the Bible 1. Sheffield: Sheffield Academic Press, pp. 225–34.

Fass, Simon M. 1995. 'Fast Food in Development', *World Development* 23 (September): 1555–73.

Faust, Beatrice. 1980. *Women, Sex and Pornography: A Controversial and Unique Study*. New York: Macmillan.

Feminists Against Censorship. 1991. *Pornography and Feminism: The Case Against Censorship*, eds Gillian Rodgerson and Elizabeth Wilson. London: Lawrence & Wishart.

Ferguson, Frances. 1991. 'Sade and the Pornographic Legacy', *Representations* 36 (Fall):1–21.

Ferrara, Patricia. 1985. 'Through Hitchcock's *Rear Window* Again', *New Orleans Review* 12 (Fall):21–30.

Fewell, Danna Nolan, and David M. Gunn. 1993. *Gender, Power, and Promise: The Subject of the Bible's First Story*. Nashville, TN: Abingdon.

Findlen, Paula. 1993. 'Humanism, Politics and Pornography in Renaissance Italy', In *The Invention of Pornography: Obscenity and the Origins of Modernity, 1500–1800*, ed. Lynn Hunt. New York: Zone Books, pp. 49–108.

Finn, Geraldine. 1996. *Why Althusser Killed His Wife: Essays on Discourse and Violence*. Society/Religion//Religion/Society. Atlantic Highlands, NJ: Humanities Press.

Fisher, William A., and Guy Grenier. 1994. 'Violent Pornography, Antiwoman Thoughts, and Antiwoman Acts: In Search of Reliable Effects', *The Journal of Sex Research* 31(1):23–38.

Flanagan, Bill. 1992. 'Shadow Boxing with Axl Rose'. Interview in *Musician* (June). http://www.students.uiuc.edu/~t-gray/music92.html

Foster, R. Spencer, Michael G. Aamodt, James A. Bodenmiller, Jeffrey G. Rodgers, Robert C. Kovach, and Devon A. Bryan. 1988. 'Effect of Menu Sign Position on Customer Ordering Times and Number of Food-Ordering Errors', *Environment and Behavior* 20 (March):200–10.

Foucault, Michel. 1990. *The History of Sexuality. Volume 1: An Introduction*. Trans. Robert Hurley. Harmondsworth: Penguin.

Fourier, Charles. 1971. *The Utopian Vision of Charles Fourier*, eds Jonathan Beecher and Richard Bienvenu. Boston, MA: Beacon.

Fox, Michael V. 1985. *The Song of Songs and Ancient Egyptian Love Songs*. Madison, WI: University of Wisconsin Press.

——. 1994. 'The Pedagogy of Proverbs 2', *Journal of Biblical Literature* 113:233–43.

Frappier-Mazur, Lucienne. 1993. 'Truth and the Obscene Word in Eighteenth-century French Pornography', In *The Invention of Pornography: Obscenity and the Origins of Modernity, 1500–1800*, ed. Lynn Hunt. New York: Zone Books, pp. 203–21.

Freeman, Paul. 1997. *Ian Roberts: Finding Out*. Sydney: Random House.

Freud, Sigmund. 1973. *The Pelican Freud Library*. Vol. 1. *Introductory Lectures on Psychoanalysis*. Trans. James Strachey. eds James Strachey and Angela Richards. Harmondsworth: Penguin.

Frith, Simon. 1981. '"The Magic That Can Set You Free": The Ideology of Folk and the Myth of the Rock Community'. *Popular Music* 1: 159–68.

——. 1990. 'Afterthoughts'. In *On Record: Rock, Pop, and the Written Word*, eds Simon Frith and Andrew Goodwin. London: Routledge, pp. 419–24.

Frith, Simon, and Angela McRobbie, 1990. 'Rock and Sexuality'. In *On Record: Rock, Pop, and the Written Word*, eds Simon Frith and Andrew Goodwin. London: Routledge, pp. 371–89.

Fuchs, Cynthia J. 1993. 'The Buddy Politic', In *Screening the Male: Exploring Masculinities in Hollywood Cinema*, eds Steven Cohan and Ina Rae Hark. London: Routledge, pp. 194–210.

Fuerst, Wesley J. 1975. *The Books of Ruth, Esther, Ecclesiastes, the Song of Songs, Lamentations: The Five Scrolls*. Cambridge, England: Cambridge University Press.

Funari, Vicky. 1997. 'Naked, Naughty, Nasty: Peep Show Reflections', In *Whores and Other Feminists*, ed. Jill Nagle. London and New York: Routledge, pp. 19–35.

Fuss, Diana. 1991. 'Inside/Out', In *Inside/Out: Lesbian Theories, Gay Theories*, ed. Diana Fuss. New York: Routledge, pp. 1–10.

———. 1995. 'Pink Freud', *GLQ: Gay and Lesbian Quarterly* 2:1–9.

Futurist (The). 1985. 'Fast Food Workers Have It Their Way', *The Futurist* 19 (February): 74–5.

Fyodorov, Alexander. 1983. 'Arkadi Strugatsky: "Man Must Always Be Man"' *Soviet Literature* 9 (426):113–23.

Gabriel, Yiannis. 1985. 'Feeding the Fast Food Chain', *New Statesman* 109 (April 12):8–9, 12.

Gagnon, Jean. 1988. *Pornography in the Urban World*. Trans. James Boake and Jeanluc Svoboda. Toronto: Art Metropole.

Gakov, Vladimir. 1982. 'A Test of Humanity: About the Work of the Strugatsky Brothers', *Soviet Literature* 1(406):154–61.

Gamson, Joshua. 1996. 'Must Identity Movements Self-Destruct? A Queer Dilemma', In *Queer Theory/Sociology*, ed. Steven Seidman. Cambridge, MA: Blackwell, pp. 395–420.

Garofalo, Reebee. 1993. 'Black Popular Music: Crossing Over or Going Under?' In *Rock and Popular Music: Politics, Policies, Institutions*. eds Tony Bennett, Simon Frith, Lawrence Grossberg, John Shepherd and Graeme Turner. Culture: Policies and Politics. London and New York: Routledge, pp. 231–48.

Garratt, Sheryl. 1990. 'Teenage Dreams'. In *On Record: Rock, Pop, and the Written Word*, eds Simon Frith and Andrew Goodwin. London: Routledge, pp. 399–409.

Garrett, Greg. 1991. 'Alfred Hitchcock and the Deviant Audience', *New Orleans Review* 18 (Winter):29–32.

Gendron, Bernard. 1986. 'Theodor Adorno Meets the Cadillacs,' In *Studies in Entertainment: Critical Approaches to Mass Culture*, ed. and introduction Tania Modleski. Foreword by Kathleen Woodward. Theories of Contemporary Culture 7. Bloomington: Indiana University Press, pp. 18–36.

Gil, Vincent E., Marco S. Wang, Allen F. Anderson, and Guao Matthew Lin. 1994. 'Plum Blossoms and Pheasants: Prostitutes, Prostitution, and Social Control Measures in Contemporary China', *International Journal of Offender Therapy and Comparative Criminology* 38 (Winter):319–37.

Gilfoyle, Timothy J. 1992. *City of Eros: New York City, Prostitution, and the Commercialization of Sex, 1790–1920*. New York, NY: W. W. Norton.

Gillet, Michel. 1990. 'La Folie de Saül', *Lumière et Vie* 39:5–21.

Goitein, S. D. 1993. 'The Song of Songs: A Female Composition', In *A Feminist Companion to the Song of Songs*, ed. Athalya Brenner. The Feminist Companion to the Bible, 1. Sheffield: Sheffield Academic Press, pp. 58–66.

Goldman, Harry. 1983. 'Introduction: In Depth: Pornography', *Journal of Popular Culture* 17 (Fall):123–8.

Gomel, Elana. 1995. 'The Poetics of Censorship: Allegory as Form and Ideology in the Novels of Arkady and Boris Strugatsky', *Science Fiction Studies* 22:87–105.

Goodwin, James. 1981. 'Conrad and Hitchcock: Secret Sharers', In *The English Novel and the Movies*, ed. and introduction Michael Klein and Gillian Parker. Ungar Film Library. New York: Ungar, 218–27.

Gopman, Vladimir. 1991. 'Science Fiction Teaches the Civic Virtues: An Interview with Arkadii Strugatsky', trans. Mark Knighton, ed. Darko Suvin. *Science Fiction Studies* 18 (March):1–10.

184

Gordis, Robert. 1974. *The Song of Songs and Lamentations: A Study, Modern Translation and Commentary*. New York: KTAV.

Gottwald, Norman K. 1962. *Studies in the Book of Lamentations*. 2nd edition London: SCM Press.

——. 1993. *The Hebrew Bible in Its Social World and in Ours*. Semeia Studies. Atlanta, GA: Scholar's Press.

Goulder, Michael D. 1986. *The Song of Fourteen Songs*. Journal for the Study of the Old Testament Supplement Series 36. Sheffield: Sheffield Academic Press.

Goulemot, Jean Marie. 1994. *Forbidden Texts: Erotic Literature and Its Readers in Eighteenth-Century France*. Trans. James Simpson. Cambridge, England: Polity Press.

Gous, Ignatius G. P. 1996. 'Mind Over Matter: Lamentations 4 in the Light of the Cognitive Sciences', *Scandinavian Journal of the Old Testament* 10:69–87.

Gracyk, Theodore. 1996. *Rhythm and Noise: An Aesthetics of Rock*. Durham, NC: Duke University Press.

Gramsci, Antonio. 1971. *Selections from the Prison Notebooks*, eds Quentin Hoare and G. Nowell Smith. London: Lawrence & Wishart.

Gray, John, ed. 1967. *Joshua, Judges and Ruth*. The Century Bible. London: Thomas Nelson.

Greenberg, David, and Marcia H. Bystryn. 1996. 'Capitalism, Bureaucracy, and Male Homosexuality', In *Queer Theory/Sociology*, ed. Steven Seidman. Twentieth-Century Social Theory. Cambridge, MA: Blackwell, pp. 83–110.

Greenberg, Moshe. 1983. *Ezekiel 1–20: A New Translation with Introduction and Commentary*. The Anchor Bible, vol. 22. Garden City, NY: Doubleday.

Greene, Diana. 1986. 'Male and Female in *The Snail on the Slope* by the Strugatsky Brothers', *Modern Fiction Studies* 32 (Spring):97–108.

Griffin, Susan. 1981. *Pornography and Silence: Culture's Revenge Against Nature*. New York: Harper & Row.

Grossberg, Daniel. 1989. *Centripetal and Centrifugal Structures in Biblical Poetry*. The Society of Biblical Literature Monograph Series, 39. Atlanta, GA: Scholar's Press.

——. 1994. 'Two Kinds of Sexual Relationships in the Hebrew Bible', *Hebrew Studies* 35: 7–25.

Grossberg, Lawrence. 1984. 'Another Boring Day in Paradise: Rock and Roll and the Empowerment of Everyday Life', *Popular Music* 4: 225–58.

——. 1990. 'Is There Rock After Punk?' In *On Record: Rock, Pop, and the Written Word*. eds Simon Frith and Andrew Goodwin. London: Routledge, pp. 111–23.

——. 1993. 'The Framing of Rock: Rock and the New Conservatism', In *Rock and Popular Music: Politics, Policies, Institutions*, eds Tony Bennett, Simon Frith, Lawrence Grossberg, John Shepherd and Graeme Turner. London and New York: Routledge, pp. 193–209.

Guns 'n' Roses, 1987. *Appetite for Destruction*. Compact Disk. Producer Mike Clink. David Geffen.

——. 1988. *G 'n' R Lies*. Compact Disk. Producer Guns 'n' Roses and Mike Clink. David Geffen.

——. 1991. *Use Your Illusion*. Compact Disk. Producer Mike Clink, vols 1–2. David Geffen.

Guy, Donna J. 1988. 'White Slavery, Public Health, and the Socialist Position on Legalized Prostitution in Argentina, 1913–1936', *Latin American Research Review* 23(3):60–80.

Gwaltney, W. C., Jr. 1991. 'The Biblical Book of Lamentations in the Context of Near Eastern Lament Literature', In *Essential Papers on Israel and the Ancient Near East*, ed. Frederick E. Grennspahn. New York: New York University Press, pp. 242–65.

Hadley, Judith M. 1995. 'Wisdom and the Goddess', In *Wisdom in Ancient Israel: Essays in*

Honour of J. A. Emerton, eds John Day, Robert P. Gorden, and H. G. M. Williamson. Cambridge: Cambridge University Press, pp. 234–43.

Hall, Donald E. 1997. 'Introduction: Queer Works', *College Literature* 24 (February):2–10.

Halperin, David. 1990a. *One Hundred Years of Homosexuality and Other Essays on Greek Love.* New York and London: Routledge.

——. 1990b. 'Why is Diotima a Woman? Platonic Eros and the Figuration of Gender', In *Before Sexuality: The Construction of Erotic Experience in the Ancient Greek World*, eds David M. Halperin, John J. Winkler, and Froma I. Zeitlin. Princeton, NJ: Princeton University Press, pp. 257–308.

——. 1995. *Saint Foucault: Towards a Gay Hagiography.* New York and Oxford: Oxford University Press.

Hamlin, E. John. 1990. *At Risk in the Promised Land: A Commentary on the Book of Judges.* International Theological Commentary. Grand Rapids, MI and Edinburgh: Eerdmans/Handsel.

Hansen, Christian, Catherine Needham, and Bill Nichols. 1989. 'Skin Flicks: Pornography, Ethnography, and the Discourse of Power', *Discourse* 11 (Spring–Summer):65–79.

Hanson, Ellis. 1993. 'Technology, Paranoia and the Queer Voice', *Screen* 34 (Summer):137–61.

Harper, Philip Brian. 1994. 'Private Affairs: Race, Sex, Property, and Persons', *GLQ: A Journal of Lesbian and Gay Studies* 1(2):111–33.

Harris, Thomas. 1987. 'Rear Window and Blow-Up: Hitchcock's Straightforwardness Vs. Antonioni's Ambiguity', *Literature Film Quarterly* 15(1):60–3.

Hartley, John E. 1992. *Leviticus.* Word Biblical Commentary, vol. 4. Dallas, TX: Word Books.

Heilbrun, Alfred B., Jr, and David T. Seif. 1988. 'Erotic Value of Female Distress in Sexually Explicit Photographs', *The Journal of Sex Research* 24:47–57.

Helberg, J. L. 1990. 'Land in the Book of Lamentations', *Zeitschrift für die Alttestamentliche Wissenschaft* 102:372–85.

Henderson, Lisa. 1992. 'Lesbian Pornography: Cultural Transgression and Sexual Demystification', In *New Lesbian Criticism: Literary and Cultural Readings*, ed. Sally Munt. Between Men/Between Women: Lesbian and Gay Studies. New York: Columbia University Press, pp. 173–91.

Hennessy, Rosemary. 1995. 'Incorporating Queer Theory on the Left', In *Marxism in the Postmodern Age: Confronting the New World Order*, eds Antonio Callari, Stephen Cullenberg, and Carole Biewener, 266–75. Critical Perspectives. New York and London: Guildford Press.

Henriot, Christian. 1995. '"La Fermeture": The Abolition of Prostitution in Shanghai, 1949–58', *China Quarterly* 142 (June):467–86.

——. 1996. '"From a Throne of Glory to a Seat of Ignominy": Shanghai Prostitution Revisited (1849–1949)', *Modern China* 22 (April):132–63.

Hepworth, John. 1995. 'Hitchcock's Homophobia', In *Out in Culture: Gay, Lesbian, and Queer Essays on Popular Culture*, eds Corey K. Creekmur and Alexander Doty, 186–96. Series Q. Durham, NC: Duke University Press.

Herman, Andrew. 1993. Review of Goodwin, Andrew. *Dancing in the Distraction Factory: Music Televison and Popular Culture* (Minneapolis: University of Minnesota Press, 1992). *Postmodern Culture* 4/1 (Sept). http://jefferson.village.virginia.edu/pmc.contents.all.html

Hershatter, Gail. 1989. 'The Hierarchy of Shanghai Prostitution, 1870–1949', *Modern China* 15 (October):463–98.

——. 1996. 'A Response', *Modern China* 22 (April):164–9.

Hertzberg, H. W. 1964. *I and II Samuel: A Commentary.* Old Testament Library. London: SCM Press.

Heym, Stefan. 1972. *The King David Report.* London: Hodder & Stoughton.

186

Hill, E. D. 1982. 'The Place of the Future: Louis Marin and His *Utopiques*', *Science Fiction Studies* 9:167–79.

Hill, Trent. 1991. 'The Enemy Within: Censorship in Rock Music in the 1950s'. *South Atlantic Quarterly* 90 (Fall): 675–708.

Hillers, Dilbert. 1992. *Lamentations: A New Translation with Introduction and Commentary*. 2nd ed. The Anchor Bible. New York: Doubleday.

Hinds, Elizabeth Jane Wall. 1992. 'The Devil Sings the Blues: Heavy Metal, Gothic Fiction and "Postmodern" Discourse'. *Journal of Popular Culture* 26 (Winter): 151–64.

Hitchcock, Alfred. 1995. *Hitchcock on Hitchcock: Selected Writings and Interviews*, ed. Sidney Gottlieb. London: Faber & Faber.

Hobson, Barbara Meil. 1987. *Uneasy Virtue: The Politics of Prostitution and the American Reform Tradition*. New York: Basic Books.

Holmlund, Chris. 1993. 'Masculinity as Multiple Masquerade: The "Mature" Stallone and the Stallone Clone', In *Screening the Male: Exploring Masculinities in Hollywood Cinema*, eds Steven Cohan and Ina Rae Hark. London: Routledge, pp. 213–29.

Howes, Keith. 1993. *Broadcasting It: An Encyclopaedia of Homosexuality on Film, Radio and TV in the UK 1923–1993*. Foreword by Ned Sherrin. Cassell Lesbian and Gay Studies. New York: Cassell.

Huang Wei. 1993. 'Local Versus Foreign Fast Food', *Beijing Review* 36 (March 15):13–16.

Hunt, Leon. 1993. 'What Are Big Boys Made Of? *Spartacus*, *El Cid* and the Male Epic', In *You Tarzan: Masculinity, Movies and Men*, eds Pat Kirkham and Janet Thumim. New York: St. Martin's, pp. 65–83.

Hunt, Lynn. 1993a. 'Introduction: Obscenity and the Origins of Modernity, 1500–1800', In *The Invention of Pornography: Obscenity and the Origins of Modernity, 1500–1800*, ed. Lynn Hunt. New York: Zone Books, pp. 9–45.

——. 1993b. 'Pornography and the French Revolution', In *The Invention of Pornography: Obscenity and the Origins of Modernity, 1500–1800*, ed. Lynn Hunt. New York: Zone Books, pp. 301–39.

——. 1993c. *The Invention of Pornography: Obscenity and the Origins of Modernity, 1500–1800*. New York: Zone Books.

Ihlanfeldt, Keith R., and Madelyn V. Young. 1994. 'Intrametropolitan Variation in Wage Rates: The Case of Atlanta Fast-Food Restaurant Workers', *Review of Economics and Statistics* 76 (August):425–33.

Irving, John. 1992. 'Pornography and the New Puritans', *New York Times Book Review* 29 March: 1, 24–5, 27.

Jackson, Lynne. 1987. 'Labor Relations: An Interview with Lizzie Borden', *Cineaste* 40(3):4–7.

Jackson, Rosemary. 1988. *Fantasy: The Literature of Subversion*. New Accents. London and New York: Routledge.

James, Dell. 1989. Interview with Axl Rose. *Rolling Stone*. 558 (August 10). http://www.students.uiuc.edu/~t-gray/axlrs89.html

Jameson, Fredric R. 1981. *The Political Unconscious: Narrative as a Socially Symbolic Act*. Ithaca, NY: Cornell University Press.

——. 1982. 'Progress Versus Utopia; Or, Can We Imagine the Future?' *Science Fiction Studies* 9:147–58.

——. 1988. *The Ideologies of Theory: Essays 1971–1986*. Foreword by Neil Larsen. Vol. 2. *Syntax of History*. Theory and History of Literature 49. Minneapolis: University of Minnesota Press.

——. 1990. *Signatures of the Visible*. New York: Routledge.

——. 1991. *Postmodernism, Or, the Cultural Logic of Late Capitalism*. Durham, NC: Duke University Press.

Jenness, Valerie. 1990. 'From Sex as Sin to Sex as Work: COYOTE and the Reorganization of Prostitution as a Social Problem', *Social Problems* 37 (August):403–20.

Jervey, Edward D. 1983. 'The Effects of a Sex History Course on Student Attitudes and Beliefs', *Journal of Popular Culture* 17 (Fall):154–60.

Jobling, David. 1978. *The Sense of Biblical Narrative: Three Structural Analyses in the Old Testament*. Journal for the Study of the Old Testament Supplementary Series 7. Sheffield: JSOT Press.

Johnson, Vida T., and Graham Petrie. 1994. *The Films of Andrei Tarkovsky: A Visual Fugue*. Bloomington: Indiana University Press.

Joll, James. 1979. *The Anarchists*. 2nd edition. London: Methuen.

Jones-Warsaw, Koala. 1993. 'Toward a Womanist Hermeneutic: A Reading of Judges 19–21', In *A Feminist Companion to Judges*. The Feminist Companion to the Bible 4. Sheffield: Sheffield Academic Press, pp. 173–86.

Joyce, Paul. 1993. 'Lamentations and the Grief Process: A Psychological Reading', *Biblical Interpretation* 1:304–20.

Julius, Marshall. 1996. *Action: The Action Movie A–Z*. Bloomington and Indianapolis: Indiana University Press.

Juni, Samuel, Robert Brannon, and Michelle M. Roth. 1988. 'Sexual and Racial Discrimination in Service-Seeking Interactions: A Field Study in Fast Food and Commercial Establishments', *Psychological Reports* 63 (August):71–6.

Kaite, Berkeley. 1995. *Pornography and Difference*. Bloomington and Indianapolis: Indiana University Press.

Kane, Stephanie C. 1993. 'Prostitution and the Military: Planning AIDS Intervention in Belize', *Social Science and Medicine* 36 (April):965–79.

Kant, Immanual. 1960. *Religion Within the Limits of Reason Alone*. Trans. Theodore M. Greene and Hoyt H. Hudson. New York: Harper & Row.

Kapsis, Robert E. 1986. 'Alfred Hitchcock: Auteur or Hack? How the Filmmaker Reshaped His Reputation Among the Critics', *Cineaste* 14(3):30–5.

——. 1989. 'Reputation Building and the Film Art World: The Case of Alfred Hitchcock', *The Sociological Quarterly* 30(1):15–35.

——. 1992. *Hitchcock: The Making of a Reputation*. Chicago, IL: University of Chicago Press.

Kasdan, Pamela. 1996. 'Fast Food for Thought', *American Demographics* 18 (May):19–21.

Katz, Lawrence F., and Alan B. Krueger. 1992. 'The Effect of the Minimum Wage on the Fast-Food Industry', *Industrial and Labor Relations Review* 46 (October):6–21.

Keel, Othmar. 1994. *The Song of Songs*. Trans. Frederick J. Gaiser. Continental Commentaries. Minneapolis, MN: Fortress Press.

Kendrick, Walter. 1996. *The Secret Museum: Pornography in Modern Culture*. Berkeley, CA: University of California Press.

Keuls, Eva C. 1985. *The Reign of the Phallus: Sexual Politics in Ancient Greece*. New York: Harper & Row.

King, Alison. 1993. 'Mystery and Imagination: The Case of Pornography Effects Studies', In *Bad Girls and Dirty Pictures: The Challenge to Reclaim Feminism*, eds Alison Assiter and Carol Avedon. London and Boulder, CO: Pluto Press, pp. 57–87.

Kinsella, Marjorie. 1982. 'The Fast Food Restaurant: Expression of Popular Culture', *Journal of Cultural Economics* 6 (June):59–70.

Kinser, Samuel. 1992. 'Everyday Ordinary', *Diacritics* 22 (Summer):70–82.

Kipnis, Laura. 1993. 'She-Male Fantasies and the Aesthetics of Pornography', In *Dirty Looks: Women, Pornography, Power*, eds Pamela Church Gibson and Roma Gibson. London: BFI, pp. 124–43.

Klein, Ralph W. 1983. *1 Samuel*. Word Biblical Commentary, vol. 10. Waco, TX: Word Books.

Kleinhans, Chuck. 1994. 'Taking Out the Trash: Camp and the Politics of Parody', In *The Politics and Poetics of Camp*, ed. Moe Meyer. London and New York: Routledge, pp. 182–201.

Klinger, Barbara. 1982. 'Psycho: The Institutionalization of Female Sexuality', *Wide Angle* 5(1):49–55.

Koehler, Ludwig, and Walter Baumgartner. 1994–. *The Hebrew and Aramaic Lexicon of the Old Testament*. Trans. and ed. M. E. J. Richardson. Leiden: Brill.

Koop, C. Everett. 1987. 'Report of the Surgeon General's Workshop on Pornography and Public Health', *American Psychologist* 42 (October):944–5.

Krasovec, Joze. 1992. 'The Source of Hope in the Book of Lamentations', *Vetus Testamentum* 42:223–33.

Kreitzer, Larry J. 1993. *The New Testament in Fiction and Film*. Sheffield: JSOT Press.

——. 1994. *The Old Testament in Fiction and Film: On Reversing the Hermeneutical Flow*. Sheffield: Sheffield Academic Press.

Kropotkin, Peter. 1939. *Mutual Aid*. Harmondsworth: Penguin. (Original 1902).

Krueger, Alan B. 1991. 'Ownership, Agency, and Wages: An Examination of Franchising in the Fast Food Industry', *Quarterly Journal of Economics* 106 (February):75–101.

Kuhn, Annette. 1985. *The Power of the Image: Essays on Representation and Sexuality*. London: Routledge.

Kutchinsky, Berl. 1992. 'The Politics of Pornography Research', *Law and Society Review* 26(2):447–55.

Lacan, Jacques. 1990. 'Kant with Sade', *October* 51:53–104.

——. 1991. *The Seminar of Jacques Lacan*. Vol. 2. *The Ego in Freud's Theory and in the Technique of Psychoanalysis, 1954–1955*, ed. Jacques-Alain Miller. Trans. Sylvana Tomaselli. Notes by John Forrester. New York and London: W. W. Norton & Company.

——. 1992. *The Seminar of Jacques Lacan*. Vol. 7. *The Ethics of Psychoanalysis 1959–1960*, ed. Jacques-Alain Miller. London: Tavistock/Routledge.

——. 1994. *The Four Fundamental Concepts of Psycho-analysis*, ed. Jacques-Alain Miller. Trans. Alan Sheridan. Introduction by David Macey. The Seminar of Jacques Lacan. Harmondsworth: Penguin.

Landy, Francis. 1983. *Paradoxes of Paradise: Identity and Difference in the Song of Songs*. Bible and Literature Series 7. Sheffield: Almond Press.

——. 1987a. 'The Song of Songs', In *The Literary Guide to the Bible*, eds Robert Alter and Frank Kermode. Cambridge, MA: Belknap, pp. 305–19.

——. 1987b. 'Lamentations', In *The Literary Guide to the Bible*, eds Robert Alter and Frank Kermode. Cambridge, MA: Belknap, pp. 329–35.

Lang, Bernhard. 1986. *Wisdom and the Book of Proverbs: A Hebrew Goddess Redefined*. New York: The Pilgrim Press.

Lasine, Stuart. 1984. 'Guest and Host in Judges 19: Lot's Hospitality in an Inverted World', *Journal for the Study of the Old Testament* 29: 37–59.

Lau, Grace. 1993. 'Confessions of a Complete Scopophiliac', In *Dirty Looks: Women, Pornography, Power*, eds Pamela Church Gibson and Roma Gibson. London: BFI, pp. 192–207.

LaValley, Al. 1995. 'The Great Escape', In *Out in Culture: Gay, Lesbian, and Queer Essays on Popular Culture*, eds Corey K. Creekmur and Alexander Doty. Series Q. Durham, NC: Duke University Press, pp. 60–70.

Lavoie, Jean-Jacques. 1995. 'Festin érotique et Tendresse Cannibalique dans le Cantique de Cantiques', *Studies in Religion/Sciences Religieuses* 24:131–46.

Lawrence, Kelli-An, and Edward S. Herold. 1988. 'Women's Attitudes Toward and Experience with Sexually Explicit Materials', *The Journal of Sex Research* 24:161–9.

Lawton, Robert B. 1993. 'Saul, Jonathan and the "Son of Jesse"' *Journal for the Study of the Old Testament* 58:35–46.

Led Zeppelin. 1968. *Led Zeppelin I*. Atlantic.

Lefebvre, Henri. 1971. *Everyday Life in the Modern World*. Trans. Sacha Rabinovitch. London: Allen Lane/Penguin.

——. 1991. *Critique of Everyday Life: Volume One: Introduction*. Trans. John Moore. Preface by Michel Trebitsch. London: Verso.

Leidner, Robin. 1993a. *Fast Food, Fast Talk: Service Work and the Routinization of Everyday Life*. Berkeley, CA: University of California Press.

——. 1993b. 'Review of *Making Fast Food* and *Dishing It Out*', *American Journal of Sociology* 98 (January):942–4.

Leigh, Carol. aka Scarlot Harlot. 1996. 'The Scarlet Harlot', In *Tales from the Clit: A Female Experience of Pornography*, ed. Cherie Matrix, for Feminists Against Censorship. Edinburgh: AK Press, pp. 134–39.

——. 1997. 'Inventing Sex Work', In *Whores and Other Feminists*, ed. Jill Nagle. London and New York: Routledge, pp. 225–31.

Leitch, Thomas M. 1986. 'Murderous Victims in *The Secret Agent* and *Sabotage*', *Literature Film Quarterly* 14(1):64–8.

Lerner, Gerda. 1986. 'The Origin of Prostitution in Ancient Mesopotamia', *Signs* 11 (Winter):236–54.

Levenson, Jon D. 1993. *The Death and Resurrection of the Beloved Son: The Transformation of Child Sacrifice in Judaism and Christianity*. New Haven, CT: Yale University Press.

Levine, Baruch A. 1989. *Leviticus*. The JPS Torah Commentary. Philadelphia, PA: The Jewish Publication Society.

Lévi-Strauss, Claude. 1989. *Tristes Tropiques*. Trans. John Weightman and Doreen Weightman. Picador Classics. London: Pan Books.

——. 1994. *The Raw and the Cooked: Introduction to a Science of Mythology*. London: Random House.

Lie, John. 1995. 'The Transformation of Sexual Work in 20th-Century Korea', *Gender and Society* 9 (June):310–27.

Light, Alan. 1991. 'About a Salary or Reality? – Rap's Recurrent Conflict.' *South Atlantic Quarterly* 90 (Fall): 855–70.

Linafelt, Tod. 1995. 'Surviving Lamentations', *Horizons in Biblical Theology* 17:45–61.

Linz, Daniel. Edward Donnerstein, and Steven Penrod. 1987. 'The Findings and Recommendations of the Attorney General's Commission on Pornography: Do the Psychological "Facts" Fit the Political Fury?' *American Psychologist* 42 (October):946–53.

Loraux, Nicole. 1990. 'Herakles: The Super-Male and the Feminine', In *Before Sexuality: The Construction of Erotic Experience in the Ancient Greek World*, eds David M. Halperin, John J. Winkler, and Froma I. Zeitlin. Princeton, NJ: Princeton University Press, pp. 21–52.

Love, John F. 1986. *McDonald's: Behind the Arches*. New York: Bantam Books.

Lüthi, Kurt. 1993. 'Das Hohe Lied der Bibel und Seine Impulse für eine Heutige Ethik', *Theologische Zeitschrift* 49:97–114.

McCaghy, Charles H., and Charles Hou. 1991. 'Family Affiliation and Prostitution in a Cultural Context: Career Onsets of Taiwanese Prostitutes', *Archives of Sexual Behavior* 23 (June):251–65.

McCalman, Iain. 1988. *Radical Underworld: Prophets, Revolutionaries and Pornographers in London, 1795–1840.* Cambridge, England: Cambridge Univeristy Press.

McCarter, P. Kyle. 1980. *I Samuel: A New Translation with Introduction, Notes and Commentary.* The Anchor Bible, Vol. 8. Garden City, NY: Doubleday.

McClintock, Anne. 1992. 'Screwing the System: Sexwork, Race, and the Law', *Boundary 2* 19(2):70–95.

——. 1993. 'Maid to Order: Commercial S/M and Gender Power', In *Dirty Looks: Women, Pornography, Power*, eds Pamela Church Gibson and Roma Gibson, 207–31. London: BFI.

McConahay, John B. 1988. 'Pornography: The Symbolic Politics of Fantasy', *Law and Contemporary Problems* 51 (Winter):31–69.

McGinn, Bernard. 1992. 'With "the Kisses of the Mouth": Recent Works on the Song of Songs', *Journal of Religion* 72:269–72.

McGuire, Patrick L. 1982. 'Future History, Soviet Style: The Work of the Strugatsky Brothers', In *Critical Encounters II: Writers and Themes in Science Fiction*, ed. Tom Staicar. Recognitions. New York: Ungar, pp. 104–24.

McIntosh, Mary. 1996. 'The Homosexual Role', In *Queer Theory/Sociology*, ed. Steven Seidman. Twentieth-Century Social Theory. Cambridge, MA: Blackwell, pp. 33–40.

McKane, William. 1970. *Proverbs: A New Approach.* The Old Testament Library. London: SCM Press.

McKeganey, Neil, and Marina Barnard. 1996. *Sex Work on the Streets: Prostitutes and Their Clients.* Buckingham, England: Open University Press.

MacKinnon, Catherine. 1989. *Toward a Feminist Theory of the State.* Cambridge, MA: Harvard University Press.

Mahood, Linda. 1990. *The Magdalenes: Prostitution in the Nineteenth Century.* London: Routledge.

Mainil, Jean. 1992. 'Pornography and Academe: Compulsory Introduction', *Fiction International* 22:335–57.

Manderson, Lenore. 1992. 'Public Sex Performances in Patpong and Explorations of the Edges of Imagination', *The Journal of Sex Research* 29 (November):451–75.

Marin, Louis. 1973. *Utopiques: Jeux d'Espaces.* Collection Critiques. Paris: Minuit.

Markos, A. R., A. A. H. Wade, and M. Walzman. 1994. 'The Adolescent Male Prostitute and Sexually Transmitted Diseases, HIV and AIDS' *Journal of Adolescence* 17 (April):123–30.

Marsh, Clive, and Gaye Ortiz, eds. 1997. *Explorations in Theology and Film: Movies and Meaning.* Oxford: Blackwell.

Marshall, Peter. 1993. *Demanding the Impossible: A History of Anarchism.* London: Fontana.

Martin, Joel W., and Conrad E. Ostwalt Jr., eds. 1995. *Screening the Sacred: Religion, Myth, and Ideology in Popular American Film.* Boulder, CO: Westview Press.

Mathews, Paul W. 1988. 'On "Being a Prostitute"' Review. *Journal of Homosexuality* 15(3–4):119–35.

Matrix, Cherie, ed. 1996. *Tales from the Clit: A Female Experience of Pornography.* Feminists Against Censorship. Edinburgh and San Francisco, CA: AK Press.

May, Charles E. 1981. 'Perversion in Pornography: Male Envy of the Female', *Literature and Psychology* 31(2):66–74.

May, John R., and Michael Bird, 1982. *Religion in Film*. Knoxville: University of Tennessee Press.

Messner, Michael A. 1996. 'Studying up on Sex', *Sociology of Sport Journal* 13(3):221–37.

Meyer, Moe. 1994. 'Introduction: Reclaiming the Discourse of Camp', In *The Politics and Poetics of Camp*, ed. Moe Meyer. London and New York: Routledge, pp. 1–22.

Meyer, Richard. 1991. 'Rock Hudson's Body', In *Inside/Out: Lesbian Theories, Gay Theories*, ed. Diana Fuss. New York: Routledge, pp. 259–88.

Meyers, Carol. 1993. 'Gender Imagery in the Song of Songs', In *A Feminist Companion to the Song of Songs*, ed. Athalya Brenner. The Feminist Companion to the Bible, 1. Sheffield: Sheffield Academic Press, pp. 197–212.

Michasiw, Kim. 1994. 'Camp, Masculinity, Masquerade', *Differences: A Journal of Feminist Cultural Studies* 6 (Summer–Fall):146–73.

Michelson, Peter. 1993. *Speaking the Unspeakable: A Poetics of Obscenity*. Albany, NY: State University of New York Press.

Milgrom, Jacob. 1991. *Leviticus 1–16*. The Anchor Bible. New York: Doubleday.

Miller, D. A. 1989. 'Sontag's Urbanity', *October* 49:91–101.

Minkoff, Harvey. 1997. 'As Simple as ABC: What Acrostics in the Bible Can Demonstrate', *Bible Review* 13(2):27–31, 46–7.

Miscall, Peter D. 1986. *1 Samuel: A Literary Reading*. Bloomington: Indiana University Press.

Modleski, Tania. 1988. *The Women Who Knew Too Much: Hitchcock and Feminist Theory*. New York: Methuen.

——. 1995. 'Rape vs. Mans/laughter: *Blackmail*', In *Perspectives on Alfred Hitchcock*, ed. David Boyd. New York: G. K. Hall, pp. 71–86.

Molitor, Graham T. T. 1984. 'From Farming to Fast Food: The Changing Look of Agribusiness', *The Futurist* 17 (December):20–22.

Moon, Michael. 1989. 'Flaming Closets', *October* 51:19–54.

Moore, George F. 1908. *A Critical and Exegetical Commentary on Judges*. 2nd edition The International Critical Commentary. Edinburgh: T. & T. Clarke.

Moore, Stephen. 1996. *God's Gym: Divine Male Bodies of the Bible*. New York and London: Routledge.

——. ed. 1999. *Semeia. In Search of the Present: The Bible Through Cultural Studies*. Atlanta, GA: Scholar's Press.

Moore, Stephen, and Janice Capel Anderson. 1998. 'Taking It Like a Man: Masculinity in 4 Maccabees', *Journal of Biblical Literature* 117 (Summer):249–73.

Morris, Meaghan. 1990. 'Banality in Cultural Studies'. In *Logics of Television*, ed. Patricia Mellencamp. Bloomington: Indiana University Press, pp. 14–43.

Mort, Frank. 1989. 'Moveable Feasts', *New Statesman and Society* 2 (January 27):18–19.

Morton, Donald. 1996. 'Changing the Terms: (virtual) Desire and (actual) Reality', In *The Material Queer: A Lesbigay Cultural Studies Reader*, ed. Donald Morton. Boulder, CO: Westview Press, pp. 1–33.

Muecke, Marjorie A. 1992. 'Mother Sold Food, Daughter Sells Her Body: The Cultural Continuity of Prostitution', *Social Science and Medicine* 35 (October):891–901.

Mulvey, Laura. 1989. *Visual and Other Pleasures*. Basingstoke, Hampshire and Bloomington: Macmillan and Indiana University Press.

Munro, Jill M. 1995. *Spikenard and Saffron: The Imagery of the Song of Songs*. Journal for the Study of the Old Testament Supplement Series 203. Sheffield: Sheffield Academic Press.

Murphy, Roland E. 1981. *Wisdom Literature: Job, Proverbs, Ruth, Canticles, Ecclesiastes, and Esther*. The Forms of the Old Testament Literature, vol. 13. Grand Rapids, MI: Eerdmans.

——. 1990. *The Song of Songs: A Commentary on the Book of Canticles or the Song of Songs*, ed. S. Dean McBride. Hermeneia. Minneapolis, MN: Fortress.

——. 1995. 'The Personification of Wisdom', In *Wisdom in Ancient Israel: Essays in Honour of J. A. Emerton*, eds John Day, Robert P. Gorden, and H. G. M. Williamson. Cambridge: Cambridge University Press, pp. 222–33.

Nagle, Jill. 1997. 'Introduction', In *Whores and Other Feminists*, ed. Jill Nagle. New York and London: Routledge, pp. 1–15.

Nash, Stanley D. 1994. *Prostitution in Great Britain, 1485–1901: An Annotated Bibliography*. Metuchen, NJ: Scarecrow Press.

Nead, Lynda. 1993. '"Above the Pulp-Line": The Cultural Significance of Erotic Art', In *Dirty Looks: Women, Pornography, Power*, eds Pamela Church Gibson and Roma Gibson. London: BFI, pp. 144–56.

Neely, Kim. 1992. Interview with Axl Rose. *Rolling Stone* (April 2). http://www.students. uiuc.edu/~t-gray/axlrs92.html

Newsom, Carol A. 1989. 'Woman and the Discourse of Patriarchal Wisdom: A Study of Proverbs 1–9', In *Gender and Difference in Ancient Israel*, ed. Peggy L. Day. Minneapolis, MN: Augsburg, pp. 142–60.

Niditch, Susan. 1982. 'The "Sodomite" Theme in Judges 19–20: Family, Community, and Social Disintegration', *Catholic Biblical Quarterly* 44 (July):365–78.

Noguchi, Paul H. 1994. 'Savor Slowly: *ekiben* – the Fast Food of High-speed Japan', *Ethnology* 33 (Fall):317–30.

Norberg, Kathryn. 1993. 'The Libertine Whore: Prostitution in French Pornography from Margot to Juliette', In *The Invention of Pornography: Obscenity and the Origins of Modernity, 1500–1800*, ed. Lynn Hunt. New York: Zone Books, pp. 225–52.

Noth, Martin. 1965. *Leviticus: A Commentary*. The Old Testament Library. London: SCM.

Nussbaum, Felicity A. 1995. 'One Part of Womankind: Prostitution and Sexual Geography in *Memoirs of a Woman of Pleasure*', *Differences* 7 (Summer):17–40.

Odabashian, Barbara. 1993. 'The Unspeakable Crime in Hitchcock's *Rear Window*: Hero as Lay Detective, Spectator as Lay Analyst', *Hitchcock Annual* 10:3–11.

Oldenburg, Veena Talwar. 1990. 'Lifestyle as Resistance: The Case of the Courtesans of Lucknow, India', *Feminist Studies* 16 (Summer):259–87.

Overall, Christine. 1992. 'What's Wrong with Prostitution? Evaluating Sex Work', *Signs* 17 (Summer):705–24.

——. 1994. 'Reply to Shrage', *Signs* 19 (Winter):571–5.

Overholt, Thomas W. 1986. *Prophecy in Cross-cultural Perspective: A Sourcebook for Biblical Researchers*. Society of Biblical Literature Sources for Biblical Study, vol. 17. Atlanta, GA: Scholar's Press.

——. 1989. *Channels of Prophecy: The Social Dynamics of Prophetic Activity*. Minneapolis, MN: Fortress.

Padgett, Vernon R., Jo Ann Brislin-Slutz, and James A. Neal. 1989. 'Pornography, Erotica, and Attitudes Toward Women: The Effects of Repeated Exposure', *The Journal of Sex Research* 26 (November):479–91.

Palmer, Robert. 1991. 'The Church of the Sonic Guitar'. In *Rock and Roll and Culture*. ed. Anthony DeCurtis. Durham, NC: Duke University Press, pp. 649–73.

Parcel, Toby L., and Marie B. Sickmeier. 1988. 'One Firm, Two Labor Markets: The Case of McDonald's in the Fast-Food Industry', *The Sociological Quarterly* 29 (Spring):29–46.

Parent-Duchâtelet, Alexandre Jean Baptiste. 1838. *De la Prostitution dans la Ville de Paris, Considerée Sous le Rapport de L'hygiene Publique, de la Morale et de l'Administration: Ouvrage Appuyé de Documents Statistiques Puisés dans les Archives de la Prefecture de Police, avec Cartes et Tableaux*. Preface by François Leuret. Bruxelles: Societe Typographique Belge, Ad. Walhen et Comp.

Parker, Simon B. 1978. 'Possession Trance and Prophecy in Post-Exilic Israel'. *Vetus Testamentum* 28 (July): 271–85.

Pateman, Carole. 1983. 'Defending Prostitution: Charges Against Ericsson', *Ethics* 93 (April):561–5.

Patton, Cindy. 1991. 'Visualizing Safe Sex: When Pedagogy and Pornography Collide', In *Inside/Out: Lesbian Theories, Gay Theories*, ed. Diana Fuss. New York: Routledge, pp. 373–86.

———. 1994. 'The Cum Shot: Takes on Lesbian and Gay Sexuality', In *Living with Contradictions: Controversies in Feminist Social Ethics*, ed. Alison M. Jaggar. Boulder, CO and Oxford: Westview, pp. 178–80.

Peele, Stanton. 1986. 'Personality, Pathology, and the Act of Creation: The Case of Alfred Hitchcock', *Biography: An Interdisciplinary Quarterly* 9 (Summer):202–18.

Pendleton, David. 1992. 'Obscene Allegories: Narrative, Representation, Pornography', *Discourse: Journal for Theoretical Studies in Media and Culture* 15 (Fall):154–68.

Perkins, Roberta. 1994. 'Female Prostitution', In *Sex Work and Sex Workers in Australia*, eds Roberta Perkins, Garrett Prestage, Rachel Sharp, and Frances Lovejoy. Sydney: University of New South Wales Press, pp. 143–73.

Perkins, Roberta, and Garry Bennett. 1985. *Being a Prostitute: Prostitute Women and Prostitute Men*. Sydney: George Allen & Unwin.

Peterson, Richard A, and David G. Berger. 1990. 'Cycles in Symbol Production: The Case of Popular Music'. In *On Record: Rock, Pop, and the Written Word*. eds Simon Frith and Andrew Goodwin. London: Routledge, pp. 140–159.

Petlewski, Paul. 1988. 'Generic Tension in *Psycho*', In *Ambiguities in Literature and Film: Selected Papers from the Seventh Annual Florida State University Conference on Literature and Film*, ed. Hans P. Braendlin. Tallahassee: Florida State University Press, pp. 50–5.

Phillips, Gene D. 1984. *Alfred Hitchcock*. Twayne's Filmmakers Series. Boston, MA: Twayne Publishers.

Pleak, Richard R., and Heino F. L. Bahlburg. 1990. 'Sexual Behavior and AIDS Knowledge of Young Male Prostitutes in Manhattan', *The Journal of Sex Research* 27:557–87.

Pleins, J. David. 1992. 'Son-slayers and Their Sons', *Catholic Biblical Quarterly* 54:29–38.

———. 1995. 'Murderous Fathers, Manipulative Mothers, and Rivalrous Siblings: Rethinking the Architecture of Genesis–Kings', In *Fortunate the Eyes That See: Essays in Honor of David Noel Freedman in Celebration of His Seventieth Birthday*. Grand Rapids, MI: Eerdmans, pp. 121–36.

Polzin, Robert. 1993. *Samuel and the Deuteronomist. A Literary Study of the Deuteronomist History. Part Two: 1 Samuel*. Bloomington, IA: Indiana University Press.

Pope, Marvin H. 1977. *Song of Songs: A New Translation with Introduction and Commentary*. Anchor Bible. Garden City, NY: Doubleday.

Potts, Stephen W. 1991. *The Second Marxian Invasion: The Fiction of the Strugatsky Brothers*. The Milford Series Popular Writers of Today 50. San Bernadino, CA: Borgo.

Price, Theodore. 1992. *Hitchcock and Homosexuality: His 50-Year Obsession with Jack the Ripper and the Superbitch Prostitute: A Psychoanalytic View*. Metuchen, NJ: Scarecrow Press.

Proudhon, Pierre-Joseph. 1970. *What is Property?* Trans. Benjamin Tucker (1876). New York: Dover.

Provan, Iain W. 1991. *Lamentations*. New Century Bible Commentary. Grand Rapids, MI: Eerdmans.

Pynchon, Thomas. 1973. *Gravity's Rainbow*. New York: Viking Press.

Queen, Carol. 1996. 'The Four Foot Phallus', In *Tales from the Clit: A Female Experience of Pornography*, ed. Feminists Against Censorship. Edinburgh and San Francisco, CA: AK Press, pp. 140–4.

Ray, Peter. 1996. 'It's not Natural', In *The Material Queer: A Lesbigay Cultural Studies Reader*, ed. Donald Morton. Queer Critique. Boulder, CO: Westview, pp. 250–3.

Regev, Motti. 1994. 'Producing Artistic Value: The Case of Rock Music'. *The Sociological Quarterly* 35 (February): pp. 85–102.

Reiter, Ester. 1991. *Making Fast Food: From the Frying Pan into the Fryer*. Montreal: McGill-Queen's University Press.

Renkema, J. 1995. 'The Meaning of the Parallel Acrostics in Lamentations', *Vetus Testamentum* 45:379–83.

Rio, Linda M. 1991. 'Psychological and Sociological Research and the Decriminalization or Legalization of Prostitution', *Archives of Sexual Behavior* 20 (April):205–18.

Ritzer, George. 1996. *The McDonaldization of Society: An Investigation Into the Changing Character of Contemporary Social Life*. 2nd edition Thousand Oaks, CA: Pine Forge.

——. 1998. *The McDonaldization Thesis*. London: Sage.

Robertson, Pamela. 1996. *Guilty Pleasures: Feminist Camp from Mae West to Madonna*. Durham, NC and London: Duke University Press.

Robinson, Kim Stanley. 1992. *Red Mars*. London: Harper Collins Publishers.

——. 1993. *Green Mars*. London: Harper Collins Publishers.

——. 1996. *Blue Mars*. London: Harper Collins Publishers.

Rohmer, Eric, and Claude Chabrol. 1979. *Hitchcock: The First Forty-Four Films*. New York: Ungar.

Rose, Axl. 1992a. Interview by *Interview Magazine*. http://www.students.uiuc.edu/~t-gray/axlint.html

——. 1992b. Interview by *Rip Magazine*. http://www.students.uiuc.edu/~t-gray/axlrip92.html

Ross, Andrew. 1993. 'The Popularity of Pornography', In *The Cultural Studies Reader*, ed. Simon During. London and New York: Routledge, pp. 221–42.

Roth, Marty. 1992. 'Hitchcock's Secret Agency', *Camera Obscura: A Journal of Feminism, Culture, and Media Studies* 30 (May):35–48.

Rothman, William. 1982. *Hitchcock – the Murderous Gaze*. Harvard Film Studies. Cambridge, MA: Harvard University Press.

Rubey, Dan. 1991. 'Voguing at the Carnival: Desire and Pleasure on MTV'. *The South Atlantic Quarterly* 90 (Fall): 871–906.

Salamon, Edna. 1989. 'The Homosexual Escort Agency: Deviance Disavowal', *The British Journal of Sociology* 40 (March):1–21.

Salvestroni, Simonetta. 1984. 'The Ambiguous Miracle in Three Novels by the Strugatsky Brothers', trans. Raphael Aceto and Robert M. Philmus. *Science Fiction Studies* 11 (November):291–303.

Satz, Debra. 1995. 'Markets in Women's Sexual Labor', *Ethics* 106 (October):63–85.

Savoy, Eric. 1995. '"In the Cage" and the Queer Effects of Gay History', *Novel: A Forum on Fiction* 28 (Spring):284–307.

Schickel, Richard. 1995. 'Hitchcock on Hitchcock: An Interview', In *Perspectives on Alfred Hitchcock*, ed. David Boyd. Perspectives on Film. New York: G. K. Hall, pp. 17–41.

Schirato, Tony. 1993. 'My Space or Yours? de Certeau, Frow and the Meanings of Popular Culture', *Cultural Studies* 7(2):282–91.

Schori, Thomas R. 1996. 'Getting the Most Out of Image: An Example from the Fast-Food Industry', *Psychological Reports* 78 (June):1299–303.

Schroer, Silvia, and Thomas Staubli. 1996. 'Saul, David, und Jonathan – eine Dreiecksgeschichte? Ein Beitrag Zum Thema "Homosexualität Im Ersten Testament"' *Bibel und Kirche* 51:15–22.

Schulte, Hannelis. 1992. 'Beobachtungen Zum Begriff der Zônâ in Alten Testament', *Zeitschrift für die Alttestamentliche Wissenschaft* 104:255–62.

Scott, Bernard Brandon. 1994. *Hollywood Dreams and Biblical Stories*. Minneapolis, MN: Fortress.

Sedgwick, Eve Kosofsky. 1994. *Epistemology of the Closet*. Harmondsworth: Penguin.

Segal, Lynne. 1990. 'Pornography and Violence: What the "Experts" Really Say', *Feminist Review* 36 (Autumn):29–41.

——. 1993. 'Does Pornography Cause Violence? the Search for Evidence', In *Dirty Looks: Women, Pornography, Power*, eds Pamela Church Gibson and Roma Gibson. London: BFI, pp. 5–21.

Seidman, Steven. 1996. 'Introduction', In *Queer Theory/Sociology*, ed. Steven Seidman. Twentieth-century Social Theory. Cambridge, MA: Blackwell, pp. 1–29.

Setel, T. Drorah. 1993. 'Prophets and Pornography: Female Sexual Imagery in Hosea', In *A Feminist Companion to the Song of Songs*, ed. Athalya Brenner. The Feminist Companion to the Bible 1. Sheffield: Sheffield Academic Press, pp. 143–55.

Shrage, Laurie. 1989. 'Should Feminists Oppose Prostitution?' *Ethics* 99 (January):347–61.

——. 1994. 'Comment on Overall's "What's Wrong with Prostitution? Evaluating Sex Work"' *Signs* 19 (Winter):564–70.

——. 1996. 'Prostitution and the Case for Decriminalization', *Dissent* 43 (Spring):41–5.

Shumway, David R. 1991. 'Rock & Roll as a Cultural Practice'. *South Atlantic Quarterly* 90 (Fall): 753–70.

Slade, Joseph W. 1982. 'The Porn Market and Porn Formulas: The Feature Film of the Seventies', In *Movies as Artifacts: Cultural Criticism of Popular Film*, eds Michael T. Marsden, John G. Nachbar and Sam L. Grogg Jr. Introduction by John G. Nachbar and Sam L. Grogg, Jr. Chicago, IL: Nelson Hall, pp. 145–60.

——. 1984. 'Violence in the Hard-core Pornographic Film: A Historical Survey', *Journal of Communication* 34 (Summer):148–63.

Sloan, Jane. 1993. *Alfred Hitchcock: A Guide to References and Resources*. New York: G. K. Hall.

Sloan, Kay. 1985. 'Three Hitchcock Heroines: The Domestication of Violence', *New Orleans Review* 12 (Winter):91–5.

Smith, Anna Marie. 1995. '"By Women, for Women, About Women" Rules OK? The Impossibility of Visual Soliloquy', In *A Queer Romance: Lesbians, Gay Men, and Popular Culture*, eds Paul Burston and Colin Richardson. London and New York: Routledge, pp. 199–215.

Smith, Julian. 1992. 'The Strange Case of Lars Thorwald: Rounding Up the Usual Suspect in *Rear Window*', *New Orleans Review* 19 (Summer):21–9.

Smyth, Cherry. 1990. 'The Pleasure Threshold: Looking at Lesbian Pornography on Film', *Feminist Review* 34 (Spring):152–60.

Soble, Alan. 1986. *Pornography: Marxism, Feminism, and the Future of Sexuality*. New Haven, CT: Yale University Press.

Somers, Paul P., Jr., and Nancy Pogel. 1981. 'Pornography', In *Handbook of American Popular Culture*, Vol. 3, ed. M. Thomas Inge. Westport, CT: Greenwood.

Sontag, Susan. 1994. *Against Interpretation*. London: Vintage Books.

Soulen, Richard N. 1993. 'The *wasfs* of the Song of Songs and Hermeneutic', In *A Feminist*

Companion to the Song of Songs, ed. Athalya Brenner. The Feminist Companion to the Bible 1. Sheffield: Sheffield Academic Press, pp. 214–24.

Spacks, Patricia Meyer. 1995. *Boredom: The Literary History of a State of Mind*. Chicago, IL and London: University of Chicago Press.

Spoto, Donald. 1982. *The Dark Side of Genius: The Life of Alfred Hitchcock*. New York: Ballantine.

Sprinkle, Annie, interviewee. 1991. 'Annie Sprinkle', with Andrea Juno. In *Angry Women*, eds Andrea Juno and V. Vale. San Francisco, CA: Re/Search Publications, pp. 23–40.

——. 1998. *Post-Porn Modernist: My 25 Years as a Multimedia Whore*. San Francisco, CA: Cleis Press.

Stadelmann, Luis. 1992. *Love and Politics: A New Commentary on the Song of Songs*. New York: Paulist.

Stam, Robert, and Roberta Pearson. 1983. 'Hitchcock's *Rear Window*: Reflexivity and the Critique of Voyeurism', *Enclitic* 7 (Spring):136–45.

Sterritt, David. 1992. 'The Diabolic Imagination: Hitchcock, Bakhtin, and the Carnivalization of Cinema', *Hitchcock Annual* 9:39–67.

Stone, Ken. 1995. 'Gender and Homosexuality in Judges 19: Subject-Honor, Object-Shame?' *Journal for the Study of the Old Testament* 67:87–107.

——. 1997. 'The Hermeneutics of Abomination: On Gay Men, Canaanites, and Biblical Interpretation', *Biblical Theology Bulletin* 27:36–41.

Straayer, Chris. 1993. 'The Seduction of Boundaries: Feminist Fluidity in Annie Sprinkle's Art/Education/Sex', In *Dirty Looks: Women, Pornography, Power*, eds Pamela Church Gibson and Roma Gibson. London: BFI, pp. 156–75.

——. 1996. *Deviant Eyes, Deviant Bodies: Sexual Re-orientations in Film and Video*. New York: Columbia University Press.

Stratton, Jon. 1983. 'Capitalism and Romantic Ideology in the Record Business'. *Popular Music* 3: 143–56.

Straw, Will. 1993. 'Characterizing Rock Music Culture: The Case of Heavy Metal'. In *The Cultural Studies Reader*, ed. Simon During. London and New York: Routledge, pp. 368–81.

Strugatsky, Arkady, and Boris Strugatsky. 1973. *Hard to Be a God*. New York: Seabury Press.

——. 1976. *The Final Circle of Paradise*. New York: DAW Books.

——. 1977a. *Monday Begins on Saturday*. New York: DAW Books.

——. 1977b. *Roadside Picnic* and *Tale of the Troika*. Macmillan Best of Soviet Science Fiction. New York: Macmillan.

——. 1978. *Definitely Maybe*. New York and London: Macmillan/Collier Macmillan.

——. 1979a. *Far Rainbow/The Second Invasion from Mars*. Trans. Antonina W. Bouis and Gary Kern. Introduction by Theodore Sturgeon. Macmillan's Best of Soviet Science Fiction. New York and London: Macmillan/Collier Macmillan.

——. 1979b. *The Ugly Swans*. Trans. Alice Stone Nakhimovsky and Alexander Nakhimovsky. New York and London: Macmillan.

——. 1980. *The Snail on the Slope*. New York and London: Bantam/Gollancz.

——. 1982. *Escape Attempt – The Kid from Hell – Space Mowgli*. New York and London: Macmillan/Collier Macmillan.

Sturma, Michael. 1992. 'The Politics of Dancing: When Rock 'n' Roll Came to Australia'. *Journal of Popular Culture* 25 (Spring): 123–42.

Sullivan, Barbara. 1994. 'Feminism and Female Prostitution', In *Sex Work and Sex Workers in Australia*, eds Roberta Perkins, Garrett Prestage, Rachel Sharp, and Frances Lovejoy. University of New South Wales Press, pp. 253–68.

Suvin, Darko. 1972. 'Criticism of the Strugatskii Brothers' Work', *Canadian-American Slavic Studies* 2:288–307.

——. 1988. *Positions and Presuppositions in Science Fiction*. London: Macmillan.

Tarlin, Jan. 1997. 'Utopia and Pornography in Ezekiel: Violence, Hope, and the Shattered Male Subject'. In *Reading Bibles, Writing Bodies: Identity and the Book*. eds Timothy K. Beal and David M. Gunn. Biblical Limits. London and New York: Routledge, pp. 175–83.

Tasker, Yvonne. 1993a. *Spectacular Bodies: Gender, Genre and the Action Cinema*. London and New York: Routledge.

——. 1993b. 'Dumb Movies for Dumb People: Masculinity, the Body, and the Voice in Contemporary Action Cinema', In *Screening the Male: Exploring Masculinities in Hollywood Cinema*, eds Steven Cohan and Ina Rae Hark. London: Routledge, pp. 230–44.

Thomas, Sheila Marie. 1996. *Speaking the Unspeakable: Annie Sprinkle's 'Prostitute Performances'*. M. A. Diss. www.dreamscape.com/elusis/thesis/thesis.html.

Trible, Phyllis. 1978. *God and the Rhetoric of Sexuality*. Philadelphia, PA: Fortress.

Trostle, Lawrence C. 1993. 'Pornography as a Source of Sex Information for University Students: Some Consistent Findings', *Psychological Reports* 72 (April):407–12.

Truffaut, Francois. *Hitchcock*, Revised Edition, ed. Helen G. Scott. London: Paladin; Grafton Books, 1986.

Trumbach, Randolph. 1993. 'Erotic Fantasy and Male Libertinism in Enlightenment England', In *The Invention of Pornography: Obscenity and the Origins of Modernity, 1500–1800*, ed. Lynn Hunt. New York: Zone Books, pp. 253–82.

Ullestad, Neal. 1987. 'Rock and Rebellion: Subversive Effects of Live Aid and "Sun City"' *Popular Music* 6 (January): 67–92.

Van Giezen, Robert W. 1994. 'Occupational Wages in the Fast-Food Restaurant Industry', *Monthly Labor Review* 117 (August):24–30.

Van Sant, Gus. 1993. *Even Cowgirls Get the Blues and My Own Private Idaho*. Film Script. London and Boston: Faber & Faber.

Van Seters, John. 1994. *The Life of Moses: The Yahwist as Historian in Exodus–Numbers*. Louisville, KY: Westminster/John Knox.

Viegener, Matias. 1992. 'There's Trouble in that Body: Queer Fanzines, Sexual Identity and Censorship', *Fiction International* 22:123–36.

Wagner, Jana L., and Richard A. Winett. 1988. 'Prompting One Low-Fat, High-Fiber Selection in a Fast-Food Restaurant', *Journal of Applied Behavior Analysis* 21 (Summer):179–85.

Waldersee, Robert. 1991. *The Impact of Manager Attributional Accuracy and Feedback on Subordinate Performance and Non Performance Outcomes*. Working Papers Series. Kensington, NSW: Centre for Corporate Change, Australian Graduate School of Management, University of New South Wales.

Waldersee, Robert, and Fred Luthans. 1991. *Feedback Sign and the Performance and Nonperformance Outcomes of High Task Mastery Employees*, Kensington, NSW: Centre for Corporate Change, Australian Graduate School of Management, University of New South Wales.

Waldrop, Judith. 1988. 'Fast Food and Family Fare', *American Demographics* 10 (June):14.

——. 1993. 'When Tulsa Burps, McDonald's Apologizes', *American Demographics* 15 (July):44–5.

Walkowitz, Judith R. 1980. *Prostitution and Victorian Society: Women, Class, and the State*. Cambridge: Cambridge University Press.

Washington, H. 1994. 'The Strange Woman (אשה זרה/נכריה) of Proverbs 1–9 and Post-exilic Judaean Society', In *Temple and Community in the Persian Period*, eds T. Eskenazi and K. Richards. Second Temple Studies 2. Sheffield: Sheffield Academic Press, pp. 217–42.

Waterman, L. 1948. *The Song of Songs: Translated and Interpreted as a Dramatic Poem*. Ann Arbor: University of Michigan Press.

Waters, Elizabeth. 1989. 'Restructuring the "Woman Question": *Perestroika* and Prostitution', *Feminist Review* 33 (Autumn):3–19.

Watney, Simon. 1987. *Policing Desire: Pornography, AIDS and the Media*. London: Methuen.

Watson, Wilfred G. E. 1995. 'Some Ancient Near Eastern Parallels to the Song of Songs', In *Words Remembered, Texts Renewed: Essays in Honor of John F. A. Sawyer*, eds Jon Davies, Graham Harvey, and Wilfred G. E. Watson. Journal for the Study of the Old Testament Supplement Series 195. Sheffield: Sheffield Academic Press, pp. 253–71.

Waugh, Thomas. 1995. 'Men's Pornography: Gay vs. Straight', In *Out in Culture: Gay, Lesbian, and Queer Essays on Popular Culture*. eds Corey K. Creekmur and Alexander Doty. Durham, NC: Duke University Press, pp. 307–27.

Weaver, Mary Jo. 1989. 'Pornography and the Religious Imagination', In *For Adult Users Only: The Dilemma of Violent Pornography*, eds Susan Gubar and Joan Hoff. Everywoman. Bloomington: Indiana University Press, pp. 68–86.

Webb, Peter. 1982. 'Victorian Literature', In *The Sexual Dimension in Literature*, ed. Alan Bold. London and Totowa, NJ: Vision; Barnes & Noble, pp. 90–121.

Weeks, Jeffrey. 1996. 'The Construction of Homosexuality', In *Queer Theory/Sociology*, ed. Steven Seidman. Twentieth-Century Social Theory. Cambridge, MA: Blackwell, pp. 41–63.

Weinstein, Deena. 1991. *Heavy Metal: A Cultural Sociology*. New York: Lexington Books.

Weis, Elisabeth. 1982. *The Silent Scream: Alfred Hitchcock's Sound Track*. Rutherford, NJ: Fairleigh Dickinson University Press.

Wendland, Ernst R. 1995. 'Seeking the Path Through a Forest of Symbols: A Figurative and Structural Survey of the Song of Songs', *Journal of Translation and Textlinguistics* 7:13–59.

Werner, Dennis. 1984. 'Paid Sex Specialists Among the Mekranoti', *Journal of Anthropological Research* 40 (Fall):394–405.

Westermann, Claus. 1967. *Basic Forms of Prophetic Speech*. Philadelphia, PA: Westminster.

——. 1994. *Lamentations: Issues and Interpretation*. Trans. Charles Muenchow. Edinburgh: T. & T. Clark.

Wilcox, Brian L. 1987. 'Pornography, Social Science, and Politics: When Research and Ideology Collide', *American Psychologist* 42 (October):941–3.

Wildavsky, Ben. 1989. 'McJobs: Inside America's Largest Youth Training Program', *Policy Review* 49 (Summer):30–7.

Williams, Daniel H. 1994. 'Proverbs 8: 22–31', *Interpretation* 48:275–9.

Williams, Linda. 1989. *Hard Core: Power, Pleasure, and the 'Frenzy of the Visible'*. Berkeley: University of California Press.

——. 1993a. 'Second Thoughts on *Hard Core*: American Obscenity Law and the Scapegoating of Deviance', In *Dirty Looks: Women, Pornography, Power*, eds Pamela Church Gibson and Roma Gibson. London: BFI, pp. 46–61.

——. 1993b. 'A Provoking Agent: The Pornography and Performance Art of Annie Sprinkle', In *Dirty Looks: Women, Pornography, Power*. eds Pamela Church Gibson and Roma Gibson. London: BFI, pp. 176–91.

——. 1994. 'Learning to Scream', *Sight and Sound* 4 (December):14–17.

Wilson, Elizabeth. 1987. 'Interview with Andrea Dworkin', In *Looking On: Images of*

Femininity in the Visual Arts and Media, ed. Rosemary Betterton. London: Pandora, pp. 161–9.

Wilson, Robert R. 1972. 'An Interpretation of Ezekiel's Dumbness'. *Vetus Testamentum* 32 (January): 91–104.

———. 1979. 'Prophecy and Ecstasy: A Reexamination'. *Journal of Biblical Literature* 98: 321–37.

———. 1980.*Prophecy and Society in Ancient Israel*. Philadelphia, PA: Fortress.

Winter, Marcel, *et al.* 1976. *Prostitution in Australia: A Sociological Study*. Balgowlah, NSW: Purtaboi Publications.

Wood, Robin. 1989. *Hitchcock's Films Revisited*. New York: Columbia University Press.

———. 1995. 'The Murderous Gays: Hitchcock's Homophobia', In *Out in Culture: Gay, Lesbian,and Queer Essays on Popular Culture*, eds Corey K. Creekmur and Alexander Doty. Series Q. Durham, NC: Duke University Press.

Worden, Steven. 1995. 'Review of *Fast Food, Fast Talk*', *Journal of Contemporary Ethnography* 23 (January):523–6.

Yang Ji. 1996. 'Domestic Fast Food Catches Up', *Beijing Review* 39 (August 19–25):25.

Yee, Gale A. 1995. '"I Have Perfumed My Bed with Myrrh": The Foreign Woman in Proverbs', In *A Feminist Companion to Wisdom Literature*, ed. Athalya Brenner. The Feminist Companion to the Bible 9. Sheffield: Sheffield Academic Press, pp. 110–26.

Zalduondo, Barbara O. 1991. 'Prostitution Viewed Cross-Culturally: Toward Recontextualizing Sex Work in AIDS Intervention Research', *The Journal of Sex Research* 28 (May): 223–48.

Zimmerli, Walther. 1979.*Ezekiel 1: A Commentary on the Book of the Prophet Ezekiel, Chapter 1–24*. Trans. Ronald E. Clements. Hermeneia: A Critical and Historical Commentary on the Bible. Philadelphia, PA: Fortress.

Zirnite, Dennis. 1986. 'Hitchcock, on the Level: The Heights of Spatial Tension', *Film Criticism* 10 (Spring):2–21.

Žižek, Slavoj. 1991a. *Looking Awry: An Introduction to Jacques Lacan Through Popular Culture*. October Books. Cambridge, MA: MIT Press.

———. 1991b. *For They Know not What They Do: Enjoyment as a Political Factor*. Phronesis. London and New York: Verso.

———. 1992. 'In His Bold Gaze My Ruin is Writ Large' In *Everything You Always Wanted to Know About Lacan (But Were Afraid to Ask Hitchcock)*, ed. S. Žižek. London: Verso, pp. 211–72.

———. 1994. *The Metastases of Enjoyment: Six Essays on Woman and Causality*. Wo Es War. London: Verso.

———. 1996. *The Indivisible Remainder: An Essay on Schelling and Related Matters*. Wo Es War. London: Verso.

Zuckerman, Bruce. 1991. *Job the Silent: A Study in Historical Counterpoint*. New York and Oxford: Oxford University Press.

INDEX OF BIBLICAL REFERENCES

GENERAL INDEX

208